PUBLICATIONS OF THE TEXAS FOLKLORE SOCIETY
NUMBER XXXII

MODY C. BOATRIGHT, *Editor*
WILSON M. HUDSON, *Associate Editor*
ALLEN MAXWELL, *Associate Editor*

A GOOD TALE and A BONNIE TUNE

PUBLISHED BY

SOUTHERN METHODIST UNIVERSITY PRESS • DALLAS

A GOOD TALE and A BONNIE TUNE

EDITED BY

MODY C. BOATRIGHT
WILSON M. HUDSON
ALLEN MAXWELL

SOUTHERN METHODIST UNIVERSITY PRESS • DALLAS

Contents

A GOOD TALE and
A BONNIE TUNE

Fifteen Mexican Tales

RILEY AIKEN

Why Women Are Like Cats

I SHALL NEVER FORGET my uncle Aurelio. He was a little old man whose age was well on the worse side of that of the world — which is to say, somewhat beyond fifty. His weakness was women. Now don't get me wrong. *Mi tío's* good deportment was always in the clear. His only sin was an indolent levity in the presence of the ladies.

I remember one morning when some *comadres* of the hacienda were having a gabfest in the kitchen of doña Cuca.

"*Buenos días*," said a shadow in the doorway.

"Come in, *tío* Aurelio," said doña Cuca.

And that did it. The fox was in the henhouse, so to speak, and one could not hear himself think for the screams and loud laughter.

And presently there was an argument. There was always conflict when *mi tío* mixed with the *comadres*. It is said that he loved to pick a fight with the ladies. For instance, if one should say black is black, *mi tío* would say: "*Según y conforme* [it all depends]."

Upon this particular occasion the bone of contention was the superiority of men over women.

"Why should men be superior?" asked doña Paula, who, because of her stubbornness and general knowledge, was known as *La Cabezona*. "Hasn't it been said that God was more skilful

3

when he made woman? And aren't we poor little *hembras* a chip off the block of man? Doesn't the Holy Bible say that Eve was made from a rib of Adam?"

"*Según y conforme*," said *mi tío*. "I don't go for silly sayings and fairy stories."

"How scandalous, *tío*," said doña Cuca, all aghast. "Don't you believe in . . . ?"

"I do believe," said *mi tío*, "but also, with scientific certainty, I know a few things."

"*Vamos*," said someone. "Let's listen to a *sábelo todo* and God's masterpiece, ha, ha! You should have seen *mi tío* the other morning when he got his legs tangled in the pig's rope. What poise! And what dignity! There he was on the ground. At one end of the *soga* was the hind leg of the pig. At the other end, the hind legs of *mi tío*. The pig was squealing and running in circles and *mi tío* was rolling, kicking, and swearing. *Ay, qué barbaridad!* If Satan had heard him he would have blushed. God's masterpiece, to say the least, was quite informal. Do you think that such an honorable man should have condemned the poor *maranito* to the realm of three thousand devils? It seems to me it would have been more fitting if he had said: 'Excuse me, señor Pig; I don't believe we have had the honor of sleeping together.'"

And there followed an uproar of mocking laughter.

"Calm yourselves, señoras," said *mi tío*. "Let me give you the facts in the case of the superiority of men over women, *la pura verdad*."

"*Andale*," said the ladies with affected interest and composure.

"Well, it is true that it had been God's intention to make Eve from the rib of Adam. Our father Adam was on the operating table, and the rib had been taken from his side. God placed it on a stand nearby, and had turned away to wash His hands when the wildcat came in.

"Let it be known, *señoras de mi alma*, that the *gato montés*, during the first days of creation, sported a long tail. He came into the operating room in search of food. You see, God had been too busy with man and had had no time to prepare *comida* for his innocent creatures. Well, God's back was turned, and the cat saw the rib. He pounced upon it and out the door he went. Goodbye ladies! God gave chase. The cat saw he was losing the race and was bustling up a tree when God grabbed his tail. There was so much momentum on the part of the cat that the tail came off.

"And now what have we? *Ahora verás*. High in the tree, crouching on a limb and snarling with Adam's rib between its teeth, was the *gato montés*. On the ground was Nuestro Señor with a cat's tail in His hand.

"Let it be said that Nuestro Señor is wise beyond wisdom, and furthermore, has a fine sense of humor. He smiled and looked first at the rib, well out of reach in a high tree, and then at what He held in His hand.

"At last, He said: 'Oh, well, a cat's tail is good enough to make a woman of.' And that, *amigas*, is why women are such cats and consequently, inferior to men."

And then you should have heard the noise in doña Cuca's kitchen. And you should have seen the speed with which *mi tío* took off for other parts.

This tale was told to me by the father of one of my Mexican friends at Presidio, Texas.

Prospectors in Paradise

THIS FELLOW, Pepe Perancejo, was a prospector. According to the stories about him, he had followed all the trails from Hermosillo to Chihuahua City and as far south as Colima. He found silver around Batopilas and gold at La Lluvia de Oro. Some strikes were exceptionally good, but Pepe was never satisfied. After each discovery he would invariably sell out for a song and a few bottles of tequila and move on.

It is said that one day he vaguely remembered some reference to a city with streets of gold. He went to a priest and was told the name of the place. The padre gave directions on how to reach heaven and soon thereafter Pepe took off for Kingdom Come.

Imagine the surprise of St. Peter when one bright morning he saw a calloused and wayworn man with a pack, shovels, and pick on his back coming up the path toward the Pearly Gates. The saint blocked the way and said:

"I am St. Peter. I shall have to frisk you and ask you a few questions."

"*Pues, escúlqueme,*" said Pepe.

"Do you have any money?"

"No, señor," was the reply.

"What is your nationality?"

"Mexicano, señor."

"On earth, what did you do for a living?"

"Prospector."

"Prospector? . . . Just one little moment, please."

St. Peter began thumbing through the pages of a large book.

"Now let's see," mused the saint, "carpenter, um, um, gardener, mason, painter, um, um . . . "

He closed the book, looked at Pepe, and said: "I regret to inform you that there is no mention of prospectors in the Constitution of Heaven. By the way, what is a prospector?"

"One who seeks gold, silver, and other precious metals."

St. Peter sighed with relief. "There is nothing un-Christian about that," he said. "Come in and make yourself at home."

Pepe Perancejo did just that, and ere long he had staked out claims all over the place.

St. Peter was vexed but decided to wait and watch.

Two days later there was a mighty commotion at the Pearly Gates. A score of trailweary men with packs, picks, and shovels on their backs were requesting entrance.

"The Constitution of Heaven does not provide for prospectors," said good St. Peter.

"Then why did you permit Pepe Perancejo to enter?" they countered.

Now the saying has it that St. Peter is a kind, good-natured old fellow but not overly bright. He has made many blunders while in heaven's immigration service, blunders like giving Pepe Perancejo permission to enter paradise, for instance. He was now in a touchy predicament. But he didn't worry.

"Oh, well," he sighed. "Come in and make yourselves at home."

Shortly thereafter the angels of heaven sent a committee to Nuestro Señor to complain about the badly cluttered condition of the streets.

"Once they were smooth, beautiful, and clean," said the committee. "You should see them now. They are badly littered with mounds, slag-heaps, and shafts everywhere. Prospectors are to blame, Señor. We request that they be banished."

"Granted," said Nuestro Señor. "Tell St. Peter to get rid of them."

"This is impossible," said St. Peter when he was approached by the committee. "I let them in and I shall lose face if I run them away."

"That is your worry," said the committee.

And worry he did, days and days of worry. At last he hit upon a plan. He went to Pepe Perancejo with his problem and suggested a solution. The latter shook his head and said it wouldn't work.

"Prospectors are a peculiar sort," said he. "They are never satisfied with well-enough, and all of them without exception have the wanderlust. This is their weakness. I believe we can arrange a trap for them and they will take themselves away; thereby you will save face. Now this is what I would do if I were you . . . "

The next morning a telegram from hell, that had been faked

by Pepe and St. Peter, was read to a group of angels from a balcony.

"A gold strike in hell," said the telegram. And that was all.

The following day there was only one prospector left in heaven and that was Pepe Perancejo.

He chuckled about this for a while but not for long. He became gloomy. He no longer worked his claims.

"This is a good place," he began repeating to himself. "Placers and lodes are everywhere. It is hard to imagine a better land for prospectors. Ah, my unfortunate friends! They have been gone a long time now and not one has returned. I wonder why. Could it be that . . . Could it be that . . . Ah, that's it!" he exclaimed. "The grade of ore in hell is better."

The next morning he picked up his pick and shovel, left through the Pearly Gates, and took off at a trot down the trail toward hell.

Since then prospectors have not been permitted to enter paradise.

I had this story from an Austrian prospector, Herr Mensch, in 1930, on the western slopes of the Sierra Madre del Occidente.

Candida

JUAN AND PEDRO were the sons of wealthy *hacendados*. And, despite the fact that one was calm and good-natured and the other constantly obsessed with conniving intentions, they were friends.

They were in the capital city of the province one evening from their respective haciendas nearby, enjoying a *paseo*. Seated on a bench facing the walks of the plaza, they watched the procession of boys and girls. Suddenly, Juan exclaimed: "Look, Pedro, at the girl in green. What a dream! I am going to make her my wife."

"You can't be serious, Juan. Don't be a *pazguato*. I know her family. Her father is as poor as a mouse," said Pedro.

"All the better reason why I should marry her," said Juan.

"Let me pick a wife for you," said Pedro. "Do you see the one in blue over there? She is pretty, and better yet, she is rich. Marry for money and in that way you won't stand to lose."

Juan refused to take his friend's advice and within a few months he had married Cándida, the one in green.

His young wife was beautiful, and her eyes were divine. Her friends spoke of her as *muy lista* (mentally vivacious), and her parents were grateful that God had given them this one and only child, who, seemingly, had no faults at all.

Time passed, and one day, like a bolt of lightning from a clear sky, Pedro said to Juan: "Pardon what I have to tell you. I have heard that your wife is unfaithful to you."

Juan paused for a long moment and then, measuring his words, he replied: "Pedro, if anyone else had told me that, I would have killed him. However, since you mean it for my own good, I shall simply say that it should be your duty to produce proof."

People wondered how two young men could be so unlike in character and yet so close in friendship. Some thought that Juan, because of his supine goodness, was incapable of seeing faults in a friend. And Pedro, indeed, had his faults. He was selfish and given to the exploitation of any virtue or vice in others, friends included, if he could gain a few pesos in so doing.

"Juan, I have no proof at this time that Cándida is unfaithful; but I shall bet my all against all that is yours that I can get proof. Will you bet?"

"For two reasons, no," said Juan. "The first of these is that I know my wife is faithful; and the second, some things are too sacred to be used as a pawn in a game of chance."

"The first of your reasons proves you don't know women, and the second shouldn't disturb your scruples since marriage is primarily a human institution and a gamble, and you have taken that gamble already," said Pedro.

"All right," said Juan, "I will take your bet, but your evidence against Cándida must be convincing."

Pedro went immediately in search of an old *trota conventos* (woman matchmaker) whose services he had used in his philanderings.

"*Oiga* Zorra," he said to her. "Would you like to possess a home of your own and ten *talegas* [5,000 pesos] in coin?"

La Zorra was too startled to answer. Pedro proceeded to explain the nature of his bet with Juan, and added: "I know that no one can match you in cunning, and for that reason you can get the evidence I need to win this fortune."

The next day La Zorra went to see Cándida at a time when Juan was not at home. She said that she had had no food for days, and would the good señora give her a bite to eat and a few little bits of money — *una caridad* — for God's sake.

Cándida knew the meaning of poverty and not only did she give her money but invited her into the house for food and rest.

Then La Zorra pretended to faint. Cándida called her servants, who carried the old *mendiga* to a bed in a back room and laid her down.

"Go on about your work," said Cándida to the servants. "I shall watch over her."

She lay down on a couch near the bed where La Zorra had been placed. After observing the old woman for some time, Cándida went to sleep. Then, La Zorra, cautiously opening an eye, realized the time was ripe for action. She took a small bottle from the folds of her shawl. In this bottle were dozens of *corrucos* (*piojos*, lice) she had caught and placed there for this evil purpose. She emptied the bottle on Cándida and waited. Presently the latter awoke and called a servant.

"Why do you call a servant?" asked La Zorra. "I am all right now. May I help you?"

"I am itching all over," said Cándida. "I want a change of clothes and a bath."

"I will prepare a bath while you undress," said the *mendiga*.

Cándida was undressed and reaching for a robe when the old woman returned suddenly. It was then the latter saw a black mole on the young woman's right thigh.

"I am feeling much relieved now, señora," said the *trota conventos*. "With your permission, I shall hurry home and prepare food for my grandson. *Adiós;* you have made me very happy."

She went immediately, not home, but to the plaza where she found Pedro.

"*Albricias*, Pedro," she said. "I have what you need to win your bet. Now, *daca* [hand over] that deed and the ten *talegas* of *plata*."

She explained in cruel detail what had happened when she entered Cándida's home. "The black mole couldn't have been placed more to our advantage," she said, giggling.

It took a few days of cautious maneuvering to arrange a deed for the *mendiga* and to get the money he promised her. After that he went to Juan and said: "*Amigo*, I don't know how to tell you this except to say that bread is bread and wine is wine. In short, to put it bluntly, you have lost the bet." He told the unhappy young man about the black mole.

"*Ya todo se acabó* [that's the end of everything]," said Juan as he left in a stupor.

The young husband didn't go home that night. The next morning he had his *mayordomo* saddle two horses and leave them hitched to a post near the big house. He then went to Cándida and explained that he had urgent business in a city two days' ride from the hacienda, and that it was his desire that she accompany him.

After having traveled in a mountain wilderness for hours, he suggested they rest for awhile. He dismounted and helped his wife from her horse. Then, quickly, he swung into his saddle, and catching the reins of the other animal, hurried away, leaving her to die of starvation.

Cándida, after days of wandering and with her last bit of

energy, dragged herself to a small house near a river. She was without shoes, her clothes were torn to tatters, and her face was the picture of agony. An old woman helped her into the house and put her to bed.

It was while working in a small garden near the old woman's home some days later that Cándida sensed that someone, somewhere, was spying on her. She looked about her and saw an Indian standing still like a post not thirty feet away. Indians had come to her hacienda often and she was not afraid of them. Yet, this old man did not come to her to ask for *ni-the-mua* (tobacco) or *escu-pua-a-pua* (salt). He stood there and stared with an expressionless face. Suddenly, he turned and ran into the brush.

That afternoon horsemen surrounded the little home of the kind old *nana* (grandmother). Among them was Juan de Miranda, Cándida's husband.

"Cándida, Cándida, at last we have found you, thanks to God and this Indian tracker. Yes, my wife, it was all a horrible nightmare, something I should like to forget. But let me tell you now that an old *mendiga,* claiming that Pedro was cheating her, stabbed him and before he died he confessed the whole dirty business to me. The old woman is in custody. Come, let's go home. I shall have to spend the rest of my life praying for your forgiveness."

"This old *nana* here saved my life, Juan. Let's see to it that her years end happily."

"Your wish is mine," said Juan.

Recorded at Batopilas, Chihuahua.

Jovita and Manuelito

ERA QUE ERA and once upon a time there was a wealthy family that lived in a land far away. Strange though it may seem, in addition to the man, his wife, and his young daughter, there was only one servant who had been reared a *criado* with the girl.

And there came a time when the father and mother of the family died. Thus it was that Jovita, the daughter, and Manuelito, the servant, were left alone in the world.

One day Jovita said to Manuelito: "Now what are we going to do? My father and mother are dead."

Then she said impulsively: "You know what? I shall have my picture taken and many copies made and I shall have them sent out over the world to see if someone might be interested in me."

Time passed and there was no reply to her pictures. One day she said to Manuelito: "Now let's try something else. Would you like to make a bargain with me? Manuelito, let's you and me get married."

"Oh, no," said Manuelito. "Remember those pictures. Some day someone would take you away from me."

"No, no," said Jovita. "Nothing like that will happen."

Then Manuelito was willing and they were married.

One day of so many happy days Jovita said: "Listen, Manuelito: If I should die would you be willing to be buried alive with me?"

"Yes; why not?" he said.

"And how would I know that you would fulfil this promise? Let us sign a compact with the blood of our bodies. We shall say: Whoever remains after the death of one of us will be buried alive together with the one that died. And, so? Are you willing?"

"Yes; why not?" he said.

And at last a time arrived when Jovita died. And Manuelito complied with his promise. He had a mason build a large vault, and he followed his beloved dead into the tomb. He arranged that a keeper of the dead should bring him food every day.

One day as he sat eating beside the coffin of his wife he noticed a small mouse that was busy gathering the crumbs that fell at his feet. And this small mouse became a companion.

Once he observed that the mouse had brought a small flower into the vault as a plaything. He was amused; he picked up a small pebble and thoughtlessly tossed it toward the *animalito. Ay, Dios;* he should not have done that! The pebble hit his little friend and killed it.

Not knowing what he was about to do, he picked up the flower and placed it at the nose of the mouse. The latter sprang to its feet and ran away.

"I wonder," said Manuelito. "Could this small white flower be *La Flor de la Vida?*"

And then he opened the coffin at his side and said: "Jovita, my little mouse came alive. Oh, to Allah and to God that you too may now return from the dead. Look, what a beautiful flower!"

He passed the flower beneath her nose and her lips began to move. He continued in his prayer to God until she was awake. He made no mention of where they were.

Then she said: "Where are we?"

"We are here in a tavern," he replied. "A gentleman looks after our interests."

At that instant the guardian of the dead came to the vault.

"With whom are you talking, Manuelito?" he asked.

"I am speaking with Jovita."

And then, with a look of pity on his face, the guardian asked: "Do you wish for something to eat?"

"No," replied Manuelito. "I want you to open the door of this vault and leave it open."

The guardian refused.

"If you will leave the door open," said Manuelito, "I will give you certain riches that I have hid in my house. Here, these are the keys to the house. Go, see for yourself."

That night the two, Jovita and Manuelito, left the tomb. They walked through the dark until they came to an inn. Here they asked for lodging.

Days passed and Manuelito was taken to bed with a fever.

Some girls came to the inn one afternoon and asked if Jovita would accompany them to the shore. "A foreign king in a large ship is coming to visit," they said.

And though he felt no good would come from their request, Manuelito consented and Jovita left him there, alone and ill.

The king in all his splendor stood on the deck of his ship with a picture in his hands. He looked at this picture and at the girls on the shore.

"There she is! There she is! The one on the end of that line of girls."

There was no delay. Jovita was carried away.

The girls who had accompanied Jovita to the dock returned to Manuelito's room. "We are unhappy, Manuelito. They have taken your wife away."

Manuelito was very sad. However, within a few days he was on his feet again. He walked along the beach and learned that the king who had stolen his wife had given an order that no one, under the penalty of death, was to follow him across the sea.

Manuelito returned to his room and began to tear and repatch some of his clothes. He now looked like a beggar or a very poor man. He bribed a friend and had him close him in a barrel and roll him into the sea.

Ere long he was in a foreign land. He pretended to be looking for work, but he knew well the object of his search. He arrived at the home of an old woman who had a son who was employed in the palace of the king.

"Look, son, this young man wants work at the palace. Tell the king that he is your brother who has lived down the coast for some time."

"What is your name?" asked the young man.

"My name," said Manuelito, "my name is Juan Soldadillo."

The young man went into the presence of the king and said: "I have with me a young man."

"Yes?" responded the king. "Where are you from?"

"I am a relative of your servant here. I am his brother who has been living down the coast for a bit. My name is Juan Soldadillo."

"Do you want work?" asked the king.

"Yes, Your Majesty; I am at your command," said Manuelito.

This Manuelito, who is now known as Juan Soldadillo, was given work in the kitchen. He went about his chores in a dull way with a large hat pulled down over his eyes.

Once, while the queen was inspecting the kitchen, she noticed the new servant.

"What is your name?" she asked.

"*Pos,* Juan Soldadillo," he drawled.

The queen was curious and continued to visit the kitchen day by day. There was something about this servant that reminded her of her husband. And before long and after asking many questions, she discovered that indeed Juan Soldadillo was her husband Manuelito.

Ere long the king noticed that the queen was upset and badly disturbed. "Listen, my queen," he said, "why are you sad?"

"Why shouldn't I be sad," she replied, "since the one we have serving as kitchen sweeper is my husband?"

"Ah," said the king. "So, *qué bueno.* This is fine, yes, very fine."

Later the king, very angry, called Manuelito into his presence and said: "Juan Soldadillo, tonight you are to guard three ounces of my gold. If any of it is lost I shall have you executed."

The king tricked Manuelito by having two other servants steal the gold. Manuelito rushed to his pseudo brother and said:

"After I am executed you are to claim my body. Watch over it throughout the night. Then get a horse, the most *ladino* of those in the king's stable. Hitch this horse to a hack. Look; I want you to listen well to this that I have to say. I have a flower. At four o'clock in the morning you are to pass this flower back and forth beneath my nose and petition God that I be returned to life. After I have departed go to the door of the king's room and shout: 'All the devils of hell have taken Juan Soldadillo away!'"

On the morning of the execution the king said to his queen Jovita: "Come and watch the execution of your husband."

After the execution the friend did all that he had promised Manuelito to do. After the resuscitation he saw to it that his friend should be spirited away to another city. This city was in mourning over the death of the favorite daughter of the emperor.

Manuelito went to the palace of the emperor and asked: "Your Majesty, what will you give me to return your daughter to life?"

"Whatever you wish," replied the emperor, weeping.

"With the death of a certain king I shall name I shall restore your daughter to life," said Manuelito.

"Be it as you request," said the emperor. "The only thing I ask is the life of my daughter."

Manuelito went to the dead princess, passed the flower back and forth beneath her nose, and prayed to God. The girl awoke. The emperor was amazed. He ordered the execution of the king immediately.

Just before the death of the king, Manuelito said to Jovita: "Come and see the execution of your husband."

Manuelito and Jovita are still in this world and are living together happily.

This story I heard in Marfa, Texas, in 1930, from the blind daughter of Santiago Garza.

Julio

JULIO WAS an orphan. His father was a poor man, one of *los de abajo*. All he possessed when death came upon him was twenty pesos. This money was left to Julio. After the funeral the latter said:

"I have no father. I have no mother. This silver is the only thing I possess. Now that there is nothing to keep me here, I shall wander. I can't wait around for whatever future there is in life for me."

He took to the road. After much uneventful and aimless trekking, he encountered two individuals and one said to him: "Where goest thou, young man?"

And Julio responded: "Señores, let it be known to you that I I travel the trail of life in search of my destiny."

The stranger replied: "Very well and good; yet, on the other hand, it isn't so good and well, for you have chosen a path that has led you to the secret hideout of a gang of thieves. Right here and now your travels have ended as they have for all who tried to pass this way."

Julio said: "Señores, don't kill me. All that I can give you is these twenty pesos my father left me when he died. You may have them, but please spare my life."

"Well," said one of the robbers, "hand over the money and move on. However, I warn you. Tell no one what has happened here; otherwise we will follow and kill you."

After leagues of further wandering Julio came on the body of a young man that lay beside the path.

Then Julio mused: "Poor chap, he wasn't so fortunate as I. His only need now is a grave."

Julio worked hard with only a sharp stick for a spade. He placed the body in a shallow trench and covered it with dirt and the leaves of a prickly pear.

Soon after this, as he rested beside the road he saw a young man approaching.

"*Para dónde?* [where are you going?]" asked the stranger.

"Just seeking adventure," said Julio.

"My name is Antonio," said the young man. "You are Julio, if I remember well. Shall we travel together?"

After five days of walking, they came to a city. Neither had so much as a centavo.

"Now we shall enter an inn," said Antonio. "We need rest and food."

"And with no money?" asked Julio. "How long would we stay there, and what would we eat without *plata*?"

"Leave that to me," said Antonio. "Listen; tonight we shall have money."

"Well, all right," said Julio. "You lead the way."

"No, upon second thought," said Antonio, "I shall go to the inn and you run down to the municipal palace and ask for permission to give a play tonight. After you get the permit, look for a place where this drama can be presented."

Julio went immediately to the *presidencia* and greeted the alcalde.

"How may we serve you?" asked the latter.

Julio gave a *pagaré* (an IOU) for the official document. The price was three pesos.

Then he went in search of a corral and after an hour or so he found what he wanted. He gave the proprietor of the place his *pagaré* for five pesos. Thereupon he went to the inn to report to Antonio.

"Now," said Antonio, "go and find us some music. We shall need the best orchestra available."

Julio was told by a violinist in a saloon where he could get an orchestra. He presented himself to the conductor and they came to terms. Julio gave this man his *pagaré* for twenty pesos. Julio told him to put up a front of music at the corral at seven o'clock that evening.

"Make all the pleasant music you can," said Julio. "We want a large attendance."

He felt that luck had been with him up to this point, yet he began to have a few doubts about Antonio. "How did he know my name when we first met on the road?" he thought. "Furthermore, if this wild dream about a drama comes to naught, who will pay the twenty-eight pesos I owe in *pagarés*? And who is to give this *comedia*? For my part, I don't know a jot about acting. *Quién sabe?* I shall speak to Antonio about this."

He was almost breathless from haste and worry when he encountered Antonio.

"*Amigo mío,*" he blurted out. "Where are the actors for our *comedia?*"

"They are awaiting us at the corral," said Antonio.

By eight o'clock the corral was full to overflowing with people eager to see the show. Antonio and an actress presented the first *auto.* Then Julio and a younger girl gave the second. It seemed as though he recited by magic. What beautiful words! What charming sentiments!

Then a third *auto* was given and Antonio rose and thanked the crowd for the favorable reception. "Now, my amiable *audiende,*" he continued, "señoras and señores, this orchestra is yours for the remainder of the night. Dance and be happy, for no one knows what tomorrow will bring."

The following morning Julio paid his debts and he and Antonio left the city.

After two weeks of travel they came to the foot of a high mountain. They climbed to the top and paused on a peak.

"Julio," said Antonio, "from here we see the world. With our money and directions wherever one looks, what else is there to wish for? Where shall we go from here?"

"*Pues, no le hace,*" said Julio. "Wherever you say is all right with me."

"Thanks for your confidence," said Antonio. "However, Julio, don't you think you are a bit too trusting? Don't be too innocent, *amigo.*"

After they had descended halfway down the peak Antonio stopped suddenly and said: "Do you see that large house at the base of the canyon?"

"That is no house," said Julio. "It is only a canyon wall in many colors."

"Yes," said Antonio, disregarding the words of Julio, "it is

not only a large house but a city of houses. Let's spend the
night there."

"*Pues, está bueno,*" shrugged Julio, "but we shall be lucky
to find a cave in which to sleep tonight."

"Look, *amigo,*" said Antonio. "Man is endowed with sight,
some more, some less. There are those who see with the eyes
of animals, and others can glimpse the supernatural. Wake up,
amigo, and clear your eyes for we are soon to enter an enchanted
city. Already I see the king's castle, and, by the way, there is
some writing on the door, and this writing says, 'My daughter
the princess shall marry the man who can read her thoughts.'
Go, Julio, and see this *rétulo* for yourself, and tell the king that
you will guess the thoughts of his daughter."

With a world of misgivings Julio descended into the canyon
and to his amazement found himself reading the inscription
on the castle door.

"Why are you here, young man?" asked the king.

"I," said Julio, "I have come to explore the mind of the
princess, Your Majesty."

"My young friend," said the king, "that has never been done
since the day of the tragic enchantment ages ago. Be it known
to you that a wicked sorcerer holds my daughter and my city
in a spell. However, if you wish to try your luck you may do so;
but mind you, the price of failure is death."

"I shall read your daughter's thoughts," said Julio. "*Hasta
mañana.* I shall return then."

That night the sorcerer spoke with the princess and said:
"Tomorrow a young man will come to tell you what you think.
Remember, you are to meditate upon yourself, then ask him:
'Can you guess my thoughts?'"

In the meantime Antonio had said to Julio: "When the
king's daughter asks you to reveal her thought, you are to say:
'You think about yourself,' and then without another word you
are to return to me, for that *mal genio* is going to demand two
more trials and we want to be prepared for him. He is a sly

one, *muy ladino,* and I don't trust him. Tomorrow, the second time you are tested, you are to say: 'You think about your shoes.' "

"And the day after that?" asked Julio.

"*Poco a poco,*" said Antonio. "I am preparing a surprise for this *mágico poderoso.*"

The second test was as easy as the first, and Julio without so much as a courteous farewell returned to Antonio.

The third day Julio faced the princess with a sack containing the head of the *genio.* "You were told," said Julio, "to concentrate upon the head of the sorcerer. Here is his head."

The king was overjoyed at Julio's success. He said to him: "Tonight, my son, you sleep here in my castle."

In this enchanted city there had been no sounds for ages. Julio had heard nothing further than the words of the princess and her father. That night, however, while in a dull half-sleep he awoke to the distant tolling of a bell. This was followed by the dismal wail of a dog. And then burros and roosters began braying and crowing. Now a *sereno* called out: "Twelve o'clock and all is well." Thereupon, people began shouting: "*Viva la vida!*" There were parades, and marching of soldiers and bands on the streets. With unrestrained emotion the people were shouting over and over again: "*Viva la vida! Viva la vida!*"

At dawn the streets were silent again. The inhabitants of the city walked about as if in a dream.

"Julio," said Antonio, "we have more to do. Go now to the king and tell him you want his daughter in marriage. He will consent, for that was a condition of the *rétulo.* But, first, you must insist on taking a walk with the girl. Take her to the lagoon in the brush near the suburbs and tell her to strip and bathe. She will refuse and then you are to whip her with a willow switch. Hit her hard and force her into the water. When she leaves the lagoon a young mare will come to the bank for water. Whip this filly into the lagoon. When she leaves a dove will settle upon a branch near you. Catch this dove and whip it into the lagoon as you did with the princess and the mare. After this your marriage will be a happy one, for your wife will obey you. She will not be giddy and wild, and best of all, she will not go about sighing. Now, my friend Julio, *adiós*."

"No," said Julio, "you are not leaving. I shall provide for you in my castle."

"*Amigo*, you must be a bit more *desconfiado*. You don't know me," said Antonio. "I was in your home twice and there I learned your name."

"But I had never seen you before our chance meeting upon a path three weeks ago."

"Do you remember the body you buried the morning before we met? I am that body. I am Death."

With this Death departed. Julio bathed his princess, the mare, and the dove in the lagoon. For years and years he and his queen lived happily. Indeed, there is no recorded history that Death ever came again to the disenchanted city.

This story comes from Francisco Agüero in Coahuila, Mexico.

Juan and the Bony One

THIS WAS A TIME of scarcity in a land far away many years ago. A mother called her three sons and said to them:

"My sons, as you well know, times are hard. We must have food, and that means one of you must seek work."

The oldest boy, a vain and presumptuous young man, said: "Mother, we must think of our honor. But since you suggest it, I shall leave for some distant land where I am not known and get a job."

After much travel this young man came to the castle of a king and was enlisted to help guard the palace. Weeks and months passed, and he sent no word to his family.

Now, with only three mouths to feed instead of four, the family should have fared better, but food was scarce. For breakfast there was for each a cup of *atole* made by grinding up old tortillas and mesquite beans. At noon the meal consisted of one tortilla and a small serving of beans for each. And for supper, when there was anything at all to eat, it was a tortilla.

One day the second son left home, presumably in search of work. He, too, by chance, went to the king's palace and was hired as a page. He did not write home to tell the mother that he had found his brother and that each had a job.

Finally the mother said to Juan, her youngest son: "Juanito, you are now a big boy. I want you to go in search of your brothers. I fear they have come to harm in some land far away."

Thus it was that Juan asked for the blessings of his mother and departed. After much wandering, he, too, came to the castle of the king and was placed in the stables as a *caballerango*. And by pure chance he met his brothers. The latter were displeased that he had taken employment as a stableboy. An argument followed and one of the two said to him: "We are ashamed of you. If people here learn that you are our brother, we shall see to it that the king sends you home."

Juan was a good boy and wept at their insults. But also, Juan was a stubborn boy and refused to quit his job.

The king had a *remuda* of fine horses, and Juan fed and brushed them daily. One of these horses, though, had been losing weight.

"Juanito," said His Majesty, "this horse has been the best in my stables, but now he is nothing but skin and bones. Also, he has begun to balk and lie down whenever he is saddled. I would give my daughter in marriage to anyone who can cure him."

It was about this time that the queen died, and the king forthwith issued a *bando* in which he asked that some brave man cross the waters of the sea and bring back a beautiful princess who lived there.

"I must have a queen immediately," he said.

The older brothers, that is to say, the page and the guard, read this *bando* and plotted to destroy Juan. They went to the king and told him that Juanito had boasted that he could fetch the princess.

"Juanito," said His Majesty, "I was told that you have been bragging about how easy it would be to cross the sea and bring the princess to us."

"No, Your Majesty, I have said nothing of the sort."

"All the same, Juanito, you are going to make good your boast, or I shall see to it that you are hanged as a stupid fool. Think it over and give me your answer in three days. I like you, my boy, and would hate to see you hanged."

Juan returned to the stable, his face all *pucheritos* and a sea of tears.

"What's wrong?" asked the poor horse, who by now had taken a liking to Juan.

"No, nothing," said Juan, "only that the king has threatened my life if I don't bring him a princess from abroad."

"Don't worry," said the horse, who now was known as the Bony One. "We shall manage to carry out his command."

On the third day Juan went to the king and agreed to go over the sea for the princess.

"How much money will you need?" asked the king.

"I will need no money. Arrange that food be prepared for me and grain for my mount, and I shall leave immediately," said Juan.

The following morning the king and his noblemen were at the corral when Juan saddled for his journey.

"You fool!" shouted His Majesty. "Why ride the Bony One? Get the boy a good horse. On that *penco* he will go perhaps a league, and then the *mañoso* will balk and lie down."

"Either I ride this horse or I refuse to go," said Juan.

At midday he came to a small meadow in the mountains, and in the very center of this meadow was a tall pine, and high in the tree sat a bird singing.

"We shall rest here," said the Bony One, "and by the way, as we eat, feed that bird. He may fit in our plans later."

The bird ate and said: "If you should ever need me, just call out: *'Aquí de mi pajarito.'*"

The horse and his rider spent the night near the sea. At dawn a fish came to the shore. The horse said that it should be fed.

"He may fit in our plans later," he said.

After the fish had eaten it breathed bubbles through the water, and said: "Should you ever need me, just call: *'Aquí de mi pescadito.'*"

"We should be on our way," said the Bony One. "Mount now, blindfold yourself, lift the reins, and we shall cross the sea."

When they reached the distant shore the horse had changed to a high-spirited animal of seven colors. They proceeded to the plaza of a large city. "Now, Juan, we shall do a *vuelta* around the square so the princess can see us. Straighten your back and ride with pride. Leave the rest to me."

The princess saw them and asked her father if she might ride the beautiful horse of seven colors. The king sent for Juan and explained that the princess wanted to ride his horse a couple of *vueltas* around the square. Juan said he felt greatly honored that so beautiful a girl should want to ride his horse, but he said this particular animal would permit no one other than himself to mount him.

The king laughed and said: "Young man, I have *jinetes* in my cavalry that can ride anything on four legs. Leave the riding to us."

He sent for a *domador*. The latter approached the horse of seven colors and *allí fue Troya*. The horse backed his ears, bared his teeth, and would have killed the breaker had Juan not calmed him down.

"If it should please Your Majesty," he said, "let the princess mount behind me."

While soldiers were taking security measures by blocking all exits to the square, the horse of seven colors told Juan that after they had completed the second *vuelta* with the princess, he should then close his eyes and lift the reins.

Thus it was that the princess was kidnapped and brought to the king who wanted to marry her. After she was informed of the king's intentions, she said: "I lost a *tumbaga* while crossing the sea. I shall marry no one until it is found and returned to me."

Again the brothers, motivated by their criminal hatred, devised a new plan to destroy Juan. They went to the king and told him that Juanito had boasted he could find the ring.

"Likely the rogue stole it on the way over," said the king. "Send him to me."

"Juanito," said he, "I hear you have been boasting again, and just for that, I am demanding that you, within three days, produce a ring the princess lost while crossing the sea. If you fail, you will be hanged."

Juan returned to the stables, and his friend, the one of seven colors, observed his sadness.

"Is the king demanding the impossible again?" asked the horse. "Don't worry, we shall manage somehow. Remember our friend the fish?"

They went to the shore and Juan called out: "*Aquí de mi pescadito.*" The fish appeared and was asked to help find the ring. And in less time than it takes to say *santiamén*, Juan held the *tumbaga* in his hand. And when it was presented to the princess the king was overjoyed and cried out: "Now we shall marry!"

"No," said the princess. "I shall marry no one until I have been given a small flask of the Water of Life."

And again the king issued a *bando*, but no one knew where to seek the Water of Life. And again Juan's brothers sought to destroy him. The king sent for him and gave him three days to find a flask of *el Agua de la Vida*.

Juan took his sadness to the horse again. "We shall manage somehow," said the latter.

They went to the tall pine in the small meadow and Juan called: "*Aquí de mi pajarito.*" A small flask was tied to the bird's foot, and it flew away to the mountains that spent the time bumping their heads together just to make the boulders roll. Zigzagging and darting hither and thither to avoid the rolling stones, it filled the flask at the Spring of Life, and returned.

"Ah," said the king, "the third time charms. Now, to be sure, we shall marry."

"Yes," said the princess, "but first, I must have permission of the *Pájaro Cu.* I shall marry no one without its consent."

Again the king issued a *bando.* And again the brothers sought to destroy Juan. And the king gave the latter three days to bring the *Pájaro Cu* to the princess.

"The bird is in the land of the Moors," said the horse. "The *Paisano* and the *Tecolote* have been looking for it for ages. Mount, close your eyes, lift the reins, and we shall go fetch the fine-feathered bird. Now, when we get to the *morisma,* we shall give a few *vueltas* about the plaza. When you see the Moors with their eyes closed, beware. They see when they seem to sleep."

They went about the square until all the Moors had their eyes open. Then Juan stole the *Pájaro Cu,* golden cage and all *(con toi jaula de oro),* closed his eyes, lifted the reins, and was soon home again at the palace.

The king was in the corral when Juan returned. "Take the bird to the princess," he ordered. And then he approached the horse. "What a beautiful animal!" he said as he came near. Suddenly, the horse of seven colors wheeled and kicked the king dead.

"Now, Juan, go marry the king's daughter, for it is generally known that he promised the princess in marriage to anyone who could fatten me and cure me of balking and lying down," said the one of seven colors.

After the wedding, the foreign princess was returned across the waters of the sea to her father. A regal *bando* was issued

to the effect that Juan's brothers be dragged to death by wild
mules. The mother was brought to the palace to live with Juan
and his queen, and the Bony One, who is no longer bony, but
rolling in fat, never balks and never lies down, not even while
asleep.

*This story was told me in 1930 in Piedras Negras by an old man who
had been a friend of General Alberto Guagardo.*

Klis-to E-e-ki Ta-u-ue-a

I-NI, WELL, you know in your heart that buzzards are a slow-
thinking sky-people who eat dead things. Yet, once upon a time
they were clean and beautiful. Even it is said that they were
captains of all sky-people.

I-ni, well, that was before the time Ta-u-ue-a (buzzard) left
Klis-to (Christ) hanging on the horn of the moon.

Klis-to needed blue paint for his face. He gazed at the blue
of the sky and wondered how he could get there. It was then
that Ta-u-ue-a came to Klis-to and they understood. Ta-u-ue-a
said: "As you wish, I shall carry you to the blue of the sky."

Ka-pot-ue, then, he said: "Get up here on my back."

Ta-u-ue-a went flying away, up and up, and left Klis-to on
the horn of the moon. "You wait here," he said, "while I look
for something to eat. When I come back we shall return to the
earth."

Ta-u-ue-a forgot to come back and Klis-to was tired. He
called over and over again: "Hey, *ne-ci-the* [my uncle], I am
tired. Come and get me."

No one came and Klis-to was angry.

Klis-to said: "He doesn't come back. I have been here for
ten hours and can stand this hanging and waiting no longer.
I am going to let go."

He changed to a leaf and fell earthward. He prayed to God
that he not fall on the ground. "Let me fall in a hollow tree,"
was his supplication.

And here he is in a hollow tree waiting and wondering what to do next. He changed back to Klis-to from a leaf.

A *pa-ci-to* (little old man) and a *me-che-mo-a* (little old woman) were in the forest looking for firewood and small game. The *me-che-mo-a* carried an ax and the *pa-ci-to* a bow and arrows.

It was then the *me-che-mo-a* found the hollow tree and began to chop. Klis-to heard and wondered who made the noise. "Perhaps it is my younger brother *a-me-kua* [beaver]," he said.

"Let me out," called Klis-to. "In here I can neither go up nor down. Cut a bigger hole."

The *me-che-mo-a* was frightened. "He talks our language," she said, "and he talks Castilian. He is not an animal. He is a man."

Klis-to came from the hollow tree and spoke to them. "I wish you pleasure," he said. "You thought I was a bear in that tree. *Na-hi*, all right, I have three bears for you, a mother and two cubs. *Nu-ui-nu ma-kue-he* [come out, bear]," he said.

The *pa-ci-to*, while running this way and that behind trees and bushes, made ready with his bow and arrows. The *me-che-mo-a* climbed a tree. The animals came out, one by one, and were killed.

"I give you these," said Klis-to. "I have just arrived here from the sky. When you speak of me to the *me-to-se-ne-ni* [Indian people] they will want proof that you saw me. Since some do not believe what their eyes can't see, I have provided you with *ma-kua* meat. That should be convincing since the bow and arrows of *pa-ci-to* are not for bear but are for small game."

I-ni. Now about Ta-u-ue-a. Klis-to was still angry and wondered how he could trap and punish Ta-u-ue-a for leaving him so long on the moon.

"When I was on his back, he smelled bad," said Klis-to. "I believe he has been with dead animals."

Klis-to threw himself on the ground, changed to a dead fox, and bloated his belly. Ta-u-ue-a was flying high when he saw this animal.

"*Ku!*" he said. "Something is dead."

Ta-u-ue-a came to earth not too close to the dead fox. "I must take care," he said, "for he may be alive."

He stopped and stared with one eye and then with the other. Then, with much caution, he came closer still. He looked to the sky and all about.

The fox, now Klis-to, sprang to his feet and caught him.

"You forgot me," said Klis-to to Ta-u-ue-a. "You left me to hang ten hours on the moon. Even sky-people are punished for their faults. I shall hold you captive for ten years. Even on the day of the dance I shall hold you. I shall strip you of your honor among the sky-people and no longer will you be known as Ui-na-kue-e, but simply as Ta-u-ue-a [buzzard]."

And this is why he is as he is.

I-ni-me-ke-kui-ke-ke-ne-ma-ki. (This is as far as I know.)

This story was told to me by a Kickapoo woman, known as La Pachita, in Nacimento in Coahuila.

Seein' Snakes

> Pan para los muchachos,
> Cebada para los machos
> Y vino para los borrachos.

ONE EVENING after supper, while in Músquiz, Coahuila, Mexico, I sat at a table in a saloon working on my Kickapoo notes, when an uninvited guest showed up at my side.

"Wad chu do?" he asked.

"Oh, nothing in particular," I answered.

He leaned low over my paper, closed an eye, and studied the words. The odor of his breath was like sour sorghum. It was evident that he was a bit high on something, and that something was not water.

"*Quiere una copa de añejo?*" I asked.

"I no like tequila," he said. "I take a wheeskley. I like a dark dreenk an' a white woman. Wad chu do; you write a somethin'?"

"I am gathering folklore," I told him. "Do you know a *cuento* you would like to tell?"

"Chu wan' me tell a story, wan thaz no lie?"

"*Cuento o historia; no le hace.*" (A story or a bit of history; it doesn't matter.)

His eyes seemed to focus for an instant and he said: "Chu know wan time som' boys they wanna peek feegs. The tree, he ees tall. Wan boy, he don' know wad ees a feeg. A boy, he climb in the tree and throw feegs down an' the odder boys, they peek um op and eat um. The boy wad don' know whad ees a feeg, he ask: 'How many legs does have the feeg?' The boys say: 'The feeg no have a leg.'

" 'Hah,' say the boy who don' know wad ees a feeg. 'I chos eat wan weeth four legs.' Wad chu know! The dam fool keed, he eat a frog. Ha, ha, thas a good story, no?"

"Fine," I said, working fast with my pencil. "Let's have another."

"Mebbe so, mebbe no, chu no like a story 'bout San Isiro? Okydokie! San Isiro, he had a girl wan time. She wanna go to a peekneek and she borrow a reeng from anudder girl. That girl she geed seek an' die. These girl, she no like to ask for reeng back from a dead girl, bot wan day she go to San Isiro an' tellum: 'San Isiro, the girl, she die I loan um reeng. I like to geed the reeng.' San Isiro, he look an' canna fin' the reeng. San Isiro he say: 'Chu wait.'

"San Isiro he go to the grave an' pray. He ask the girl where ees the reeng, and the girl tellum from the grave where ees the reeng."

"Ah; mebbe so chu like anoder. Thees ees about . . . wad chu callum? . . . ah . . . ship man."

"A sailor," I prompted.

"No, no, ship man, ship man, wan man who goes in mountains weeth the ships."

"Sheep man?" I gambled.

"Yes, ship man." (Why he insisted on a short *i* instead of a long *e* sound in the word sheep, I shall never know.) "A ship man an' a nun...no...a man...wad chu callum, San Isiro, wad chu callum...ah, a monk, thaz what, a monk, San Isiro.

"The ship man, he work out. San Isiro he paz that way. He say: 'Wad chu doin'?' The ship man, he say: 'I make a leevin' for the keeds. I heet on the rocks, break um op, sell um, make money.'

"A snake, she ron by. San Isiro peek um op and she is torn [turned to] gol'. 'Take a snake to three ball shop, an' the *gachupín*, he geeve chu some leetle money,' say San Isiro.

"The ship man, he tak' a snake waz now gol'. The *gachupín* he see the snake she is all gol'. When ship man wanna leetle money the *gachupín* sholers [shoulders] they go op. He's glad to geeve leetle money for gol' snake.

"Later, the ship man, he go to getta snake and the *gachupín* he say: 'No gottum. Somebody stealum. She's gone.'

"Ship man, he go back to San Isiro. San Isiro he tellum: 'Chu go anoder time.' Ship man he go anoder time. And the *gachupín* he say: 'No gottum snake. She get away.' Ship man, he go to San Isiro anoder time. San Isiro he say: 'Chu go thir' time. Tellum chu chos wanna see snake, an' not to takeum, chos to see um.'

"The *gachupín*, he open box where ees the snake an' the snake no longer gol'. She's chos snake."

"*Qué cuento tan curioso* [what a curious story]," I said.

"Thaz no *cuento*," said my tipsy friend. "Thaz no lie. I see um weeth the two eyes."

Destiny

Two BROTHERS, Juan and Pedro, had inherited the family *granja*. This was a good farm, very fertile and well located with regard to market and water; but it was small.

"Our homestead," said the father before he died, "is large

enough for both of you if you will work it together. Whatever you do, don't divide it."

But Juan, a dreamer, wasn't satisfied. "It is not right that I get as much of this land as Pedro," he said. "I, a *soltero*, need little, while Pedro with his large family needs much. I shall never feel right about this, and there is only one thing to be done—I shall sell my part and leave."

Pedro, with his good heart and level head, tried to dissuade Juan from his purpose, but for all his goodness, he got nowhere. Juan received cash for his interest in the farm and left the old homestead.

Within a few years he had lost all his money in wild investments and get-rich-quick schemes. Then he was forced to work at odd jobs. He did not complain until he began pondering over the big problem of *mine* and *thine*. "Destiny," he said, "Destiny has dealt badly with me, yet, I deserve what I have come by. My brother said once that gold was to be had from the soil of the *granja*, and that '*a veces el oro no resplandece*' [sometimes gold doesn't glisten]. I wonder how it goes with Pedro now."

He wandered back toward the family farm. Eventually, he came to a large wheat field. He asked a passerby who owned it and was told that a certain señor Tal para Cual was the proprietor. Later he saw a beautiful orchard, and still later a rich vineyard. These too, he was informed, were owned by the same señor Tal para Cual, who was none other than Pedro himself. Suddenly, Juan became bitter, not against Pedro, but against his own *mala suerte* (bad luck, fate).

"I have tried, *según mis miras*, to make a go of life," he complained. "Something somewhere, is wrong, and I can't get my hands on it to correct it."

Just then he spied a beautiful old woman seated beneath an arbor. "Who owns this?" he asked.

"It belongs to your brother Pedro," answered the woman.

"How does it happen that you know me?" he asked.

"For the simple reason that I am your brother's *suerte*."

"*Dispénseme,* but will you tell me how I am to find the one who holds my fortune in her hand?"

"Seek and thou shalt find," she said.

Feeling somewhat relieved, Juan went to his brother's house. Here he was welcomed as a prodigal. He was fed and clothed and asked to make the *granja* his home. However, he was intent on finding his *suerte,* and one morning, at early dawn, he set out on his search.

He hadn't proceeded far when he came upon an old hag near a gutter. She was asleep and seemed the worse off for drink. He nudged her awake with his foot and asked, "Who are you?"

"I am your *suerte,*" she said. "You can thank my long siesta for those fine clothes you wear. If I had been awake you wouldn't have them."

"Do you hate me so much as all that?" he asked.

"Don't blame me. You should speak to El Destino [Destiny]."

"How do I find El Destino?"

She directed him to a hermit who lived in a cave some leagues away. This old man referred him to one older yet; and the latter, in turn, sent him farther into the mountains to the oldest hermit in the land.

"I have come to ask you the directions to El Destino," said Juan.

"Young man, I have lived in these parts for a mighty long time and I'm sorry that I can't help you. Yet, I rule the birds of the air; and if you will wait until sunup I'll call them in; and, perhaps, one of them knows about this El Destino," said the third and oldest hermit.

At dawn, the following morning, this old man with the long white beard whistled three times; and the birds of the air, all except one, came to him. He whistled again and again. Far on the distant horizon they saw an eagle. At last he lit near his master and said, "I heard you call, but I was attending a festival given by El Destino. I regret my delay."

"Very well," said the hermit. "Take this man on your back and return to El Destino."

When Juan and the eagle reached the home of Destiny, the bird said, "When you enter there, do as others do. If they eat, you eat; if they sleep, you sleep; and above all, speak only when spoken to."

Juan had been in the house of Destiny three days before he was noticed, and then Destiny said to him, "Do you have a complaint?"

"Yes," said Juan. "I want the same *suerte* as possessed by my brother, Pedro."

"Predestination rules against that," said El Destino. "Yet, since you have gone to so much trouble to get here, I will help you. Return to your brother's home and ask him for his sister-in-law in marriage. Thanks to Pedro, she now has a *granja* in her own name. But there is one condition: after the wedding you must never refer to the property as belonging to you. You must always say: *'Es de mi mujer'* [it belongs to my wife]." With that, Juan was dismissed.

He married the sister of his brother's wife.

One day while out looking over the *granja* he met a stranger. "Whose land is this?" asked the man.

"It belongs to my wife," said Juan.

Days later some men were admiring this property. "It is an ideal farm," they said.

Then turning to Juan, who stood near, they asked, "To whom does this beautiful farm belong?"

"It is mine," said Juan.

These men went on their way. Suddenly, Juan realized that the field of ripe wheat was ablaze. He was quick to gather the reason for this and ran after the strangers. "Listen!" he called, "Listen! I lied. This field belongs to my wife."

The fire lifted and was out immediately.

Never, after that, did Juan forget. His Destiny was that he was to live all the rest of his life tied to the apron strings of his wife.

Told by Avelina Dóñez, Zacatecas, Mexico.

Silbado

THIS WAS A YOUTH who was so restless and disobedient that his mother found it necessary to turn him over to an *ayo* for his training and education. The new order in his life had hardly begun when he ran away.

He followed a road out of town and then entered the mountains. After two weeks of wandering with no recommendation whatever either to God or the devil, he came to the shore of a large body of water. He made a raft and set sail for nowhere in particular. Ten days and nights had passed before he reached land. This country was covered with a growth resembling bamboo. Some of it reached fourteen meters high. He found a trail and was following it, all the while wondering where it led, when he heard the trot-trot of a horse. He dropped to the ground and hid.

A giant on a giant-size horse came along the trail. He stopped near where Silbado was hidden. The latter heard him mumble something about a good wheat harvest, and then it dawned on him that he was not in a canebrake but in a wheat field.

The horse became restless and the giant looked to the ground, doubtless thinking of a snake. He saw Silbado, leaned from his saddle, and picked him up.

"What a curious little plaything," said the giant. "I shall take this *monito* to my daughter."

This girl was fourteen years old and fourteen meters tall. She was thrilled with her new toy, and presently she and her father began making a cage in which to keep Silbado. It was large and more like a house than a cage. Before supper the giantess took him to a bathtub to wash him, and he almost drowned. The tub was several meters long and the water was over his head. At supper he was given a bowl of broth. He had to stand on tiptoes to reach into the bowl. The girl took him to a piano and placed him on the keys. She was amused by the noise he made running and skipping along, back and forth, from one end of the instrument to the other.

The governor of a city nearby sent a request to the effect that the strange little *monito* be brought to him so the people could see for themselves the unusual creature that had been found in a wheat field. The girl picked up the cage, placed it on her shoulder, and, accompanied by her father, went to the city.

The people were so amazed they decided to celebrate for three days. These giants stuffed their lunch baskets and went to a nearby forest, where they prepared camp. Silbado's mistress hung his cage from a limb of a large tree and the music, eating, and dancing began.

During the celebration a large eagle swooped down, clutched the cage in his claws, and flew away. Finally the cage, or house, was dropped in the sea. Luckily, Silbado floated toward another shore some days away where his house was thrown on land by a tidal wave and Silbado escaped.

"This is what disobedience has brought me," said he. "If ever I get home I shall listen more to my mother."

After much wandering, *a la buena de Dios,* he finally arrived home.

The friends of his *camada* (age) asked Silbado many questions and were carried away by the narrative of his amazing adventures.

"We want to see all this for ourselves," they said.

It was very evident that they did not believe what they had been told, and Silbado felt so compromised he agreed to take them to the territory of the giants; however, his mother said he needed school more than new adventures.

Ten years drifted by and there was never a day that someone did not remind him of the wild story he had told about seeing giants. They began calling him Catorce.

"Listen, Catorce," they would say. "Tell us that tale again. Now let's see; that *chamaca* was fourteen years old and she was fourteen meters tall, and the wheat was fourteen meters high, and surely the height of the horse was fourteen meters. Ay, Catorce!"

Finally, since his mother had passed away and he was not needed around the place, he told his ten friends that he was tired of being called a liar.

"We shall leave within a week on that adventure you have asked for, if it so please you, and if you have the *agallas* [guts]," he said.

After two weeks of travel over the mountains they came to the sea, where they built a large raft and shoved off, hoping for all sorts of thrills.

Once ashore again, they followed the beach. At last they saw a large house. Upon approaching it they found it closed. However, the corral was open and they entered, sat down in a corner, and rested.

Suddenly, there were noises like claps of thunder. They were caused by a giant who slammed doors when he came into the corral from the house. He saw them. He immediately shut the gate to the corral and built a large fire. One of Silbado's friends was picked up, put on a spit, and roasted alive. Then the giant, after eating the man, returned to the house but forgot to close the door.

"We are in a bad fix, Silbado," said one of the men. "We must find a way out of here. Sh . . . come; let's follow him."

They found the giant asleep on a mat. Returning to the corral, they heated an iron bar until it glowed; then they went to the monster, and stabbed him through the heart. When they were sure he was dead, they fled to their raft on the beach.

They reached the raft just in time, since another giant was

hot on their heels. This big fellow took two steps into the sea after them, struck the raft a side-blow with his hand, and three of the men were drowned.

Out at sea again, the raft ran into a storm and all aboard were lost except Silbado.

Reaching land, he began wandering and came to a city where all the vaqueros rode bareback. He asked why they didn't use saddles.

"*Pues, no es la costumbre*," was the answer he received to his question.

He made a saddle and persuaded a man to try it out. The vaquero liked it He made more saddles and sold them. And after that he made bridles.

He had become rich as a saddlemaker and decided to get married.

"That is all very good," said a friend, "but there are some things you need to know. Here in our country a *matrimonio* [a married couple] is buried together should one of them die. Are you willing to be buried alive should your wife die?"

"Yes," said Silbado.

He had been married two years when his wife died. He was placed in a box and was carried into a large cave with the body of his wife. After some hours he took out his knife and cut a hole in his box.

He escaped and after much groping he found an opening to the cave. In the dark of the night that followed, Silbado reached the sea, where he found a small boat.

Many days passed on the water and in the mountains before he reached home again.

"*Gracias a Dios*," he said. "Never, if it be God's will, shall I leave this place again."

Told to me by Santiago Garza in Marfa, Texas, August, 1929. (The indebtedness of this cuento to Gulliver's voyage to Brobdingnag and to Odysseus' adventure with Polyphemus is obvious. — Eds.)

Satan and the Boy

ONCE UPON A TIME there was a boy who, while seeking work, met Satan himself.

It was on the outskirts of a town that this boy encountered a well-dressed man and, after greetings, told the stranger that he was seeking employment.

"I have been looking for a *mozo*," said the señor. "Do you know how to read?"

"Sí, señor," answered the youth.

"That is too bad; I want a boy who cannot read," said the man.

Then the boy said: "In that case, possibly, you will give work to my brother. He is *muy listo,* but hasn't learned to read yet. On up the way you will likely meet him."

The youth proceeded along in the direction he had taken, and when out of sight of the man, he doubled back, cut across a chaparral, stopped, put his poncho and hat on backward, and by running fast, came into the road ahead of the stranger. And presently they met.

The señor, or Satan, for indeed it was he, greeted him, presuming this youth to be the brother of the one he had just met, and asked where he was going.

"I am out looking for work," said the boy.

"Can you read?" asked Satan.

"No, señor," answered the youth.

"I have been looking for a *mozo* to keep my office and library clean," said Satan.

After taking over his new job the boy, by stealing glances at the titles of the books on the library shelves, realized for the first time who his master was, and whenever the latter was away from home, he read with deep interest one book after another, and became a master in diabolical arts.

However, one day Satan discovered him reading and was furious. He was preparing to flog him when the boy, using his newly acquired skills, changed into a jackrabbit. Immediately, in order to catch him, Satan became a greyhound, and was about to pounce upon him when his intended victim changed into a dove. Not to be outdone by a mere youth, Satan metamorphosed into a hawk. The race was swift and desperate with much darting about on the part of both of them. The hawk, by maneuvering skilfully, was gaining on the dove when the latter changed into a pebble and fell to the earth. Thereupon, the hawk became a grain of rice. The pebble immediately changed into a rooster who found the rice and ate it.

Since then, Satan has always kept a weather eye out for tricks when in the presence of boys.

From José Dóñez, Zacatecas, Mexico.

Solomon the Wise

IT IS SAID that Solomon wasn't always discreet in the way he illustrated a truth.

Once he was walking along a street pondering over the weakness of human nature. One of many in a crowd that followed him asked, "Are women good or bad?"

"There are as many kinds of women as there are women," said Solomon; "but in general they are selfish, untruthful, and bad."

"In that case would it be right to point out any one of them as an example?"

"Yes," said Solomon, "we will begin with my mother." He called his mother, who was following at a distance. "*Mamá*," he said, "there is a question that bothers us. We would like to know whether you are bad or good."

"Son, I am good. Do you doubt it?"

Solomon turned to the crowd and asked if anyone felt any wiser, now that his mother had made her comment.

Later that day the shrewd king called one of his servants and said, "Have no fear of consequences. Tomorrow I want you to walk with my mother into the mountains. She won't care to listen to all that you have to say; but regardless of her anger, you are to tell her that she is beautiful, young, and lovely. Shower her with *piropos* [flattery]. Remember, half a word won't be enough. In short, make love to her and tell me later what she said to you."

That afternoon the mother came to Solomon and said, "My son, I have brought you this servant. He has been provoking me. He has insulted you, his king, by saying things to me that I prefer not to mention."

"What would you have me do with him?" asked Solomon. "Let's let him go. I will take care of him later."

"Don't ask me again to associate with anyone so uncouth. This I ask as a favor," said the mother.

"But I want you to go out again, with another servant. I command it."

This time she was accompanied into the fields. They came to a stream and sat on the bank. Later, when she found her son, she said to him, "Son, you are a *cornudo* [pander]. Is there no limit to you? That servant should be hanged, for he wanted to put his arms about me. He was worse than the last."

"Just one more, *mamacita*, and this will be all."

"I shall go only because you have the power to command me to do so," she said.

Solomon's mother and his servant walked along a boulevard. They came to a bench and sat for awhile to rest. This man commented on the spring flowers and particularly on the lilies of the field; he quoted poetry in which there was much mention of love. He made casual reference to this and that girl who passed by, but seemingly ignored the woman by his side.

Then she took the initiative, and before it was over she had invited him to her bedroom after night had drawn over the city. "Knock on my door three times," she said, "and I shall let you in."

The servant reported all this to Solomon. The latter changed clothes with the servant and kept his appointment for him. He knocked on the mother's door and was told to come in; but he refused, saying in a muffled voice that she should open for him.

"My son!" she gasped when he entered.

Then she began to weep, and Solomon asked what she would have him do with the servants for their part in the trick that had been played on her.

"Nothing," she said. "Let them go in peace."

"Mother," said Solomon, "only a few days ago you told me you were good. This nature of forgiveness on your part proves that. On the other hand, it was not a good woman who invited a man to her bedroom at this hour of the night. We don't need God's help for our goodness, Mother, but we do need it to protect us from evil. Keep that in mind and we will understand each other."

From Ojinaga, Chihuahua.

El Caballero Porfiado

THIS WAS A KING who was told by a dream spirit that he would soon lose his one and only daughter. In order to be sure that nothing should happen to the princess, he had her moved to a large and luxurious chamber beneath the castle. Here she was placed behind seven locks; and the keys were handed over to a trusted housekeeper with instructions that she was to serve the girl three meals a day, make her bed of a morning, and keep the place clean.

The princess, who was beautiful, modest, and intelligent, seemed little concerned with the mandate of her father the king. She painted, practiced her music, did embroidery, and was contented until one night when she was touched by an invisible hand. The following morning she had the servant fetch the king.

"Father," she said, "last night a Christian came to my room and placed his hands upon me."

"Don't be foolish," said the king. "It is impossible for a Christian, Moor, or anyone else to enter here. You are behind seven locks, and these have one key each. Surely you were dreaming."

The following morning she sent for him again and said she was positive some man had come to her bed and placed his hand upon her brow.

"Listen, my child," said the king. "Would you have me believe that you are losing your mind? Don't bother me again, or I shall flog you."

The father called the maid and they searched every nook and corner of the underground chambers for evidence of someone's having entered the place. Nowhere was there any indication that a stranger had been there.

The following night, as the princess lay awake, she felt a movement on the covers of her bed; and presently a hand rested upon her brow. She did not scream, but calmly asked, "Who are you?"

"Don't fear," said a voice. "It is I, the one destined to take you from this place to Los Llanos de Apa, a long sleep from here. As for my name, it will be your name in marriage within ten years."

Dawn had removed the stars from heaven and had covered the eastern sky with gleams of a new day when the maid opened the last of the seven locks and entered the chamber of the princess.

"*Válgame Dios!*" she gasped. "She is gone! *Válgame Dios!* What is to become of me?"

The father was called. He faced defeat with dignity and vented no rage upon the servant. It was as though he had known all the while that seven locks and seven keys could not prevent the constant and forward strides of time and destiny.

"I should have known," he said. "I should have known. The dream spirit spoke the words of fate."

For weeks past, a venturesome young knight had been

writing to the princess. A bribe had smoothed the way for this. Letters of love had led to their engagement, and the young man had studied and schemed in order to find some way to free the girl, but all to no avail. So it was that when he learned of her mysterious disappearance, his dilemma was so deep he felt unequal to cope with it and took to his feet and wandered away.

A voice came to him from a cabin near his path. "Where goest thou, young man?" it asked.

"I go nowhere," he answered. "I drift *a la buena de Dios.* Be it known unto you, old man and old woman, that the girl I love has been spirited away. A strict father, seven locks, and seven keys could not hold her. There is no hope of happiness for me. Thus it is that I have placed my lot in the hands of blind fate and shall drift until I die."

"Don't be despondent," said the old woman from where she stood with her husband in the doorway of the cabin. "If you knew where to find the girl what would you do?"

"I would go to her immediately," said the youth.

"I can tell you where to find her," said the old man. "She and the magician who freed her stopped by here in their flight to Los Llanos de Apa. Follow on toward the south and you will reach these plains, and let's hope, by good chance, that you come to a small hut with a large door of oak wood."

The young knight bought three tortillas from the old woman and with many thanks for their favor, he left and continued toward the south.

After some hours of travel he came to a tree and while he was resting and eating in its shade three small ants came to where he sat. He dropped crumbs for them and was surprised when one addressed him as follows: "We are grateful for the food. Here is one of my feet. If you should ever need to become an ant hold this foot between your thumb and index finger and say, *'Dios y hormiga.'* And when you wish to be yourself again, you are to say, *'Dios y Cristiano.'* "

After more wandering he came to a lagoon, where he drank

and rested. A hawk that had been soaring above him came down and lit nearby. The young knight took his second tortilla from beneath his blouse and gave part of it to the bird. The latter ate, sat still for a moment, and then asked: "Good young man, why are you traveling over this wide desert?"

"I am looking for Los Llanos de Apa," he answered. "I hope to find there a girl who wandered away from home."

"I have much ill-boding for you, my young friend. You take dire chances with your life. Seeking afoot you will get nowhere and eventually you will die of thirst. Look, I present you with this feather. If, by chance, you should like to fly as a hawk, hold it between your thumb and forefinger and say, 'Dios y gavilán,' and when you wish to become yourself again, say, 'Dios y Cristiano.'"

For two days he continued his journey from dawn to dusk. On the third day he met a lion.

"I am too near death to care what happens to me," thought the young man. "This lion will kill me and that will be the end of all, so why worry."

He walked up to the lion and placed a tortilla on its nose. The animal ate and said, "You have killed my need for food. May I ask where you are going?"

"I seek Los Llanos de Apa," answered the knight.

"Los Llanos are alive with wild beasts," said the lion. "They will kill you."

"That makes little difference," said the youth.

"But you are going to need help," said the lion. "Here, accept this claw. When things seem hopeless, hold it between your thumb and index finger and say, 'Dios y león,' and when you wish to change back to yourself once again, say, 'Dios y Cristiano.'"

The knight continued on his way and presently he heard voices from somewhere within himself and they were saying, "Dios y león, Dios y gavilán, Dios y hormiga, have faith."

Thereupon he took the feather and held it in accordance

with the advice of the hawk. And like a child's kite, he was swooped into the air and went flying over the desert.

Shortly thereafter he found a small hut, and the door was of oak wood. Yet it was closed tight and locked from within. He took the small foot of the ant between his thumb and forefinger and said, "*Dios y hormiga.*"

Presently he found a small crack beneath the door and crawled through, and barely had he caught his breath and changed back to his natural self when he heard a loud voice that sang:

> Jo, jo; carne y hueso huelo aquí,
> Si no me la das, te como a tí.
> (Ho, ho; flesh and bone I smell here,
> If thou doest not give it to me I shall eat you.)

A girl's voice was heard to ask, "Whom do you suspect? No one can enter here."

The *mal genio* picked up a wand, struck a table with it, and within a wink of the eye, he and the missing princess were eating supper. After the meal, the *genio* went about the place closing doors. He turned, said good night, and disappeared.

The ant changed back into a knight and the latter touched the shoulder of the girl. She was startled. "If the magician finds you here he will kill you," she said.

"Not before I have learned the secrets of this place," said the knight. "How can such a little hut have so much room? How did you get here, and how do we leave?"

"When you entered what you thought was a small hut, you came into a large cavern. I don't know how I got here nor how we are to leave," said the girl.

"When you dine tomorrow," said the young man, "see what you can find out. Remember, I shall be near you all the while in the form of an ant."

Then they heard the slamming of doors about the place and presently:

> Jo, jo; carne y hueso huelo aquí,
> Si no me la das, te como a tí.

"Dios y hormiga," said the knight. And he changed to an ant and crawled into the hem of the girl's skirt.

The magician was in a talkative mood; and before long the girl had learned that his soul was in an egg, and the egg was in a dove that was in a room guarded by a large bear. Also she learned that if the egg was broken before the magic time had expired the magician would die immediately.

The *genio* went to his room, the ant changed into a knight again, and the knight changed to a lion and killed the bear. After becoming a young man again, the knight found the dove, got the egg, broke it on the forehead of the magician, and thus destroyed him.

The knight and the princess soon found their way out of the cavern, returned to civilization, and were married.

Told by Jesús Cepeda Barrera from the Sierra Mojada, Chihuahua. He thought he had heard it as early as 1884.

Br'er Rabbit and Br'er Coyote

'MANO CONEJO was feeling out of sorts and combative. This condition of his personality was quite unusual. Possibly, by mistake, he may have peppered his lettuce with gunpowder, or thoughtlessly nibbled at a fermented leaf of sotol. However this may have been, when he met a wax-baby in his private entrance to a *frijolar* (bean patch) that night, he swaggered right up to him and threatened: *"Te quitas o te pego una pescosada* [get away or I'll whang you on the neck]." And without waiting to count ten he began swinging, and ended up, you guessed it, stuck fast to a smirking little wax-baby.

'Mano Coyote had been trailing 'Mano Conejo for over an hour and had had no supper. When he found him stuck to the wax-baby and completely helpless, it was too much for his cautious composure. He began yipping and wailing with laughter. "Now 'Manito Conejito *de mis entrañas* [of my heart and soul], I am going to eat you up, but first, please explain just how you managed to get your hands, your feet, and even your mouth in such a trap."

'Mano Conejo tried to speak but could not say a word. Then 'Mano Coyote caught him by the ears and pulled until his mouth was free.

"I don't care to talk about it," said 'Mano Conejo. "And I know what you intend to do with me." Then he began to weep.

"Listen, 'Manito, your sadness touches my heart," said 'Mano Coyote. "Don't be a crybaby. You are not the first rabbit who has fallen victim to a coyote."

"It isn't that," said 'Mano Conejo. "This getting stuck to a *monito* is a blow to my pride; and that isn't the half of it. Do you know what the owner of this bean patch told me just now? He said . . . ay . . . ay, he said he was going to keep me here for eight days . . . ay . . . ay . . . and feed me nothing but chickens. Ay . . . ay. He should know rabbits don't eat chickens." (Sniff, sniff.) "Oh, it is terrible."

"Listen," said 'Mano Coyote. "We will put one over on the Indio. Quit crying; I'm going to pull you loose. I've an idea."

'Mano Coyote freed the rabbit and stuck himself to the wax-baby and waited impatiently to be served chicken.

The Indio came from his *jacal* with a large bucket of scalding water and drenched 'Mano Coyote in such fashion as to cause him to lose all his hair. However, the hot water melted the wax, and then, 'Mano Coyote, as angry as a wet wasp, went hunting for 'Mano Conejo.

He found him bedded down comfortably beneath a *nopal* and eating *tunas*.

"Now, Conejito," he snarled, "what do you have to say for yourself before I eat you?"

"No, *nada*," said 'Mano Conejo, "only that these *tunas* are delicious. Will you have one? Open your mouth and I shall toss you this one that I have just peeled."

'Mano Coyote caught it and ate it.

"Do you want another? I have a large one here that looks tasty. It is very large so you will have to open your mouth wide."

'Mano Coyote opened his mouth so wide that his eyes were closed. 'Mano Conejo pulled off a leaf covered with dozens of sharp-pointed, needle-like thorns and tossed it into the coyote's mouth. The latter, in a fit of agony, was clawing at his face and rolling over and over when 'Mano Conejo slipped away.

Some days later 'Mano Conejo had found a nest of bumble-bees and he had placed a small, flat rock over the hole and was holding it there when 'Mano Coyote appeared on the scene.

"Now, 'Mano Conejo, we will make this brief and painless."

"Don't be *mal cria'o*," said 'Mano Conejo. "Don't you know it is bad manners to interrupt one's meal?"

"What are you eating?" asked 'Mano Coyote.

"Tamales," was the reply. "I keep them here so others won't find them. To show you that I am a gentleman I shall ignore your threat and ask you to dine with me."

"Are there some made of pork?" asked 'Mano Coyote.

"*Sí, hay*," answered 'Mano Conejo.

"Are there any made of chicken?"

"*Hay.*"

"Are there any that are still hot?"

"*Hay.*"

Then 'Mano Coyote, unable to restrain himself longer, rammed his hand into the hole and immediately jerked it out and began crying, "Ay, ay, ay, ay!"

"*Caramba, hombre*, why the surprise? You act as if I didn't warn you three times!" And the conejo left for safer places.

'Mano Coyote, by now, was really in a bad mood. He trailed 'Mano Conejo with such skill that eventually he found him in a canebrake playing a *jarana* (small guitar).

"*Buenos días*, 'Manito," he said. "Will you play me a piece, say something on the order of table music? I am about to dine on rabbit."

"After the wedding procession has passed," said 'Mano Conejo. "They promised me a lot of good food if I would add happiness to the occasion with my *jarana*. By the way, 'Manito, you with your soprano voice should make a big hit with them. Your specialty is the *huapango*, I know; but you should be able to contribute something that would please them. Take this *jarana* and give them your best with a bit of staccato now and then. Ah, you are superb with staccato. I lie awake at night listening to you."

'Mano Coyote began playing and singing. 'Mano Conejo slipped away and set fire to the canbrake. 'Mano Coyote heard explosions like the popping of firecrackers and began singing louder. Suddenly, he looked about him and saw he was about to be burned alive. After a good scorching he made his escape.

One moonlit night, some days later, he found 'Mano Conejo gazing into a pool. "I am tired of your pranks, 'Mano Conejo. This is your last hour on earth. Do you have anything to say before your execution?"

"No, *nada*," said the 'Manito. "I was sitting here trying to catch my breath before diving for that large, round piece of cheese you see down there in the pool."

The water was clear and the moon was so full and round that we can pardon 'Mano Coyote's mistake, and mistake it was, his last on earth.

"How are you going to manage to dive so far down?" asked 'Mano Coyote.

"I have it all figured out," answered 'Mano Conejo. "I shall tie this large rock to my neck; I shall dive in and it shouldn't be at all hard to tear that cheese loose from the bottom of the pool and bring it up. What a feast we'll have!"

"It's a mighty big cheese for such a little rabbit," said 'Mano Coyote. "Here, tie that rock to my neck and let me bring it up."

The rock was tied tight to the neck of 'Mano Coyote; he dived into the pool and never came to the surface again.

I had this story from a Huastic Indian in Tanquín, Tamaulipas, Mexico.

Don Cacahuate

ONE DAY Don Cacahuate (Peanut) was strolling about a plaza when he met a señorita who wasn't hard to look at.

"*Escucha tu, señorita*," he said. "What is your name?"

Timidly, she blushed and then replied, "*Pos*, Flora Rosa Rosales."

"Come, Flora Rosa," he teased, "let's you and me start a flower garden."

It is said they were married some time thereafter.

A friend took him to task for his laziness.

"Don't you ever have a desire to work?" he asked.

"*Cómo no?*" was the answer from our hero. "I have the desire but *lo aguanto* [I tolerate it].

Often Don Cacahuate was late getting home from his carousals. Flora, his wife, began locking him out. One morning, about three o'clock, he tried the door, and when he found it locked he began screaming: "Flora, open the door for me, open the door, I've been cut."

Flora came running from the house in her nightgown. "Where, where have you been cut?"

"Out, stupid, out from a bunch of horny roughnecks. Come, it is late; let's go to bed."

Civic authorities never permitted Don Cacahuate to settle at any place for long. Like Till Eulenspiegel, he generally left a town just a hop and a half ahead of an officer of the law, or a mob that had been the butt of his pranks. However, upon one occasion, the *presidente municipal* generously gave him one hour in which to leave the region. Don Cacahuate rushed home and shouted: "*Oye vieja*, we are leaving on the railroad. Get your things together in a hurry; we have to be at the station within thirty minutes."

Going places by train was Flora's weakness. She ran about the place in a happy flurry, gathering her few little possessions in a *morral*, and hurried after her husband, who reached the station ahead of her and kept walking with long strides down the track.

"*Epa* [listen]," Cacahuate," she called, "people catch the the train at the station."

"What train, by my father," said Don Cacahuate as he kept right on hotfooting it down the track. "I didn't tell you we were going by train, but on the *ferrocarril* [railroad]; hurry, walk faster or the syndicate will be charging us for the use of the tracks."

Once he tried his luck in Texas. He learned to wear a Stetson and levis. Also he learned a smattering of English. When he returned to Chihuahua he began showing off his new language. One day, as he followed a wagon road, riding his famous horse Pinto Verde, he met a man driving six burros hitched to a heavy wagon. Our Don, trying hard to look and act the part of a *tejano*, rolled himself a cigarette and approached the wagon; and holding his unlit *pita* before him, he said: "Alo, compadre, you gottie maeches [matches, understood as *machos*, mules]?"

"*No, señor*," responded the driver, "*son puros burros* [just burros]."

He and Pinto Verde were following a narrow trail in the mountains one day when they found it blocked by a dead animal. Don Cacahuate couldn't make out what it was, so he dismounted for a close inspection.

"*Válgame Dios!*" he exclaimed. "I wonder what killed this mosquito!"

Flora Rosa Rosales de Cacahuate was very coquettish. She flirted around so much that Don Cacahuate eventually began to doubt the paternity of his three sons. One morning he invited the boys to ride with him into the mountains. At a place overlooking a canyon, he stopped and said: "Do you see that doe over there across the canyon?"

"Where?" asked the oldest boy; "I see no doe."

"Where?" asked the second son; "I see no doe."

"*Ay, caray!*" said the third and youngest boy. "There are a doe and a fawn."

"How do you see a doe and a fawn when the rest of us don't even see a doe?"

"I didn't say I saw them," said the little boy, "but I hear the fawn sucking its mother."

"That's my boy!" exclaimed the father. "You, at least, are my son."

Once while herding cattle in a rainstorm our great man and hero crossed his leg over the pommel of his saddle and rolled himself a cigarette. Then he felt for matches. He found none and began cursing his luck. Pinto Verde heard him and appreciated the embarrassment of his master. The horse watched the thundercloud, and at the proper time and split second, he sprang skyward into a thunderhead. Don Cacahuate lit his *pita* on a flash of lightning.

He went to Zacatecas to attend a convention. When he reached the city Pinto Verde became aware of the glad-happy rhythm made by his hoofs on the cobbled streets, and he put on such a show of fancy singlefooting à la equestrian terpsichore that his feet sounded a merry tune—Za-ca-TE-cas, Za-ca-TE-cas, Za-ca-TE-cas. But he overdid it and broke square dab half in two. And then there was no other sound from his shoes except—Za-ca, Za-ca, Za-ca, Za-ca.

"Whoa," said Don Cacahuate, "there is something missing. *Dónde estarán las te-cas* [where could the *tecas* be]?"

He stopped, looked back, and saw the rear of Pinto Verde a half-block away. But that didn't bother him. He simply waited until the *te-cas* caught up with the *Za-ca,* and continued on down the street with more caution, saying ZA-ca-*TE*-cas, ZA-ca-*TE*-cas, ZA-ca-*TE*-cas.

Once he put a few peaches in a *morral,* picked up his old muzzle-loader, and went deer hunting. While working his way through a meadow where the grass was waist-high, he saw a large buck. After much nervous fumbling he succeeded in getting powder and *taco* down the muzzle of his gun. Then he quickly reached into his shot-pouch, but found nothing. He had just finished eating a peach, so he rammed the seed into his gun, took a jittery aim, and fired. The deer fell. Don Cacahuate ran to the buck, but before he reached him the animal had gotten to his feet and had run away.

Three years later he was in the same meadow hunting and this time the grass was up to his shoulders. He found no deer but did find a peach tree laden with ripe fruit. He climbed into the branches, and was picking and eating peaches, when, by chance, he looked down. Imagine his amazement when he realized his tree was running across the meadow with him high on a limb. This was the same animal he had shot in the head with a peach seed three years before. Gently he climbed down, killed the deer with his *daga,* took it home, and had venison and peach preserves for supper.

Do you doubt this? Well, we can take care of that. He planted one of the seeds in his patio, and the tree came up and stands as evidence of the truth of this tale and the unquestionable honesty of Don Cacahuate.

From Chinati (formerly San Jose), Texas.

Two Treasure Tales

J. FRANK DOBIE

His Favorite Phantom Pursue

I AM NOT INTERESTED in the chameleon-changing legend of twenty jack-loads of gold from a church in Mexico that Catholic missionaries, overwhelmed by Kiowa Indians, are credited with having buried in the region of Kiowa Peak in Stonewall County —or maybe the Kiowas buried it—or maybe nobody. I am interested in Frank Olmstead, who forsook everything else in life to follow alone, for years and years, through unremitting deprivation and unfading belief, the gleam that a tale of gold emblazoned upon his consciousness. He saw that gold—twenty jack-loads of it—while he dug on in wilderness aloneness; he saw it in the dreams of fitful sleep. He died only when the vision faded, leaving him nothing to live for.

All I know of Frank Olmstead is from Lee Weldon Norman, who some years ago sent me a singular account of this singular character from the town bearing the singular name of Old Glory. The details and much of the language that follow are Mr. Norman's. Frank Olmstead "baptized" him into the lost treasure game. He used to buy his meager supplies from the Norman grocery store in Rule. His purchases varied from those of other country people on one item. He bought birdseed—for the birds.

Before and during World War I, Frank Olmstead was a prosperous stock-farmer near Peoria, Illinois. He owned the land he and his family lived on. He had expanded on credit and owned too many mortgaged cattle when the big break of 1920-21 came in cattle prices—more severe on stockmen than the Great Depression was. He was an educated man and a great reader. He turned to teaching for a living and, restless, energetic, unsatisfied, was teaching in a small college when he read or heard of Spanish gold on the Salt Fork of the Brazos— in the Kiowa Peak country. He could have come to that legendary lode through looking into *Legends of Texas,* a Texas Folklore Society book, long out of print, that I issued forth in 1924. He sold what property he had left in Illinois and brought his wife and two small children to Old Glory (in Stonewall County), where they lived until he, after considerable investigation, decided that "the core of prospectus" was about six miles northeast of town.

Sure that he was on the right trail, he built, of scrap lumber and pasteboard, a half-dugout hut, consisting of one room with one door and one window, in the side of a cliff and moved his family into it. He had already spent most of what money he brought with him; the pursuit of his particular phantom was not a gainful occupation. Before long wife and children left for Illinois, never to return. She had never shared his illusion; she said he was crazy. He seemed not to miss her, or the children either. Occasionally in digging he uncovered an Indian grinding stone, a bone that he declared to be human, or some other object to inflame his hope and fortify his confidence. He wrote the Vatican for information on a book and a ring that had allegedly belonged to a priest in Mexico. The days were not long enough for him to prospect and dig in. Often he went hungry. He might shoot wild meat now and then, but he did not like to disturb nature. Once in a while he got an odd job on a farm; in season he picked cotton. Somehow he managed to subscribe for so many magazines that on occasion his mailbox, six miles from his cabin, would not hold them and the mail carrier had to place some on the ground beneath.

He preferred solitude and most people respected his preference. His reading habits added to the country's idea of his queerness. The Speck Cox family came nearer being neighbors than anybody else. Mrs. Cox once gave a "forty-two" party to which she invited Frank Olmstead, mainly to show him off to some gossips who had never so much as glimpsed him. He turned up in a tuxedo, white shirt, black tie, top hat, gloves—everything but a cane. He was altogether at ease in his role of sophisticated college professor. In time he installed a radio—secondhand—but that did not alter his lone existence.

According to testimony he gave after he was snakebit, rattlesnakes had moved into his half-dugout, and even got in bed with him. A certain old rattler lived in his cabinet for years, and somehow he could not ferret him out. At night he could hear the creature's staccato rattling. It "bothered his rest" so much that he set a trap and caught a huge diamondback. One night not long after this he reached out of bed in the darkness toward the floor and was fanged by another diamondback. He lanced the bite, sucked poison out, thought he was going to die, but lived to dig on.

At the age of sixty-six he contracted pneumonia and was forced to go to the hospital in Aspermont. He had dug his own grave, six by three, near his dugout before this. Recovered, he came back to live beside the grave, but somehow the phantom of his pursuit had died into nothingness. One day a man, curious over not having seen him, looked into the dugout cabin and found him hanging dead by a lightcord tied around his neck, absorbent cotton stuffed into his nostrils.

He had died alone—as he had lived. Respectability buried him in a graveyard with a hymn and a prayer. Most of the people around said he was plain crazy. Some said he had received inside information on the twenty jack-loads of gold from an old Kiowa chief—and that if his energy, which is life, had not played out he would have dug it up. He was not the last to follow, follow the phantom.

The Blue Egg of Silver and the Golden Hope

IN 1929 I almost missed a midnight train to the north out of
El Paso while C. B. Ruggles held me enthralled with his story
of the Lost Tayopa Mine down in the Sierra Madre. Two weeks
later I was back in El Paso from a panther hunt in New Mexico,
and Ruggles again held me until I barely caught a midnight
train to the east. A few weeks later I outfitted with him and we
rode with pack mules for ten days across the Sierra Madre—
without going through a gate or seeing a wheel, except on a
little oxcart that had never been out of the miniature mountain
valley where it was made. We were going to fabulous Tayopa,
for which Ruggles had been prospecting for six years and
which he thought he had finally located near a rancheria in
Sonora named Guadalupe de Santa Ana.

We were out nearly a month and in all that time Ruggles
never palled as a storyteller.

"If Tayopa gives up its gold," I asked him, "what are you
going to do?"

"I'm going to find La Gloria Pan."

The Gloria Pan, in Durango or somewhere else, is another
of the legendary lost mines of the Sierra Madre. I wrote the
story of Tayopa for a magazine and finally put it into a book.
Four or five years after I rode the trail to it, I heard from
Ruggles in Oklahoma. He was married and just back from
Alaska, where he had had extraordinary experiences. He was
expecting to have more. Then I lost track of him. I knew that
Tayopa had not panned out. Over the years I have heard from
various men who "knew" where it is, always at another location
from that made by Ruggles.

Ten years ago in a hotel in Tucson, my telephone rang.
"This is Mrs. C. B. Ruggles," the voice said. "C. B. and I read
in the paper that you are to make a talk at the University of
Arizona. We have come up from Arivaca to see you."

Twenty-five years had passed since I had seen him, but
Ruggles was himself, seventy-three years old now. He told

me of two mining claims staked out near Arivaca, not far
from the Arizona-Sonora line—and they will pay when the price
of gold goes up enough. Meanwhile Ruggles was expecting to
set off for something unbelievably rich. This is the story he told,
for he did not disappoint me.

Years ago on an expedition down into the Ocampo country
of Chihuahua he took along an El Paso mining engineer named
Noble. Each had his own mount and pack mule, but they had
in common a *mozo*—the servant, guide, part cook, and altogether
handy man so necessary for travel in the Sierra Madre.

In that country every trail goes down a canyon, up a canyon,
or over a mountain to another canyon. One day Ruggles and
Noble stopped in a canyon at the mouth of a side-canyon, and
while they were halted Ruggles walked two or three hundred
yards up this side-canyon until he came to a waterfall over
a ledge. There was not much water in the stream; beneath the
ledge was a shallow pool. In it Ruggles saw something that
looked like an enormous blue egg. It was too big to have been
laid by any bird on earth, maybe two feet long, oblong and
shaped all over like an egg. The blue was almost indigo. There
it was in the shallow water. He got down near it and stooped
to pick it up. He could not budge it. The underpart was covered
with slime that made a handhold difficult. He crossed his legs,
got a firmer hold, and still could not raise the "egg."

Looking about, he saw a large ball of the same color. He
picked it up but was astounded at the weight. It was solid
something. Then he picked up a smaller ball. The balls, mani-
festly, were not rocks. He knew that they had come from some
formation nearby. Examining the ledge more closely, he saw
that it was made of some kind of gneiss attached to a vein of
the blue substance. He tried to break off some of the blue
substance but could not. He followed the vein for maybe a
quarter of a mile up one side of the canyon and saw that it
lay exposed up the other side. Then he took the two balls and
carried them to camp.

He showed them to the mining engineer, Noble.

"I don't know what it is," Noble said, "but it is worthless. I know that." And he threw the larger ball, which he had taken in his hands, down.

Ruggles picked it up and put it in the *morral* (fiber bag) hanging to the horn of his saddle. He put the smaller ball in a saddle pocket. Noble remonstrated with him for carrying so much weight, though the horse that carried it belonged to Ruggles. On the way out of the canyon he kept harping on the weight until, finally, Ruggles discarded the large ball, but kept the smaller one.

He had it when they got back to El Paso. Whether the heavy stuff was worthless or not, he wanted to know what it was. He knew an assayer named Millar who had an office downtown but taught in the College of Mines (now Texas Western).

A little before eight he reached the office. And there Noble was.

"You've brought your little blue ball, I guess," Noble taunted.

Talking to the assayer in private could not be very well managed. Ruggles handed him the small ball.

"I don't know what it is," the assayer said, "but if you will let me, I will take it with me up to the College of Mines and find out. You won't mind if we cut off a slice for assaying?"

Ruggles did not mind. About three o'clock that afternoon, Ruggles was back at the office.

"Nobody," the assayer said, "ever saw anything like this. It assays 98.9 per cent pure silver. I can't imagine what sort of formation it is out of. That color is unknown to silver."

Ruggles got back what was left of the ball. Just as he stepped out into the street, another man associated with the College of Mines accosted him. He had just been fired, but Ruggles did not know it. The assayer had shown him the blue ball, and now he asked to take it for further examination. Ruggles let him have it—and that night the fired man left for South America.

"But Ruggles," I said at this point of his narrative, "prospectors have been all over the Sierra Madre for hundreds of years. Why wouldn't some of them have discovered long ago such an exposed vein of pure silver?"

"They were just like Noble," Ruggles replied. "They saw it and did not recognize it. And it's still there, where it's been for thousands of years. There's a good automobile road into Ocampo now. All a man needs is two jeeps, a crowbar, and a metal saw. A hunk of that blue stuff no bigger than an old-time case of canned tomatoes would make a jeep load. There'll be no milling involved. The stuff can be taken straight to the mint at Chihuahua City. 98.9 per cent pure silver."

Two or three years before this Ruggles made a trip into Chihuahua to bring out some of the blue silver. When he got to the canyon where it is located, he found eight or ten feet of dashing waters. The rainy season was on. He stayed for nine days waiting for the water to run down, but rains kept adding to it. His time was limited and he had to come back to Arizona.

While he was telling of his plans to go back again, he said that he might take a modern metal detector, go to the church at Guadalupe de Santa Ana in Sonora—his location for Tayopa—and find all the ancient treasure supposed to be buried under it.

"But, Ruggles," I said, "why fool with unknown treasures when that great vein of silver, 98.9 per cent pure, is there for the taking?"

"I guess you are right," he said. "Come and go with me."

Shivarees and Charivaris: Variations on a Theme

E. BAGBY ATWOOD

MOST RURAL ADULTS in the United States, particularly those of an older generation, are familiar with the *shivaree*—a raucous, noisy, discordant mock serenade inflicted on newly married couples, usually on the wedding night. Neither the etymology of the term nor the origin of the practice is the business of the present study. *Shivaree* clearly derives from the French *charivari* (still in use), which goes back to a Medieval Latin term given by Du Cange as *carivarium,* probably best regarded as of unknown origin.[1] The custom itself had certainly developed in western Europe by medieval times, and some elements of it no doubt go back to antiquity.[2] In Europe the practice is associated with the expression of popular disapproval, or even with the meting out of popular justice.[3] In the United States, however, it is usually devoid of real animus, although some of the nineteenth-century literary descriptions picture demonstrations that are sufficiently rowdy to arouse a good deal of resentment.[4]

Research for the Linguistic Atlas[5] has provided the means of determining the distribution of the lexical variants in use for this custom in the different geographical areas. Hanley,[6] and later Davis and McDavid,[7] demonstrated the incidence of a number of regional synonyms. To sum up briefly, we may say that, so far as the eastern states are concerned, *serenade* prevails in eastern New England and the South Atlantic states;

horning in the Narragansett Bay area and in upstate New York; *callathump* in western Connecticut; *skimmilton* in the lower Hudson Valley; *bullband(ing)* in eastern Pennsylvania; and *belling* in Ohio, West Virginia, and western Pennsylvania. To the west of these areas, as well as in northernmost New England, the term *shivaree* is in almost universal use wherever the custom itself is known. The prevalence of this term is interpreted by Davis and McDavid (rightly, in my opinion) as indicative of an influence exerted by the early French settlers in various inland portions of the country.

My observations with regard to Texas and adjoining states are the outgrowth of a systematic vocabulary survey which has been in progress for the last ten or twelve years. The method was dependent on the actual interviewing of informants—over 460 of them—with the use of a standardized questionnaire based primarily on the work sheets for the Linguistic Atlas. The interviewers were for the most part advanced and graduate students in southwestern colleges and universities—"Baker Street Irregulars" as I have called them—who went forth to interview acquaintances or kinsmen in many remote areas. Questions were asked indirectly as far as possible; for example, "What do you call a very heavy rain that doesn't last long?" — not "Do you use the word *gully-washer?*" Interviewers were requested to record not only each word that was found to be in use, but also any remarks by the informant that threw light on the meaning of the word or on its status in the community. A full account of the methodology will be found in my recent book, *The Regional Vocabulary of Texas.*[8]

Nearly 80 per cent of the southwestern informants are familiar with the custom of the shivaree and give one term or another for it. Among these terms, *shivaree* is overwhelmingly predominant. Only ten informants give the South Atlantic term *serenade,* and some of these occurrences may result from only partial familiarity with the custom. Some six or eight persons of German background carry over the term *Katzen-*

musik. Only two Texas informants respond with the French form *charivari,* which, as we will see, is considerably more frequent in the Acadian region of Louisiana.

In addition to the required lexical data, about ninety of the field workers recorded information concerning the general nature of the shivaree or certain details of its observance. From these records we may derive a composite picture of the practice as well as a large number of variations that occur in one community or another. In the following summary, the numbers in parentheses will indicate the number of informants who agree on a specific detail; sometimes also I have noted the county or parish in which a detail was recorded.

THE WEDDED COUPLE. In general there is no restriction on the type of couple who may be given a shivaree. One informant (Eastland) specifies "very popular couples"; another (Brazoria), couples who run away to get married. Only two Texas informants (both of Louisiana background) indicate that the demonstration is limited to the remarriage of a widow or widower. In the Acadian area of Louisiana this limitation is quite general, as will appear later.

THE SERENADERS. There is no indication that the serenaders are a hostile group, although some of their antics (see below) might seem to verge on cruelty. The group is ordinarily thought to be made up of friends (4), or neighbors (3), or in some instances the wedding guests (3). One informant (Travis) describes them as "a friendly, happy group of neighbors." There is no mention of masquerading or concealment of identity, but one informant (Travis) states that the men used to wear their coats turned inside out so that the white sleeve linings would gleam in the darkness.

THE TIME. The shivaree is ordinarily held on the wedding night, rather late, often after the couple is thought to have gone to bed (7). One informant in Texas (Brazoria) and one in Louisiana (Lafourche) indicate that in the case of a couple

that has gone away to be married the serenade may be post-
poned until their return.

THE PLACE. The demonstration is always held outside
the house of the newly married pair. Sometimes the serenaders
circle about the house a number of times (6). There is no
mention of what happens when a couple follows the modern
practice of spending the wedding night at a hotel or motel;
but it is certain that many Texas couples nowadays conceal
their whereabouts on the first night in order to avoid the atten-
tions of their friends.

THE NOISEMAKERS. The implements which the serenaders bring with them are designed to produce a hideous din
which bears little resemblance to music. The devices that are
most often mentioned are bells, including cowbells (15), pots
and pans (10), tin cans (7), washtubs (5), shotguns (3), and
dishpans (2). Some also mention pails (1), drums (1), whistles
(1), and the sweep (triangular blade) of a cultivator (1),
which may be beaten to produce a loud clang. Sometimes there
is a kind of "singing" (3); if musical instruments, such as
guitars (1), French harps (1), or fiddles (1) are used, they
are out of order or out of tune. Two informants describe what
in my childhood I knew as a *tick-tack;* one of them (Falls)
explains it thus: "They'd get a string, a good stout string . . . ,
and they'd put a lot of resin on it and they run things up and
down this. . . . And the way they do it just makes an awful
sound—a just terrible sound. You'd think the world was falling
apart."

PRANKS PLAYED ON THE COUPLE. There is adequate
evidence that the shivaree is often combined with the equally
common custom of hazing the bridegroom by crude tricks and
pranks. These are extremely varied and some show a perverse
inventiveness, but most are very simple forms of annoyance.
The serenaders might burst in on the couple (1) and take
them out of bed the way they are attired (1), or they might
dress the pair in "funny looking clothes" (1). Sometimes the

groom is "kidnapped" (1) or otherwise separated from the bride (2), after which he may be "dunked" in a pool or tank (2), or rolled in the snow (1), or locked in the cellar (1), or even ridden on a rail (2). One informant (Comanche, Oklahoma) mentions the practice of forcing the groom to push the bride in a wheelbarrow; another (Angelina) tells of stringing a bell to the bedstead beforehand and presumably listening for the tinklings. Somewhat more ingenious is the trick of currying the horses and putting the brushings into the bridal bed (Grant, New Mexico).

THE TREAT. In some cases the serenaders, rather than merely creating annoyances, expect to be invited in for refreshments. The nature of these is rather vague: some informants mention food in general (4), others specify cake(s) (4). Some kind of drink (4) must be provided, often coffee (3) but sometimes alcoholic drinks (2). The food may occasionally be brought by the guests themselves (1) or by the relatives of the wedded pair (2). The party usually appears to be brief and simple, but one informant (Grant, Arkansas) states that music and dancing are expected. After the treat the bride and groom are usually spared further annoyance.

As has been mentioned, the French original of the word *shivaree* is *charivari*. This is in frequent use in Louisiana French and is sometimes carried over into English.[9] About 17 per cent of the southern Louisiana informants give the response *charivari;* the others use the anglicized form. No other words are current in the area. A feature of the custom that is mentioned by a large number of Louisiana informants (at least 25) is the restriction of the demonstration to weddings in which one of the pair has been married before. This is a traditional French practice which has been followed for centuries,[10] and it must formerly have prevailed in various frontier areas with a heavy French population. Indeed, one of James Hall's French characters (in a village along the Mississippi) expresses great surprise at the incongruity of giving a *charivari* after the wedding of a bachelor and a spinster.[11]

In the past, the "treat" demanded of a widow or widower in the French-dominated area must have been regarded as something in the nature of amends made to society for a departure from convention or strict purity. Thus the parties or other forms of tribute to the crowd were often very substantial and involved the expenditure, or downright payment, of a considerable sum of money.[12] Nowadays there appears to be little or no bad feeling on the part of the populace, but still the shivaree parties described by the Acadians seem to be a good deal more elaborate than those mentioned by the Texas informants, particularly if the groom is known to be a person of means. In order to exemplify the Acadian usage, I append a portion of a tape-recorded interview with a middle-aged woman of French background who lives in Lafourche Parish. It demonstrates the occasional lavishness of the celebrations, a well as an admirable persistence on the part of the serenaders.[18]

[Were you familiar with the custom of making a loud noise, beating on pans or blowing horns after a wedding?]

Well, that was done when a man . . . that had been married would marry a single girl or a woman that had been married would marry a single man. That was called *charivari.*

[. . . Could you describe one? . . .]

Oh, yes. They would come there, especially if the party hadn't invited his own party, 'cause he had a choice of inviting his own party. And if he invited his own party they would come there and beat on any old things, just as you say, making a loud noise. And then he'd come out and ask them what they wanted and they'd keep on beating. And the third time when he'd come out, well, whatever they wanted, if it was a dance— usually they'd ask for a dance or they'd ask for a *collation* . . . or something like that, you know. And then it was all over . . . ; they couldn't go around following him. But if he didn't come out, they had the rights to follow him as long as he wouldn't give them what they wanted. No matter where he went, even on his honeymoon, they had the right—and at the end, whenever he would come out and ask what they wanted they would charge him with all the expenses. . . . I have been told (now,

I didn't see this but I have been told) that there were some that followed them as long as eight days on trains and everything, and finally [they] had to give in, and *by law* they had to pay the expenses.

[That was because they didn't approve of remarriage? Is that the idea?]

I don't know. I don't know why. If they didn't approve of that—it was just a custom, I guess, like a lot of other things that they had in this area.

[And what was the collation . . . ?]

Well, that was . . . bringing a lot of drinks and something to eat, but sweets, cakes—things like that—and that was making merry with everybody that was invited, after the wedding. But this *charivari* only occurred when a man that had been married already would remarry a single girl . . . or a girl that had been married would marry a single man.

[If they had both been married before, then they wouldn't have it?]

Oh, no. Then they wouldn't have it. I remember when old _____, young _____'s father, remarried. Well, so the people wouldn't give him a *charivari* . . . she came to church and he came and met her there and they got married [and went] to the train and left right away. But the people were waiting for them, and they knew that they had been married. They were waiting for 'em, so the minute he got down from the train when he got back from his honeymoon, he didn't give them a chance; he asked them right away what they wanted. So they said that they wanted a big dance and *collation* at _____. And I mean, he had to *pay*. It was like a fair, they tell me. I didn't go, but they tell me a big fair couldn't have been worse than this. . . . Oh, yes, musicians and everything—whatever they'd asked for. Of course, the people knew about the means, you know, of the man that was marrying.

1. C. Du Cange, *Glossarium Mediae et Infimae Latinitatis*. Edited and published by Léopold Favre (Niort, 1883). Most dictionaries give no origin for the Medieval Latin term; however, *Webster's Third New International Dictionary* (Springfield, Mass., 1961) derives it from Late Latin *caribaria*, "headache," from Greek *karē*, "head" and *-baria*, "heaviness." I do not know the documentary evidence on which this etymology is based, but it seems dubious to me.

2. See Violet Alford, "Rough Music or Charivari," *Folklore*, LXX (1959), 505-18, esp. p. 507.

3. *Ibid.*

4. In *The End of the World* by Edward Eggleston (New York, 1872), the serenaders seem relieved when the groom does not open fire on them (pp. 295-96). In *The Valley of Shadows* by Francis Grierson (reprinted New York, 1948), the bride chases the serenaders away with a rawhide whip (pp. 111-12). For comment on some of the early shivarees, see Mamie Meredith, " 'Belling the Bridal Couple' in Pioneer Days," *American Speech*, VIII (1933), 22-24; and John T. Flanagan, "A Note on 'Shivaree,' " *American Speech*, XV (1940), 109-10.

5. The Atlas is based on the direct interviewing of informants and the recording of their usage. Only the materials pertaining to New England have been published in full: Hans Kurath and Bernard Bloch, *Linguistic Atlas of New England*, 3 vols. in six parts (Providence, R.I., 1939-43). For a full account of the methodology and of the progress of the work in other parts of the country, see Raven I. McDavid, Jr., "The Dialects of American English," in W. Nelson Francis, *The Structure of American English* (New York, 1958), pp. 480-543.

6. Miles L. Hanley, " 'Serenade' in New England," *American Speech*, VIII (1933), 24-26.

7. Alva L. Davis and Raven I. McDavid, Jr., " 'Shivaree': An Example of Cultural Diffusion," *American Speech*, XXIV (1949), 249-55.

8. University of Texas Press, 1962.

9. Most of the materials from southern Louisiana were gathered by the late Mima Babington, who died on December 30, 1960. She had intended to incorporate these materials into a doctoral dissertation, to have been presented at the University of Texas in 1961.

10. Du Cange thus restricts the term *carivarium*: "Ludus turpis tinnitibus et clamoribus variis, quibus illudunt iis, qui ad secundas convolant nuptias." Émile Littré records a similar limitation in the nineteenth century (under *charivari*): "Concert ridicule, bruyant et tumultueux de poêles, de chaudrons, de siflets, de huées, etc. qu'on donne en certaines localités aux femmes veuves et âgées et aux veufs qui se remarient, et aussi à des personnages qui ont excité un mécontentement." *Dictionnaire de la langue française* (Paris, 1873). Littré also records a number of extended or figurative meanings.

11. See "The French Village," in *Tales of the Border* (Philadelphia, 1835), pp. 102-28. The groom expostulates: "Gentlemen: pardonnez-moi. If I understan dis custom, which have long prevail vid us, it is vat I say—ven a gentilman, who have been marry before, shall marry de second time—or ven a lady have de misfortune to loose her husban, and be so happy to marry some odder gentilman, den we make de charivary—but 'tis not so wid Mam'selle Duval and me. Upon my honour we have never been marry before dis time" (p. 123).

12. The diarist John F. Watson, recording events at New Orleans in 1804 and 1805, makes mention of the "sherrievarrie" of a widow who had contracted an unpopular marriage—a demonstration which lasted three entire days, and which was attended by "thousands of the people of the town." In this instance the widow "had to compromise by giving to the outdoor mass three thousand dollars in solid coin," an exaction which later "was honorably given to the orphans of the place." See "Notitia of Incidents at New Orleans, in 1804 and 1805," *American Pioneer*, II (1843), 227-37, esp. p. 229.

13. The portions in brackets are my own questions and proddings, and occasionally words which I have supplied in a slight abridgment of the original.

Freud's Myth of the Primal Horde

WILSON M. HUDSON

In RECENT YEARS it has often been asserted that myth is far more prevalent in modern life and thought than we had supposed it to be. Some who have found myth in unsuspected places have been able to do so by making use of relaxed or peculiar concepts of myth. Without analyzing the various meanings given to the term *myth* in current discussions, I believe it can be shown that Freud's primal horde theory, or primal parricide theory as it will be referred to alternatively, satisfies most of the "orthodox" criteria for the identification of myth; in other words, that it is a bona fide instance of modern myth devised to explain social, religious, and moral origins. I should like to consider Freud's theory as myth, to show its pervasiveness in his thought relating to society and culture, and to indicate the extent of its acceptance in a field of study combining psychoanalysis and anthropology.

The primal horde theory involves dramatis personae and a drama. This drama occurred a long time ago and was preserved by a kind of group psyche. It marked the beginning of society, religion, and morality. It originated and sanctified the primitive customs of totemism and taboo. Periodically the drama was re-enacted in commemorative rites and ceremonies, some of which survive in disguised form today. The primal horde theory is for society what the Oedipus myth as interpreted by Freud is for the individual; in fact, the primal horde theory is the Oedipus myth with one father and a multiplicity of wives, daughters, and sons. The drama consists in the murder of the primal father by the sons, who have been denied access to the women, and their reaction to the deed. The participants are not divine beings in Freud's view, of course; but in the minds of the sons the primal father acquires, after being murdered, a sacred status as the totem animal and is eventually transformed into the god of monotheism.

In primitive myth the founders of the world order and the customs of man are gods or semidivine beings such as "the old ones" or "ancestors" who perform archetypal acts which are henceforth imitated by men. A construct which has the configuration and function ordinarily ascribed to myth but which lacks the supernatural element might be called sophisticated myth. In this sense, the drama of the framing of the social compact is sophisticated myth, whether in the version of Hobbes, Locke, or Rousseau. Freud's primal horde theory is sophisticated myth in that it is *Urdrama* explaining socio-religio-moral origins without supernaturalism. The basic explanations are natural—specifically, the concepts of Freudian psychoanalysis. Some years after formulating his theory Freud himself referred to it as "the scientific myth of the father of the primal horde." This may seem to be a contradiction in terms, but perhaps it can be shown that it is not.

Freud enunciated his theory of the primal horde in *Totem and Taboo* (1913), which had as its subtitle *Some Points of Agreement Between the Mental Lives of Savages and Neurotics.* The validity of this theory is taken for granted in his later books having to do with social psychology: *Group Psychology and the Analysis of the Ego* (1921), *The Future of an Illusion* (1927), *Civilization and Its Discontents* (1930), and *Moses and Monotheism* (1939).[1] Freud held to his theory with virtually no modification, his sole concession to criticism being a very unemphatic statement in his last book that the primal parricide had occurred not once but many times.

It has been said that *Totem and Taboo* grew out of Freud's search for evidence to prove that "what was once conscious in primitive man would be 'unconscious' in modern man."[2] He had assigned this task to Jung but undertook it himself after becoming dissatisfied with the turn of Jung's inquiry. Freud brought together his psychoanalytic theory and the theories and data of evolutionary anthropologists such as James Frazer, J. J. Atkinson, and W. Robertson Smith. Freud's own thought had an evolutionary cast. In biology he held to the Lamarckian doctrine of the inheritance of acquired characters, an idea which he carried over into psychology, so that he was friendly to the belief that mental experiences, especially traumatic ones, are in some way inheritable. He was influenced by Haeckel's biogenetic law that ontogeny recapitulates phylogeny, with the result that he saw significant parallels between the psychic development of the individual and that of the race. The mind of modern man contains archaic remnants, Freud thought. The neurotic children who furnished him with the clue to an understanding of totemism he presented as cases of reversion to a primitive totemic stage. He applied to savages the same explanations that he had devised for the mentality of neurotics. His theory of the libido (energy deriving from the sexual instinct), with the Oedipal complex as the nucleus of all neuroses, served for both. In thus providing answers to "some unsolved problems of social psychology,"[3] Freud felt that he had demonstrated the value of psychoanalysis for the study of man in his social as well as in his individual aspect.

Freud followed the theories of the evolutionary anthropologists as far as they would take him in his direction. Atkinson accepted Darwin's belief that men must have first lived together in small bands or hordes dominated by an older and stronger male who kept the females for himself and drove out his sons as they matured. The younger males would have to be exogamous, that is, find women for themselves outside the father's band. The brothers would sometimes kill the father, but they would disintegrate as a group when they fought among themselves to obtain the father's place. The rest of Atkinson's theory need not be stated, for Freud parts company with him immediately after the parricide. Freud drew on Robertson Smith for the theory that the totem meal is a sacrificial feast of kinsmen and that the animal sacrificed and the totem animal are the same. The totem animal is the god or ancestor of the kinsmen. When the totem group ritually kill and eat the totem animal, which ordinarily is sacred and untouchable, they are asserting their oneness with their god and their kinship with each other. They mourn the death of the totem animal but immediately rejoice. At this point Freud is ready to produce his psychoanalytical explanation: the totem animal is in reality a substitute for the father. The ambivalent attitude of the participants in the totem feast is identical with that found in children today and persisting in adults under the influence of the father-complex.

The primal parricide, says Freud, took place in the following manner:

One day the brothers who had been driven out came together, killed and devoured their father and so made an end of the patriarchal horde. United, they had the courage to do and succeeded in doing what would have been impossible for them individually. (Some cultural advance, perhaps, command over some new weapon, had given them a sense of superior strength.) Cannibal savages as they were, it goes without saying that they devoured their victim as well as killing him. The violent primal father had doubtless been the feared and envied model of each one of the company of brothers: and in the act of devouring him they accomplished their identification with him, and each one of them acquired a portion of his strength. The totem meal, which is perhaps mankind's earliest festival, would thus be a repetition and a commemoration of this memorable and criminal deed, which was the beginning of so many things—of social organization, of moral restrictions and of religion.[4]

Without the addition of new elements, this condensed account of the primal parricide could be readily turned into full-blown myth by providing names and details. What we have here is a dramatic representation of an ancient happening that occurred in nonspecific time, brought in a new order, and strongly influenced man forever after. Freud refers to the primal parricide as "the great event with which civilization began and which, since it occurred, has not allowed mankind a moment's rest," and, again, he calls it "the great event in human prehistory."[5]

After the murder of the primal father the ambivalent attitude of the brothers toward him became evident, for they loved and admired as well as hated him. Their love took the form of remorse and they began to feel a sense of guilt. They then "revoked" their deed by adopting an animal as a substitute for their father and forbidding the killing of this totem animal, which they thought of thereafter as their ancestor. By a process known in Freudian psychoanalysis as "deferred obedience" they also renounced the women—their mothers and sisters—whom they had won by their parricide and henceforth forbade incest. Thus arose totemism and its two fundamental taboos, the prohibition of eating the totem animal and the prohibition of incest, these taboos corresponding to the two repressed wishes of the Oedipus complex, to kill the father and possess the mother. The brothers could now live together in a fraternal clan without sexual rivalry; they found mates for themselves outside the totem group, and thus exogamy came into being. A kind of religion was developed in which the totem animal was conceived of as ancestor and protector. On occasion the brothers would ceremonially kill and eat the totem animal as a re-enactment of the triumph over their father and an acknowledgment of their common involvement in the crime and also as an affirmation of their identity with him and each other and a renewal in themselves of his attributes. The fraternal clan formed out of the patriarchal horde sanctified the tie of blood between the brothers and prohibited fratricide, so that the new form of society could continue to exist.

"Society," says Freud in summary, "was now based on

complicity in the common crime; religion was based on the sense of guilt and the remorse attaching to it; while morality was based partly on the exigencies of this society and partly on the penance demanded by the sense of guilt."[6] Freud has made his myth account for the origin of society, religion, and morality and also connect and explain totemism, taboo, and exogamy. This is indeed a high yield. The rationale of the myth is Freudian psychoanalysis, which existed before the myth and led the way to its construction.

After stating his myth, Freud shows its connection with some subsequent religious developments. The totem animal is the first form of a father surrogate and a god is a later form in which the father has regained his human shape. A longing for the father, which Freud sees as the root of every kind of religion, led the sons, after a lapse of time and a diminution of their bitterness toward him, to conceive of a god who was an ideal father image. At this stage there was a change to a patriarchal form of society, but the patriarchs, restrained by the established taboos and prohibitions, did not resume the unrestricted power of the primal father. When an animal was sacrificed to a god, the primal father was represented twice, as the totemic animal and also as the god.

Freud supposes that as time went on the sacrificial animal lost its sacred character and the sacrifice was not viewed as a totem feast but as an offering to the deity. Divine kings appeared and there was a revival of paternal authority. In this situation the subjugated sons further divested themselves of guilt feelings by assigning the responsibility for the sacrifice, which was an acknowledgment of guilt, to the god himself. It was now the god who demanded the sacrifice. This phase is reflected in myths which show the god killing the animal that is sacred to him and that actually represents the god. "Here," says Freud, "we have the most extreme denial of the great crime which was the beginning of society and of the sense of guilt."[7] The later father surrogate kills the first father surrogate; in this way the guilt of the sons is transferred to the father.

Sometimes human beings playing the role of a god were sacrificed. They were still surrogates for the father, says Freud. The explanation is simple: when the surrogate changed from animal to human shape, then a human being replaced the animal in the sacrificial ceremony. "The memory of the first great act of sacrifice thus proved indestructible, in spite of every effort to forget it," Freud declares; "and at the very point at which men sought to be at the farthest distance from the motives that led to it, its undistorted reproduction emerged in the form of the sacrifice of the god."[8]

Two driving forces in the development of religion never became extinct—the sons' sense of guilt and their rebelliousness. The sons tried to assume the place of the father-god, but they had great difficulty in overcoming their feeling of guilt. Freud attempts, very sketchily and unsatisfactorily, to interpret Attis, Adonis, and Tammuz as youthful vegetation gods who rebelliously commit incest with their mothers and whose guilt is punished by their fathers. "The mourning for these gods and the rejoicings over their resurrection," says Freud, "passed over into the ritual of another son-deity who was destined to lasting success."[9] The son-deity that he has in mind was Christ.

As Freud worked it out, Christ allayed the brothers' feeling of guilt by sacrificing his own life. He redeemed them from original sin, which was nothing less than the murder of the primal father. By his self-sacrifice he became god himself and took the father's place, and thus succeeded in supplanting the father-religion by a son-religion. The totem meal was revived as communion, in which the brothers eat the flesh and blood of the son and through this ritual are sanctified and identified with the new son-deity.

Not content with having accounted for the beginning of society, religion, and morals by means of his primal horde myth, Freud reached out for tragedy too. In Greek tragedy the hero, usually in rebellion against human or divine authority, is surrounded by the chorus, who try to advise or restrain him and sympathize with him when he is punished for his rebelliousness. Because of his tragic guilt the hero must suffer. Here we have a re-enactment of the "great primaeval tragedy" of the primal parricide. The hero is the primal father and the chorus are the sons. "The scene upon the stage," Freud explains, "was derived from the historical scene through a process of systematic distortion. . . ."[10] The guilt for the crime of rebellion—the murder of the father—has been shifted from the brothers to the father, and they, who were in reality the cause of his suffering, expend their sympathy upon him.

"At the conclusion, then, of this exceedingly condensed inquiry," Freud states, "I should like to insist that its outcome shows that the beginnings of religion, morals, society and art converge in the Oedipus complex."[11] He says that this is in complete agreement with the psychoanalytic finding that the Oedipus complex is the nucleus of all neuroses. His inquiry and the "psychoanalytic finding" are not, of course, independent lines of investigation. The inquiry produced the results demanded by Freudian psychoanalysis. Freud expresses surprise at the discovery that the problems of social as well as individual psychology should prove soluble by reference to man's relation to his father.

Freud anticipates two criticisms. First, he has assumed the existence of "a collective mind, in which mental processes occur just as they do in the mind of an individual."[12] He has supposed that the sense of guilt for the primal parricide persisted for thousands of years and remained operative in generations with no knowledge of the deed. Freud's defense is that social psychology requires the assumption of a collective mind (Brill translates Massenpsyche literally as "mass psyche") to provide psychic continuity, without which little or no development could take place from one generation to another. Just how the process of transmission operates is an unsolved problem, but Freud does not think that direct communication and tradition provide the solution. In his opinion, part of the solution seems to be that psychical dispositions are inherited and are called into play by the experience of the individual. The other criticism is that the primal parricide might have been merely desired and not really committed, since the guilt feelings of neurotics are always founded on psychical realities rather than factual ones. But because primitive men are, unlike neurotics, not inhibited, Freud is inclined to believe that the "deed which gave those who performed it the concept of 'crime' "[13] was actually committed.

Again and again in *Totem and Taboo* Freud refers to the primal parricide as if it were a deed or event that had taken place in history. He came to believe so intensely in his account of the murder of the primal father and its continuing consequences that he could hardly bring himself to present it as a hypothesis. Nor did he present it as a convenient dramatization of Freudian theory invented for the sake of exposition. He could not, of course, locate it in history, nor did he disavow its historicity. The primal parricide belongs to the time when the world and man's life were being ordered; this is mythological time, or, as Mircea Eliade would say, sacred time—that is, nonprofane time. Eliade would see the ritual of the totem feast in Freud's account as a paradigmatic, symbolic repetition of a sacred event whereby men renew and affirm the order established by this event originally—another instance of "the eternal return."[14] If, as should be expected according to Eliade's view, primitive men had had a narrative accompanying and representing the event in words, this would have been the myth. These primitives would not have been in possession of the Freudian explanation, for that is the "scientific" part. The story of the primal horde is a scientific myth—an "ancient" drama forever affecting mankind, with motives understandable psychoanalytically.

Freud's theory of origins struck many anthropologists as a fantasy. In a review R. R. Marett characterized it as "a 'just-so' story which is no better and no worse than many a savage myth on the same subject."[15] Freud's loyal disciple, Ernest Jones, has said in retrospect that the anthropologists were wrong in accusing him of "dating the whole genesis of culture from a single event."[16] Jones maintains that Freud visualized the primal parricide and its effects as having recurred repeatedly over thousands of years; this interpretation is hardly justified by Freud's presentation in *Totem and Taboo,* though he did say in a footnote that he had "abbreviated the time factor."[17] Even if the parricide had been recurrent, Freud was still involved in the Lamarckian supposition that the memory of the event was transmissible by inheritance rather than by tradition. Jones admits that the weakest link in Freud's chain of reasoning in *Moses and Monotheism* was his "theory of the unconscious transmission of historical events."[18]

A. L. Kroeber, an American anthropologist who had had training in psychology and was even to practice psychoanalysis between 1921 and 1923, reviewed Brill's translation of *Totem and Taboo* in 1920.[19] He made eleven specific objections to the primal horde theory, the last of which was that Freud had not explained how the sense of guilt for the primal parricide could remain active in generations long removed from the deed and hence ignorant of it. Kroeber did not press this objection, because Freud had anticipated it by stating that social psychologists were in the habit of assuming the existence of a mass psyche without being able to explain the process of transmission. Freud, said Kroeber, had pyramided hypotheses instead of building up larger certainties by the determination and addition of smaller ones. Though Freud's book failed to establish its thesis, Kroeber acknowledged that it was a valuable contribution inasmuch as it made clear that cultural anthropology must make use of psychological as well as historical methods. The parallels pointed out by Freud between the psychology of savages and neurotics, such as taboo customs and compulsion neuroses, are real and should be studied by

ethnologists. Kroeber stressed the significance of Freud's entry
into the field of anthropology, saying that his point of view
could henceforth not be ignored without stultification. Kroeber
concluded by advising psychoanalysts who want to follow
Freud's lead to become acquainted with genuine historical
ethnology and not to rely on such authors as Frazer, who merely
attempt to psychologize with ethnological data.

Freud read Kroeber's review, but he did not relinquish or
modify his theory of the primal horde, which he reasserted
and extended to further applications in *Group Psychology and
the Analysis of the Ego.* He attributed to Kroeber (misspelled
Kroeger) Marett's characterization of his account as a just-so
story.[20] It was a hypothesis, Freud admits with a show of candor, but its worth was proved by its ability "to bring coher-
ence and understanding into more and more new regions."[21]
With unshaken confidence, he goes on to make use of the primal horde theory to explain group psychology. In the time of
the primal horde there were two kinds of psychology, that of
the dominating and narcissistic horde father and that of the
submissive brothers whom he forced to feel and think as a
group. A group of modern men under the control of a dominating leader think and act like the primal horde, of which they
are a revival. Such a leader causes the group to revert to the
psychological condition of the sons in the primal horde. They
desired to be governed by the powerful father whom they
feared and admired; he was their group ideal in the place of
an ego ideal. Freud even supposes that the hypnotist exerts
his power by assuming the role of the primal father.

Freud proposes the question of the point at which man
advances from group to individual psychology, a process which
he regards as not yet complete. He says he will again make
use of "the scientific myth of the father of the primal horde,"[22]
an expression which should not be interpreted as a weakening
of his faith in the validity of the primal horde theory. The
totemistic community of brothers gave way to an organization

in which a number of families existed together under fathers who were strong but possessed much less power than the horde father. During this time there arose someone who aspired to take over the father's part. He was the first epic poet, the inventor of the heroic myth, in which a hero acting alone slays a monster, representing the father. Thus this poet created the first ego ideal. Though the hero seems to act alone, he has helpers (his brothers in the horde), who are suppressed in myth but appear in fairy tales, usually as animals. "The myth, then, is the step by which the individual emerges from group psychology," says Freud.[23] The epic poet identifies himself with the hero and thus separates himself from his brothers. When the brothers hear the myth related, they also identify themselves with the hero and likewise achieve individuality through imagination.

In 1921 Freud acquired an ally who, more persistently and prolifically than anyone else, was to employ the orthodox psychoanalytic approach in anthropology. In that year, Hungarian-born Geza Roheim was awarded the Freud Prize for two papers, a long one on the self and a much shorter one on a phase of Australian totemism.[24] With Freud's backing, Roheim made a trip to Australia in 1929 to study the world's most primitive men from the Freudian point of view. Before undertaking his field trip, however, Roheim used the data of others to produce *Australian Totemism: A Psycho-Analytic Study in Anthropology*, published in 1925. In this book Roheim gave the myth of the primal horde its most assured and extravagant statement; the disciple outdid the master.

By adding details not specified in Freud's account Roheim extended the explanatory power of the myth to matters not touched on in *Totem and Taboo*. The sons first hurled stones at the father and then placed a huge slab over the corpse to prevent it from rising. This slab represented a repression of the memory of the dead father, but by a return of the repressed it was placed upright and so was changed into a memorial column to the father. It became also a phallic symbol indicative of the sexual conflict that had led to the father's death and his later apotheosis. Roheim continues to invent interpretations until he arrives at the origin of the Stone Age itself in the primal parricide. This is from the analytical table of contents:

> The worship of phallic gravestones is a reaction formation against the wish to castrate the Jealous Sire who selfishly usurps all the women of the horde. The ancestor who impregnates all the women of the horde, or fertilizes the fields, is the Primeval Father regaining the very object after his death for which war was waged against him by his sons as long as he was alive. Throwing stones at a grave or a god as a symbol of procreation; the leader of the horde had to be stoned before the young males could proceed to procreation, and hence the magical power of stones as weapons of the first rebellion. The memory of the first conflict survives in the ritual use of stone, which must be regarded as the precursor of the Stone Age.[25]

There were many repeated parricides, so that the force of the memory was increased. In 1932 Roheim relinquished the idea that memories are phylogenetically inheritable.

Before Roheim published *Australian Totemism*, Malinowski had made extended field trips to the Trobriand Islands (1915-18) and studied the natives at close range. C. G. Seligman sent him some literature which stimulated him to investigate "the manner in which the Oedipus complex and other manifestations of the 'unconscious' might appear in a community founded on mother-right."[26] Thus Malinowski was led to make the first application of psychoanalytic theory to the study of a living primitive people. In 1923 he began to publish the results of his investigation in the periodical *Psyche*.[27] Ernest Jones challenged his interpretations, and Malinowski pursued his line of thought until he had completed a book, *Sex and Repression in Savage Society*, which appeared in 1927. This is a reply to *Totem and Taboo, Group Psychology and the Analysis of the Ego*, and *Australian Totemism*.

Malinowski questioned the basic tenet of Freudianism, the primacy and universality of the Oedipus complex. This complex, he said, arises in a form of the family which cannot be shown to be the first form and which does not exist everywhere. The Oedipus complex is a development of the patrilinear family. The nuclear complex in a matrilinear family must be different. The Trobriand natives are ignorant of the father's part in procreation and believe that the children belong altogether to the mother. The father helps care for the children and in general acts the part of an affectionate companion. The authority vested in the head of a patrilinear family is exercised by the mother's brother. Children are allowed free sexual play, but any kind of sexual interest between brother and sister is prohibited by a very strict taboo. In the Trobriand family the son experiences ambivalent feelings of love and hate toward his uncle and develops a repressed incestuous attraction only toward his sister.

Jones disagreed with Malinowski, of course. The complex in the Trobriand family is a transformation of the Oedipus complex made for the unconscious purpose of deflecting the growing boy's hate from his father to his uncle.[28] Jones held that the Oedipus tendency was primordial; he alluded to without accepting or rejecting Freud's "hypothesis" that impulses dating back to the primal horde have been inherited and his "suggestion that the inherited idea of the primal father is still actively alive in our unconscious."[29] Jones said that in Malinowski's data he could detect evidence that the Trobrianders are unconsciously aware of the fact of paternity. They have substituted the sister for the mother and the uncle for the father; in psychoanalytical language, the love for the mother is displaced upon the sister and the hatred for the father is displaced upon the uncle. Thus the boy and his father are saved from rivalry and hostility. This type of matrilineal family, Jones says, decomposes "the primal father into a kind and lenient actual father on the one hand, and a stern and moral uncle on the other."[30]

In replying to Jones and broadening the discussion to

include Freud's theory of cultural origins, Malinowski repeated
that he could not accept the Oedipus complex as absolute or
primordial, since the nuclear family complex depends on the
structure of the society. Culture could not begin with a primal
parricide expressing the Oedipus complex and surviving in
racial memory. The theory of the primal parricide is not tenable
even conjecturally. If man behaved in a primal horde as sim-
ians do, young females as well as young males would leave it
upon reaching maturity; there would then be no motive for
killing the father. If the primal parricide occurred in a state
of nature, as required by Freud's theory, there would have been
no means by which its consequences could have been fixed in
cultural institutions. Culture is a matter of slow growth extending over long periods of time; it could not have been created
by a single act. If the primal parricide is regarded as a historical fact, did culture spread all over the world as the result of
a single occurrence or did it appear independently in many
places as a result of many occurrences? The alternatives are
equally hard to imagine, Malinowski said. The more he looked
at the hypothesis, the more inclined he was to think of it as a
"just-so story." Malinowski went on to construct his own theory
of social origins, which he summarized thus: "We have developed a theory of the plasticity of instincts under culture and
the transformation of instinctive response into cultural adjustment."[31] Continuity comes from the framework of the culture
and personal contacts, not from a "group mind" or a "collective
unconscious."

The myth of the primal horde is functionally present in *The
Future of an Illusion,* which was published in the same year
as Malinowski's book. The illusion in question is religion, with
which Freud is concerned primarily as providing the basis for
the laws of culture or civilization. His general contention is
that reason—specifically, the idea of social necessity—should
replace religion as this basis. Civilization requires that man
renounce instincts leading to incest, cannibalism, and murder.

He makes this renunciation, he supposes today, because of divine commands—that is, he is prohibited from giving freedom to his destructive instincts by religion, which has behind it God's will. Religion is an illusion in that it is founded on man's wishes; in a world filled with dangers he finds himself weak and helpless and so desires a loving and protective father, whom he creates for himself in the form of God. This statement of the less deeply hidden cause of religion, Freud says, coincides with the statement of the deeper cause in *Totem and Taboo*, that religion arises from a longing for the murdered primal father, who became the prototype of God. As a consequence of the primal parricide there came into being taboos against incest and murder (first of the totem animal as father and then of his brothers), prohibitions necessary for the existence of society. When men ascribe these prohibitions to God's will, they are in a sense right, for after the parricide the sons accepted the primal father's (i.e., God's) will by deferred obedience. Religious doctrine contains "historical truth" in disguise and preserves "historical memories."[32]

On the supposition that mankind goes through the same development as children, and for the same reasons, the formation of religion would be comparable to the formation of obsessional neuroses in childhood for the suppression of instinctual impulses. Religion would then be seen as the "universal obsessional neurosis of humanity" originating in the Oedipus complex.[33] It might be that religion can be replaced as the support of civilization only by a process like that of the child's outgrowing of his neurosis, but Freud is inclined to believe that it is now time to exert a "rational mental effort, as in the analytic treatment of neuroses."[34] Thus Freud's conclusion implies that modern man is to be psychoanalytically treated for a neurosis reaching back to the primal parricide. In *The Future of an Illusion* Freud avoids or softens the presentation of the primal parricide as a "historical" event, but the myth continues to function as a part of his thought.

In *Civilization and Its Discontents* Freud seeks to show that culture (or civilization) is the product of two primal instincts, love (which he often calls Eros) and death (which he does not call Thanatos), which oppose one another. Eros binds men together, but the death instinct, through aggression, its derivative and main representative, resists the efforts of Eros. The chief means by which aggression is kept in check is a process of internalization whereby it is turned back upon the ego. The super-ego, in the form of conscience, subjects the ego to aggression. The tension between the super-ego and the ego is called the sense of guilt, which severely demands punishment for impulses that are never actualized. The super-ego heightens the sense of guilt and so diminishes man's happiness; this is the price which culture pays for progress. How does the sense of guilt, which is so important to the evolution of culture, come into being and exert its influence? In answering these questions Freud has recourse to his myth of the primal parricide.

Before mentioning the primal parricide, Freud offers a "new theory" of the development of the sense of guilt. There are two sources and two corresponding stages. In both stages, one superimposed on the other, guilt feelings force the renunciation of instinctual impulses. In the first stage the sense of guilt is founded on dread of aggression by external authority—i.e., a dread of the loss of love, which is a protection against the aggressions of authority. The appearance of the super-ego marks the beginning of the second or internalized stage. Here the sense of guilt depends on dread of this internal authority, or conscience, which is not satisfied with instinctual renunciation, but goes further and demands punishment for mere impulses, since nothing is hidden from it. Every succeeding renunciation intensifies the severity of conscience.

According to the "new theory" the sense of guilt may be the consequence of an uncommitted act of aggression; this seems to contradict the account of its "historical beginning"[35] in the murder of the primal father. But there is no contradiction, Freud says. Immediately after the murder the sons felt remorse, and the sense of guilt coincided with remorse before the appearance of the super-ego. The love of the sons for the murdered father created in them a super-ego resembling the father and having his power to punish. After the super-ego came conscience. When in later generations aggressive impulses toward the father were repeated, the guilt feelings were reinforced with every new suppression. Whether or not actual deeds are committed, the sense of guilt is made inevitable by the conflict of ambivalent emotions, hate that leads to aggressive impulses and love that leads to the super-ego and conscience. Another point of apparent contradiction is whether the aggressive energy of the super-ego is only the energy derived from external authority and preserved in the mind or whether this energy originates in the self by being turned away from the external inhibiting authority and back upon the self. The first view, Freud says, accords better with "the history of the sense of guilt, the second with the theory of it."[36] The resolution is that in both cases aggression has been turned inward.

The two versions of the origin of the sense of guilt are not presented as alternates, one of which must be preferred to the other; Freud wishes to show that they are perfectly harmonious. Indeed, they are basically the same; the "new" theory simply lacks the "historicity" of the earlier one. In formulating the "new" theory Freud often referred to the development of the child or individual; all along he was working under the assumption that the history of the individual recapitulates the history of the race, so that in the end it was easy to bring the two versions together. This assumption is made explicit and emphatic in the final pages: "When . . . we compare the cultural process in humanity with the process of development or upbringing in an individual human being, we shall conclude without much hesitation that the two are very similar in nature, if not in fact the same process applied to a different kind of object."[37] The struggle between Eros and death, the instinct of love and the instinct of death (expressed through aggression), is deeply involved in general cultural evolution as well as in individual development. Eros and death, represented by the ambivalent emotions of the sons, presided at the birth of civilization in the primal parricide, and to this day they have continued to shape individual lives; in scientific language, they are phylogenetically and ontogenetically determinative. If Freud had personified death as Thanatos besides personifying love as Eros, he might have created a larger mythological structure enveloping the myth of the primal parricide, which would have been a dramatic and fateful event in their age-old struggle.

In *Moses and Monotheism* Freud advanced a very daring thesis. Moses, a noble Egyptian estranged from his countrymen because of having embraced a new monotheistic religion which the Pharaoh Ikhnaton had tried to introduce, gave monotheism to the Jews, whom he chose as his people and led out of captivity; the Jews murdered Moses, fell away from his god, and finally returned to him. Freud distinguished a Midian Moses whose god was Jahve from the Egyptian Moses whose god was Aton; Jahve, originally a volcanic god, was a tribal god thought to be superior to the gods of other tribes, but Aton was the one true god, spiritualized, disdainful of ceremonial, and insistent upon an ethical life. The second concept of God triumphed eventually. The myth of the primal parricide is important in Freud's exposition of basic causes and processes.

When Moses revealed his god to the Jews he reunited them with the father that they had long missed and yearned for. He made them feel that they had been chosen by God, whom they identified with the primal father by an ancient memory-trace. "There was admiration, awe and gratitude that the people had found favour in His eyes...."[38] They were like the sons of the horde father again, convinced of the irresistibility of the father-god's power and completely subject to his will. But they rebelled against Moses and murdered him. "The great deed and misdeed of primaeval time, the murder of the Father, was brought home to the Jews, for fate decreed that they should repeat it on the person of Moses, an eminent father substitute."[39] This repetition of the primal parricide should have reawakened the unconscious memory of the killing of the *Urvater*. At this point Freud encounters one of the most difficult questions in his psychoanalytical exposition: why did not effects like those of the primal parricide appear sooner in Jewish history? Much time elapsed between the murder of Moses and the firm establishment of his father-religion. Freud finds the answer in the existence of a latency period in the Jewish people similar to that observed in individuals between a traumatic experience and its later psychic effects. The Jews wished to forget the murder of Moses and so suppressed its memory, and to some extent they also suppressed what was associated with it, the memory of Moses the Egyptian and his teachings. But these persistent memories gradually transformed Jahve into the god of Moses and brought about a restoration of the religion of Moses centuries after his death.

"When Moses gave to his people the conception of an Only God," says Freud, "it was not an altogether new idea, for it meant the re-animation of primaeval experience in the human family that had long ago faded from the conscious memory of mankind."[40] This experience, of course, was the primal parricide and the resultant formation of totemic religion, between which and the murder of Moses there had been a very long latency period. The murder of Moses connects the primal parricide and the murder of Christ. If the feeling of guilt for the murder of Moses stimulated the "wish-phantasy"[41] of the Messiah and if Moses was the first Messiah, Christ became his substitute. In this sense Paul could say that the Messiah had appeared and been murdered. Christ is Moses as well as the son who leads the rebellion against the primal father, and he becomes also the father by transformation after his sacrifice.

In rejecting Christ the Jews rejected redemption for the murder of the primal father, which Freud identifies as the meaning of Paul's "original sin." Their religion did not provide for the alleviation of this burden of guilt, which their prophets kept alive and which helps explain the strictness of their religious precepts and the demand for greater and greater instinctual renunciation. By retaining the religion of Moses, which is the religion of the primeval father, the Jews have maintained a source of self-confidence arising from the feeling of having been chosen by God. Moses instilled in them this feeling, which they still possess. Besides giving them confidence in themselves, it has turned others against them in the course of history. Among the people of the ancient world, Freud says, the Jews thought of themselves as occupying the position of the favored son of the dreaded father, and it was no wonder that the other children were jealous. This jealousy has continued to exist unconsciously from ancient times. The high degree of spirituality attained by Jewish monotheism, beginning with Moses' prohibition of idolatry, was another source of confidence. The religion of Moses has been a strong influence on Jewish character and on the attitude of others to the Jews.

In this last of his books Freud is very definite about the inheritance of memories. As the individual preserves memories of the past in the unconscious, so also does the race. "I hold that the concordance between the individual and the mass is in this point almost complete. The masses, too, retain an impression of the past in unconscious memory-traces."[42] And again he asserts that "the archaic heritage of mankind includes not only dispositions, but also ideational contents, memory-traces of the experience of former generations."[43] The memory of the primal parricide, after a lapse of thousands of years, has been phylogenetically preserved. Freud improves his case only slightly by saying, unemphatically in a single sentence, that the primal parricide must have been repeated and "forgotten" many times in man's prehistory.[44] He did not like Jung's term "collective unconscious,"[45] but his final position is hardly distinguishable from that of his defected disciple. Even Ernest Jones, whose loyalty Freud never had cause to doubt, attempted, unsuccessfully, to persuade his master to omit a passage in *Moses and Monotheism* expressing belief in the biological inheritance of acquired characters.[46]

In an article that appeared shortly after Freud's death in 1939, Kroeber re-examined *Totem and Taboo*.[47] He had not read *Moses and Monotheism* before writing this article. Freud, Kroeber said, had vacillated between history and psychology. He should have given up his seeming claim to historic authenticity and concentrated on a timeless explanation of the psychology underlying recurrent historic phenomena or institutions such as totemism and taboo. Without its historicity and gratuitous assumptions, Freud's thesis would have been "that certain psychic processes tend always to be operative and to find expression in widespread human institutions." And Kroeber specifies these processes. Anthropologists and sociologists would like to have a means of explaining both the repetitions and the variations of culture. Restated in a usable form, "Freud's hypothesis might long before this have proved fertile in the realm of cultural understanding instead of being mainly rejected or ignored as a brilliant fantasy." Three obstructions have prevented fruitful restatement. First, Freud has neither repudiated nor affirmed the historicity of his hypothesis. Second, Freud and his disciples have not cared whether their conclusions integrated with the totality of science. Freud has adhered to the principle of the inheritance of acquired traits, though biologists have discarded it. Third, most avowed psychoanalysts, operating within a closed system, take an all-or-nothing attitude. This can be seen in Ernest Jones and Geza Roheim. Kroeber added a postscript noting Freud's reaffirmation of the thesis of *Totem and Taboo* in *Moses and Monotheism,* which he had read after writing his article. He also noted Freud's slight concession to the effect that the primal parricide was a repeated event.

The founder of one school of psychodynamics, Abram Kardiner, who had studied under Freud in 1921, evaluated Freud's social psychology in a book that appeared in 1939, *The Individual and His Society: The Psychodynamics of Primitive Social Organization.* One of Kardiner's principal criticisms is that Freud, following the pattern of evolutionary thought, went too far in drawing a parallel between ontogenetic and phylogenetic development. If the individual has an Oedipus complex caused by childhood experiences, society also has an Oedipus complex deriving from some prehistoric occurrence that has been preserved somehow in the memory of the race. "The assumption of a primal Oedipus situation in the remote past, the myth of the primal horde, and 'primal parricide' were, therefore, inescapable."[48] Freud's version of the discredited recapitulation theory (the history of the individual recapitulates the history of the race) permitted only limited use to be made of anthropological data; it focused attention on the inherited Oedipus complex to the neglect of all cultural features not related to the complex and provided no way of dealing with differences between primitive cultures or of considering the influence of external realities on the institutions of a particular group. Furthermore, as Erich Fromm had pointed out, Freud's patients, whose development he saw as reflecting the development of mankind in general, were products of a specific culture in which "human nature" had been influenced by institutions belonging to that culture. Another error involved in the recapitulation theory was that instinct and repression do not operate in society as they do in individuals. In criticizing Roheim's effort to find evidence for the primal parricide in primitive myths, Kardiner said that the present and past are linked by institutions, not myths, recollections, or unconscious memories. "In short, we abandon the quest for origins as an explanation of society, and substitute for it a study of the dynamic relationship between man and institutions."[49]

After a period of field work from 1928 through 1931, Roheim experienced a weakening of faith in the preservation of the primal parricide as an inherited unconscious memory and moved toward an ontogenetic theory of culture stressing man's prolonged infancy. He continued to believe that men had been organized in primal hordes and that the primal parricide had occurred many times; the evidence for this, he thought, was to be found in certain myths and in historical narratives from central Australia. In 1942 Roheim wrote, "In recent years I have upheld a somewhat modified form of Freud's Primal Horde Theory."[50] References to the primal horde frequently occur in the 15 books and 150 articles that he produced before his death in 1953. In *Psychoanalysis and Anthropology* (1950) he says, "I do not assume that the Oedipus complex is universal because we inherit our Oedipus complexes from hypothetical events that may have taken place in primeval mankind (Freud, Primal Horde theory)."[51] Such an ultra-Lamarckian point of view is untenable, he acknowledges. "But," he continues, "it is evident that the Oedipus complex is a direct derivative of our partly premature, partly conservative (prolonged or retarded) rate of growing up." He never doubted the primacy and universality of the Oedipus complex, which he defended against Malinowski, Erich Fromm, and all other disbelieving anthropologists and nonorthodox psychoanalysts. As for the general socioanthropological question raised by the controversy stemming from *Totem and Taboo*, whether universal elements exist among the great variety of cultures in the world, Roheim's view was that cross-cultural parallels, though they may have additional meanings determined by the cultural context, have an independent, underlying meaning that can be uncovered by the methods of Freudian psychoanalysis. The latent content is universal though the manifest content is local.

In 1951 Clyde Kluckhohn, an anthropologist then taking a leading part in the culture-and-personality movement, gave notice that he had found his position moving steadily closer to that of Roheim. He said he used to believe that psychoanalysis was strongly culture-bound (that is, it had originated in a particular culture and was not applicable to other and different cultures); he thought, for example, that Malinowski had correctly interpreted the Oedipal situation among the Trobrianders. Kluckhohn's field work had led him to conclude that Freud and other psychoanalysts had "depicted with astonishing correctness many central themes in motivational life which are universal."[52] He went on to say, "The styles of expression of these themes and much of the manifest content are culturally determined, but the underlying psychologic drama transcends cultural difference." Anthropologists have been overindoctrinated with cultural relativism; they have been looking for differences instead of likenesses. Kluckhohn made these statements in a contribution to *Psychoanalysis and Culture*, a volume published in honor of Roheim in 1951; the next year he quoted himself in an address on "Universal Categories of Culture,"[53] delivered at the International Symposium on Anthropology, held under the presidency of Kroeber. In the discussion period Kroeber commented on Kluckhohn's paper.[54] The universals mentioned by Kluckhohn, he said, exist, but they exist on a subcultural rather than a cultural level. What culture rests on is not the same as culture. Kluckhohn's universals are biological, psychological, or social constants. The anthropologist must take them into consideration, but his proper business is to describe the content of culture. Kroeber was opposed to "reductionism," the resolution of cultural anthropology into some allied science such as psychology or psychoanalysis.

In spite of Kroeber's limitation on the role of psychology in anthropology, Kardiner's psychodynamics has provided some illuminating results when applied to a variety of cultures.[55] In making his studies and working out his methodology Kardiner had the collaboration of several anthropologists, Ralph Linton in particular. When Kardiner attempted to use psychoanalysis for the solution of sociological and anthropological problems, he found that he had to revise and modify the Freudian approach. Freud's work in the social sciences, Kardiner says in his latest book (1961), suffered because of two false assumptions, that ontogeny recapitulates phylogeny in cultural evolution and that instinct is the guide to all psychological processes.[56] The "new synthesis" of Freudian theory employed by Kardiner emphasizes adaptation rather than instinct. Kardiner lists five tenets which distinguish his application of psychodynamics to anthropology from other psychodynamic procedures such as those of Roheim; the first two are counter-Freudian, the next two are non-Freudian, and only the last permits, with restrictions, the use of Freudian methods to investigate the relation between the individual and his social institutions.[57]

Before turning to group psychology and the development of culture or civilization, Freud had constructed an individual psychology in which instincts and the Oedipus complex were basic. *Oedipus Rex* provided a ready-made drama to which he could key his individual psychology. The myth of the primal horde or primal parricide was invented to perform the same function for group psychology. If in the childhood of the individual there is a psychic experience that leads to and explains later formations, there must be something similar in the prehistory of mankind. This is true provided that the recapitulation theory is sound and that ancient memories are somehow transmissible in the race. Freud's critics were unwilling to grant these premises, which were based on discarded or obsolescent evolutionary ideas. Another point of vulnerability was Freud's presentation of the primal parricide as if it were a historical event; his very late defense, that the primal parricide had occurred repeatedly, was made in vain. Malinowski shook the Freudian view of cultural origins to its foundations when he questioned the universality of the Oedipus complex; Jones did not argue him down in a way convincing to all psychoanalysts (Fromm, notably, sided with Malinowski), and Roheim's attempt to prove him wrong by collecting and interpreting field data of his own convinced very few anthropologists besides Kluckhohn. If, according to Kardiner, emphasis should be shifted from instincts to adaptation as the prime element to be considered in cultural development, not much remains of Freudian methodology or interpretation in this area. But there will always be, no doubt, loyalists who will say, for example, that Kilroy, of "Kilroy was here" fame, is the most daring of the brothers who murdered the horde father.[58]

1. The dates given are for publication in book form. Parts of the books appeared earlier in *Imago*, the periodical founded by Freud.

2. Abram Kardiner and Edward Preble, *They Studied Man* (Cleveland and New York, 1961), p. 232. See also Ernest Jones, *The Life and Work of Sigmund Freud*, II (New York, 1955), 351.

3. *Totem and Taboo*, trans. James Strachey (London, 1950), p. ix.

4. *Ibid.*, pp. 141-42.

5. *Ibid.*, pp. 145, 152.

6. *Ibid.*, p. 146.

7. *Ibid.*, p. 150.

8. *Ibid.*, pp. 151-52.

9. *Ibid.*, p. 153.

10. *Ibid.*, p. 156.

11. *Ibid.*

12. *Ibid.*, p. 157.

13. *Ibid.*, p. 159.

14. See *The Myth of the Eternal Return*, trans. Willard R. Trask (New York, 1954); *The Sacred and the Profane*, trans. Willard R. Trask (New York, 1959); *Myths, Dreams and Mysteries*, trans. Philip Mairet (London, 1960).

15. "Psycho-Analysis and the Savage," *Athenaeum*, Feb. 13, 1920, p. 206. This is a review of A. A. Brill's translation of *Totem and Taboo*.

16. *The Life and Work of Sigmund Freud*, III (New York, 1957), 328.

17. P. 142. Not until the publication of *Moses and Monotheism* in 1939 did Freud refer to the primal parricide as an often repeated event occurring in prehistory.

18. *The Life and Work of Sigmund Freud*, III, 369.

19. "*Totem and Taboo*: An Ethnographic Psychoanalysis," *American Anthropologist*, XXII (January, 1920), 48-55. Reprinted in Kroeber's *The Nature of Culture* (Chicago, 1952), pp. 301-5.

20. *Group Psychology and the Analysis of the Ego*, trans. James Strachey (London, 1949), p. 90.

21. *Ibid.*, pp. 90-91.

22. *Ibid.*, p. 112.

23. *Ibid.*, p. 114.

24. The second paper announced Roheim's theory that the brothers used stones to kill the horde father. It was translated into English: "Stone-Shrine and Tomb: Ethnological Remarks on Totemism and Culture Stages in Australia," *International Journal of Psycho-Analysis*, III (1922), 121-27.

25. *Australian Totemism* (London, 1925), p. 23.

26. Bronislaw Malinowski, *Sex and Repression in Savage Society* (London, 1927), p. ix.

27. "The Psychology of Sex and the Foundation of Kinship in Primitive Societies," *Psyche*, IV (October, 1923), 98-128; "Psycho-Analysis and Anthropology," *Psyche*, IV (April, 1924), 293-332; "Complex and Myth in Mother-Right," *Psyche*, V (January, 1925), 194-216. Some of this material went into *The Sexual Life of Savages in North-Western Melanesia* (London, 1929), but the major proportion of it was incorporated in *Sex and Repression in Savage Society*.

28. "Mother-Right and the Sexual Ignorance of Savages," *International Journal of Psycho-Analysis*, VI (1925), 109-30; reprinted in Jones's *Essays in Applied Psycho-Analysis* (London, 1951), II, 145-73.

29. *Essays*, p. 162.

30. *Ibid.*, p. 166.

31. *Sex and Repression in Savage Society*, p. 277.

32. *The Future of an Illusion*, trans. W. D. Robson-Scott (London, 1949), pp. 74-75 and 78.

33. *Ibid.*, p. 76.

34. *Ibid.*, p. 77.

35. *Ibid.*, p. 128.

36. *Ibid.*, p. 130.

37. *Ibid.*, p. 133.

38. *Moses and Monotheism*, trans. Katherine Jones (London, 1951), p. 210.

39. *Ibid.*, p. 143.

40. *Ibid.*, p. 204.

41. *Ibid.*, p. 144.

42. *Ibid.*, p. 151.

43. *Ibid.*, p. 159; see also pp. 204-5.

44. *Ibid.*, p. 130.

45. *Ibid.*, p. 208.

46. *The Life and Work of Sigmund Freud*, III, 313.

47. "*Totem and Taboo* in Retrospect," *American Journal of Sociology*, XLV (November, 1939), 446-51. This was reprinted in *The Nature of Culture*, pp. 306-9.

48. P. 387; the book was published in New York.

49. P. 108.

50. "The Primal Horde and Incest in Central Australia," *Journal of Criminal Psychopathology*, III (January, 1942), 454.

51. P. 424; the book was published in New York.

52. Clyde Kluckhohn and William Morgan, "Some Notes on Navaho Dreams," in *Psychoanalysis and Culture: Essays in Honor of Geza Roheim*, ed. George B. Wilbur and Warner Muensterberger (New York, 1951), p. 120.

53. In *Anthropology Today: An Encyclopedic Inventory*, prepared under the chairmanship of A. L. Kroeber (Chicago, 1953), pp. 507-23.

54. *An Appraisal of Anthropology Today*, ed. Sol Tax *et al.* (Chicago, 1953), p. 119.

55. Marquesan and Tonala cultures are analyzed in *The Individual and His*

Society, Comanche and Alorese in *The Psychological Frontiers of Society* (New York, 1945). In the second book the culture of a small American town, called "Plainville" for the sake of anonymity, is analyzed also.

56. *They Studied Man*, p. 238.

57. *Ibid.*, pp. 244-45.

58. So says Richard Sterba in "Kilroy Was Here," *American Imago*, V (November, 1948), 173-81.

Folklore of the South and Racial Discrimination

JAMES M. LACY

THOSE OF US who work and study in the field of folklore soon develop a fondness for this most intimate part of our knowledge and understanding of life. We relish this part of our education, the pleasure undimmed and unscarred by memories of long hours spent in formal study of what sometimes seemed extraneous subject matter. We have a feeling of admiration and affinity for the folk who have given us this lore.

It is with a feeling of disloyalty and sorrow that one suggests that the fountainheads of our folklore could also pour out streams of distrust and hatred toward those who differ from the majority in belief or national origin or color. Yet, the evidence indicates that the discriminations exercised against certain racial and cultural groups in this country are the results of attitudes instilled in our citizens at a very early age. These prejudiced concepts enter the minds of our youth at the same time and in the same manner as the remainder of the great body of lore which one generation passes on to the next. Thus attitudes of antagonism, feelings of racial superiority, and lack of respect for ethnic and cultural minorities can be traced directly to the same origins as the other elements of folklore which constitute our cultural heritage.

Most of us who have spent our lives in the South are proud of the regional characteristics which we possess or which have been attributed to us. But we must recognize that there has been rampant in our culture an insidious force, often unseen or unrecognized, pulling us toward racial prejudice and discrimination. We see this force strongest in that segment of our population most susceptible to folk patterns of thought and feeling. And those of us who recognize prejudice for what it is are not always completely immune to its influence. In spite of intent and desire we sometimes find it lurking tenaciously in the backgrounds of our minds, ready to reveal itself at an unguarded moment.

The child is introduced to racial prejudice early in his life. The names which he hears applied to the Negro, such as "coon," "darky," "nigger," and "burr-head," give an early impression that the Negro is an object of humor and scorn. He buys fireworks called "nigger chasers," nuts called "nigger toes," makes a toy called a "nigger shooter," and recites a jingle about catching "a nigger by his toe." He hears degrading jokes about Negroes and sees signs in public places which distinguish between "Colored" and "Whites." From earliest childhood he is conscious of the segregation of the colored race: in school, in church, in theaters, in public conveyances, and in the city in which he lives. The evidence of racial distinction is omnipresent. Sometimes it is open and brutal; more often it is subtle and veiled, ranging from an appellation of scorn and derision to an instinctive withdrawal from physical contact. These attitudes of discrimination are as deeply ingrained in the minds of children as are those of morality or patriotism.

As the child grows older and becomes active in his society, he practices these discriminations he has observed. He learns to ignore the presence of colored people, or to be condescending when association is necessary. He learns to accept their inferior status without question or twinge of conscience, and he begins to deride their most serious activities as emulations of their superiors. The youth comes to expect deference from the Negro and to resent the absence of it. The adult, through ignorance or habit, continues these discriminations, or, recognizing the nature of these prejudices, does nothing, or, little, to remedy them. The individual who has been born and reared in the South has had imbued in him throughout his life and from almost all aspects of his society an acute awareness of racial inequality.

The folk image of the Negro that has been created in the minds of southern whites has been long in the making and is firmly entrenched. Many characteristics have been attributed to the race as a whole, and these are in turn applied to the individual. The picture usually presented is that of a likable fellow with a pleasant nature but inferior capabilities. This idea in the minds of the white race that the Negro is mentally and morally inferior is the basis for racial discrimination and the chief justification for denying him equal opportunities. According to extremists holding this view, the reason for this inferiority is not environmental, but rather biological and racial. As pointed out by Maurice R. Davie in his study of *Negroes in American Society,* the doctrine of the Negro's inferiority has a history as long as his stay in America, but the basis for this concept has shifted through the years.[1] First was the question of whether the Negro was to be classed as a human being with a soul; later it was whether he had the intelligence to master the rudiments of learning; then his capability for higher educa-tion was debated; and today the question is "whether he has those high qualities of imagination, intellect, initiative, and aggressiveness characteristic of the Anglo-Saxons."

The popular stereotype of the Negro in fiction and in movies has been that of an ignorant, superstitious, lazy, irresponsible individual. This view was satirized by a Negro journalist, George S. Schuyler, in 1927:

We Ethiops, one gathers from this mass of evidence, are a childish, shiftless, immoral, primitive, incurably religious, genially incompetent, incredibly odoriferous, . . . mentally inferior people with pronounced homi-cidal tendencies. We are incapable of . . . self-restraint and irresponsible except when led by white folks. We possess a penchant for assaulting white females and an inordinate appetite for chicken, gin, and water-melon. While it is finally and reluctantly admitted that we belong to the human race, we are accorded only the lowest position in the species, a notch or two above the great apes. . . . In short, from examining the bulk of the evidence, the impartial investigator must conclude that the Negro has almost a monopoly of all the more discreditable characteristics of mankind. But at the same time one is effusively informed that he is deeply loved and thoroughly understood, especially by his pork-skinned friends of Southern derivation.[2]

Perhaps the most cherished image of the Negro in the southern mind is the "Uncle Tom" type of individual, the devoted, faithful servant whose one aim in life is to serve his master. The master, in turn, repays this loyalty with affection and protects him as one of his own. Among Negroes the term "Uncle Tom" is used to show their contempt for a member of their race who seeks favor with whites by being subservient.

At the heart of racial discrimination in this country, serving as both cause and effect, lies the lore concerning color distinc-tion. As in the other forms of prejudice, this color consciousness was learned in the true folk manner. That the pigmentation of the skin is the chief basis for racial prejudice is evident when the bias extended toward other darker-skinned minorities is considered. This awareness of color is so strong that the degree of discrimination often corresponds to the shade of darkness. The proof of white superiority given recently by a staunch segregationist was that all the Negroes who had attained prom-inence in the country were light-colored, that is, part white. We are forced to accept, not for the reason intended, but for its statistical accuracy, the correctness of this statement. Several studies made on this subject indicate that some doors are easier to open for the Negro if his skin is of a lighter color. Davie states that Negroes with lighter complexions have long enjoyed opportunities and a social status superior to those of unmixed blood, and that, with some notable exceptions, most Negro leaders have mixed blood. Davie goes on to say that Negroes themselves draw the color line, that "the lighter colored form cliques to which darker Negroes are admitted, if at all, only by wealth, education, or attainment." Davie explains the superior attitude of mulattoes, using the term regardless of degree of mixture, by asserting that a greater proportion of them derive from the free Negroes and from the favored class of house slaves, with many of them descending from the masters themselves, from even such eminent persons as Alexander Hamilton, Patrick Henry, and Thomas Jefferson. It seems natural that during the period of slavery the master of the plantation would show preference to his own or some relative's mulatto child, giving him an education or special privileges, or freeing him when he became an adult. Many accounts of plantation life in the ante-bellum South make references to the lighter-skinned house servants and the darker field workers.

In a few places in the South just after the Civil War, the mulattoes organized themselves into a little guild known as "The Blue Vein Circle," from which those who were black were excluded. One of the folk rhymes from this group shows their disdain for their darker-skinned brothers:[3]

> Stan' back, black man,
> You cain't shine;
> Yo lips is too thick,
> An' you hain't my kin'.
>
> Git 'way, black man,
> You jes hain't fine;
> I'se done quit foolin'
> Wid de nappy-headed kin'.
>
> Stan' back, black man!
> Cain't you see
> Dat a kinky-headed chap
> Hain't nothin' side o' me?

This color-consciousness in the folklore of the Negroes has been confirmed by Negro writers. Dr. Charles S. Johnson in his study of southern rural Negro youth, *Growing Up in the*

Black Belt,[4] found decided color preferences among the boys and girls who were interviewed. A simple test was devised to determine the importance of color as a factor in the personality development of Negro youth. A familiar color classification was employed: black, dark brown, brown, light-brown, yellow, and white. The individual was asked to check the color of persons toward whom he held certain favorable and unfavorable attitudes.

The results of this test seem very significant. For example, the number of boys who checked light-brown as the color of "The most beautiful girl you know" was almost ten times greater than the number who checked black. The rating of color preference by the girls was very similar in questions concerning the boys they admired or disliked the most. The association of color with moral judgments in these tests was almost as significant as was that with judgments of physical appearance.

In the list of favorable descriptions given on this test, light-brown received by far the highest ranking. Brown was second with approximately half as many votes, and "the worst color to be" was black. The color yellow was the only one of the lighter colors to receive social opprobrium, as yellowness seems to be associated with a recent mixture of the two races.

The reactions to color on the part of both races show some similarities and many differences. It would be interesting, but probably impossible, to determine the effect which nonracial associations with the colors white and black, found throughout our folklore, might have on racial discrimination. The popular concepts of white as a symbol of purity and goodness and black as a symbol of ill-favor and evil are strong in American lore. We wear white for the happiness of marriage and black for the mourning of death. Every child knows the difference between a white lie and a black one. Undesirable citizens are "black-balled" or put on a "black list," and in our society there are "black sheep" and "blackguards." The more superstitious among us fear black magic and try to avoid black cats. It seems possible that the traditional stigma placed on the color black might have contributed toward the discrimination against the Negro race.

Except for the legal restrictions which exclude the Negro from many of the activities of the whites, no aspect of folklore has been more conspicuous in its regulation of behavior than the etiquette practiced in biracial associations. The code of etiquette based on the color line had its inception during slavery. Clearly understood by all and maintained by tradition and custom, this social ritual needed little if any legislation to enforce it. Bertram W. Doyle in his study of race relations in the South maintains that there was no such thing as a race problem before the Civil War.[5] The clearly defined caste system afforded a means by which the master-slave relationship might be carried on with little friction, and the most intimate bonds could exist between master and slave on the plantation, provided the proper etiquette was not violated by either party. Part of an old Negro spiritual bears witness to one custom observed in this social ritual. The refrain, "I want to go to heaven settin' down," is possibly a reference to the fact that the slave was expected to stand whenever he was in the "Big House."

With the close of the war and the end of slavery the old way of life was gone, and with it the customs and social ritual which had governed race relations. The plantation owners were no longer the dominant force in the South, and their heirs to political authority were the masses of small landowners, tenants, and tradesmen, the "poor whites" of ante-bellum days, for whom the slaves had had little respect. An old Negro jingle shows the attitude toward the lower class of whites:[6]

> My name's Ran, I wuks in de san';
> But I'd druther be a Nigger dan a po' white man.
> I'd druther be a Nigger, an' plow ole Beck
> Dan a white Hill Billy with his long red neck.

The subsequent acts of this new force in the South did little to bring about respect. To maintain white supremacy, laws were passed to enforce the restrictions of the caste system which had formerly been maintained by custom and public opinion. Thus the caste system was perpetuated in the South and with it the etiquette of race relations, ever present but gradually being altered as the status of the Negro in the society changed. In recent years the formality of these associations has lessened considerably, and in many cases disappeared. Where interracial etiquette is still practiced it is usually in employer-employee relationships or among the less educated members of both groups who are still to a considerable extent bound by the mores of the past

Dr. Johnson, in his study of the Negro in the rural South, published in 1941, reports that he found a consistency in the racial etiquette concerning some activities, and differing attitudes in some sections about other relationships.[7] The two universally tabooed practices were found to be intermarriage and interdancing. Interdining was generally prohibited, but was permitted in some areas on special occasions. Negroes were expected to use "Mr." and "Mrs." when addressing whites, but as a rule only white salesmen or others seeking patronage used these terms when speaking to Negroes. In some counties Negroes were expected to enter a house by the back door. Some stores required Negroes to remove their hats on entering and refused to let them try on hats and gloves. A boy or girl could buy an ice cream cone in a drugstore but could not eat it until he had left the building.

At times some fine distinctions have been made in observing the etiquette of racial relations. The story is told of one white man in Mississippi who readily admitted that he had had a colored mistress for thirty years, but hotly denied that he had ever sat down to breakfast with her.

It was inevitable that the lore concerning the Negro should affect the folklore of the Negro himself. The racial etiquette imposed upon him, his position in society, and the way he was regarded by those who were prejudiced against him had to contribute to the view he had of himself. It is doubtful whether anyone outside the Negro race can fully understand what it is like to be a part of what James Baldwin calls "that fantastic and fearful image which we have lived with since the first slave fell beneath the lash." He reminds us that "the American image of the Negro also lives in the Negro's heart," and that only through an adjustment to this position created for him by others can he "secure his birthright as a man."[8] That this adjustment is not easy can be seen in Baldwin's statement that he "can conceive of no Negro, native to this country, who has not, by the age of puberty, been irreparably scarred by the conditions of his life."

The myth that the Negro is content with his lot has been strong in southern lore. Created as a balm to the southern conscience, this belief has been able to survive until recent years because of the reluctance of a majority of Negroes to press a seemingly hopeless cause. The individual also learned that an appearance of cheerful acceptance of his status was to his advantage. The true attitude of the Negro toward his position in American society can be found in his writings. One wrote that "black is a terrible color to be born." It is not surprising that some of this writing portrays desperate action taken against the ever present oppression that the writers feel. Countee Cullen, for example, wrote that ". . . one grows weary turning cheek to blow."[9]

The ultimate reaction of desperation toward an unfriendly society is seen in the main character of Richard Wright's novel *Native Son*.[10] "Bigger" Thomas sees in the white race a hated symbol of all his frustrations and all the oppressions he has suffered—a symbol also of self-hatred because he has no place in the white man's or any other society. His murder of the white girl gives him his first sense of well being, of asserting himself, not against the girl personally, but against those forces which have made him what he is.

Today in the South we can observe a phenomenon which is probably unique in our society. We can see in the process a great change taking place in the beliefs, customs, and patterns of thought of a large segment of our population. Just as Americans gave up the common belief that the only good Indian was a dead one, they are now beginning to discard the popular theory of Negro inferiority, which has been the basis for racial prejudice. Americans of both races are coming to realize that the caste structure on which racial discrimination is founded was not created by anyone living today, and that no individual or racial group of this generation is actually responsible for it.

The image of the Negro in our society is changing rapidly. One evidence of this can be seen in those media through which the earlier image was propagated. In fictional writings, in movies, and in the theater, the old stereotyped characters have all but disappeared. Today it is common for the Negro to be portrayed on the screen as an admirable or even heroic figure, and the old-time Negro minstrel has gone the way of the patent medicine show.

One by one the different facets of discriminatory practice are being displaced. The segregation of the races, unequal employment opportunities, and voting restrictions are opposed by law, but racial discrimination in the South, and in the rest of America, will come to an end, not by legislation alone, but only when there is a real change in the folklore of the American people.

1. Maurice R. Davie, *Negroes in American Society* (New York: McGraw-Hill Book Co., 1949), p. 367.

2. George S. Schuyler, "Our White Folks," *American Mercury*, XII (December, 1927), 385.

3. Thomas W. Talley (ed.), *Negro Folk Rhymes* (New York: Macmillan Company, 1922), p. 10.

4. Charles S. Johnson, *Growing Up in the Black Belt* (Washington, D.C.: American Council on Education, 1941), pp. 258-65.

5. Bertram W. Doyle, *The Etiquette of Race Relations in the South* (Chicago: University of Chicago Press, 1937), p. xxi.

6. Talley, *op. cit.*, pp. 42-43.

7. Johnson, *op. cit.*, p. 277.

8. James Baldwin, *Notes of a Native Son* (Boston: Beacon Press, 1955), p. 38.

9. Countee Cullen, *On These I Stand* (New York: Harper & Bros., 1947), p. 85.

10. Richard Wright, *Native Son* (New York: Harper & Bros., 1940).

Texas Stream Names

JOHN Q. ANDERSON

THE FOLK IMAGINATION was not as fertile in naming Texas streams as it was in naming post offices,[1] towns, and villages; but early settlers did originate a few unusual creek names, such as *Talking John, Hardshell, Fuzzy, Supple Jack, Devils Jump, Washboard, Greasy, Jawbone, Getaway, Picnitt, Purgatory, Raggedy, Rowdy, Tar Box, Hunting Shirt, One Eye, Monkey, Swampoodle, Squabble,* and *Thunder Struck.* These intriguing names are rare, however; most of the approximately four thousand small water courses in the state bear much more ordinary names—those of families, animals, vegetation, or terrain features.[2]

Despite centuries of occupation by Indians and Spaniards, relatively few of the total number of stream names reflect those cultures. Spanish names of all types form only about 5 per cent of the total, excluding the major rivers which retained their Spanish designations.[3] Names associated with Indians, one way or another, account for only about 3 per cent of the total number.[4] Thus, 92 per cent of the four thousand names of streams are Anglo-Saxon, mute testimony of the dominance of the Anglo-American culture after 1820—as foreseen by Emerson in 1844, when, in writing about the proposed annexation of Texas, he said: "It is very certain that the strong British race, which have now overrun so much of this continent, must also overrun that tract."[5] The result is that terminology applied to streams is largely English. The word *creek* is, for example, by far the most common, with a limited use of *run* in East Texas, an area most closely linked with the mountain country of the eastern United States where *run (mill run)* appears extensively. The southern word *branch*, especially *spring branch*, is widely distributed in Texas; *fork*, often with the qualifying directional *east, west, north, south*, is applied to both large and small tributary streams. The more colloquial *prong* is less common. Intermittent streams are called *draws; gully* appears in limited areas in South Texas, though *gulch* is quite rare. Spanish *canyon* and *arroyo* are widely used in far West Texas, along the Mexican border, and in a small area in the Panhandle. *Bayou*[6] appears extensively in the Gulf Coast region.

The drainage system of the state is largely self-contained, since about three-quarters of its boundaries are streams: the Rio Grande, south-southwest; Red River, much of the north; Sabine, more than half of the east. Consequently, almost all small streams begin and end in the state as tributaries to these river boundaries. No streams flow west out of Texas; none flow south into Mexico; a very few in the Panhandle flow east into Oklahoma; and a small number flow east into Arkansas and Louisiana. Generally, the land slopes gently from northwest to southeast, and the rainfall diminishes from east to west, from about fifty inches annually on the Sabine to less than ten inches around El Paso, a fact which determines that the largest number of small streams are in the eastern half of the state. The lay of the land and the rainfall that determined the nature and amount of vegetation influenced settlers who gave names to Texas streams. For convenience of discussion these names are listed in the following order:[7] names of people *(Smith, Johnson, Mary);* names of trees, shrubs, and plants *(Oak, Briar, Onion);* terrain, size, color, number *(Prairie, Big, Black, Second);* animals, birds, fish, and insects *(Horse, Duck, Catfish, Bee);* events and implements *(Camp Meeting, Ox Yoke);* rocks and minerals *(Flat Rock, Salt);* Spanish names of all types *(Charco Redondo,*

Seco); and names which are associated with Indians *(Squaw, Kickapoo).*

I

Early Texans drew heavily on their own family names to designate streams, more than fourteen hundred of them (shown in Appendix). Significantly very few of these surnames commemorate historical personages, either Texan or national, a direct contrast with county names—*Austin, Houston, Crockett, Washington, Jackson, Polk, Lee.* Too insignificant to be of concern to legislators, small streams were named for the settlers who lived on the surrounding land. It is now next to impossible to discover in written records who the Joneses, Smiths, and Wallaces were who gave their names to creeks, branches, and draws. Questionnaires sent to county librarians, local historians, and county newspapers brought only a few specific explanations.[8] For instance, *Martin Creek,* Rusk County, was named for Daniel Martin, who lived nearby; *Downie Draw,* Pecos County, bears the name of Charlie Downie, who settled there; *Iron Creek,* Waller County (easily mistaken for a mineral), recalls John Irons, an early settler; *Thut Creek,* Gray County, was named for pioneer Henry Thut; *Journigan Creek,* Hunt County, probably was named for William Jernigan, who had the first store in the area; fur trader Colonel Bent gave his name to *Bent Creek,* Hutchinson County. More prominent is Samuel Highsmith, a soldier of the Revolution and Texas Ranger, who is remembered in *Highsmith Creek,* Guadalupe County; since there is also a *Smith Creek* in that county, local residents sometimes distinguish between *Highsmith* and *"Low"* Smith creeks.[9]

These few specific explanations of family names attached to some creeks indicate that similar stories lie behind other names, but such once well-known facts escaped recording. Even more intriguing are streams that bear given names of people—*Jakes Creek, Mariana Creek, French John Creek.* Some individuals, by personality or by deeds, became associated with specific places. For instance, *Kate Creek,* Howard County, is said to be named for a woman who lost her life attempting to save a pet coon from a saloon fire.[10] *Marys Creek,* Tarrant County, was named for an Indian squaw who with her children drowned in the stream during a flood. Streams bearing women's given names number thirty-four, as compared to thirty for men's first names. Creeks and bayous in East and South Texas named *Gracie, Polly, Magie,* and *Caroline* may recall wives of settlers or widows, but probably streams called *Lucy, Lola,* and *Rose,* located in the ranch country where women were scarce, may be for dance-hall girls or perhaps cowboys' sweethearts back in the settlements. *White Woman Creek* in the upper Panhandle doubtless recalls the greatest of all horrors to pioneer women, captivity by the Comanches. *Big* and *Little Sister* creeks, Kendall County, derive not from specific women, but from the fact that they meet below the town of Sisterdale. Even more anonymous are the victims who gave names to the nine *Deadman* creeks, draws, and branches. In Guadalupe County *Toms Creek,* named for William Tom, became *Bell Creek,* and then about 1861 was changed to *Deadmans Creek* for reasons not now obvious.

Nationalities and races are remembered in a few stream names: *Dutchman, Dutch* (for a German trader who drowned in that Rusk County creek), *Paddy, Mexican,* and *Negro.* Satan himself is honored in *Devils Creek* and *Devils Draw, Devils Jump Creek, Big* and *Little Satan,* and *Devils River,* which supposedly was renamed by Texas Ranger Jack Hays, who, when told that it was called *San Pedro's,* said that it looked more like the Devil's.[11] The Rangers themselves are commemorated in *Rangers Branch,* Kendall County, because they once headquartered at the spring which heads the creek.

II

Like the American Indian before him, the American pioneer was greatly dependent upon trees for housing materials, implements, and sometimes food. The first settlers in Texas found timbered regions in the eastern part of the state not unlike those they had left behind, and named streams for surrounding trees. Later arrivals in the higher and drier parts of the state found fewer trees but named streams for those they did find. Indirectly, then, streams named for trees reflect the rainfall and the original pattern of timber. Statistically, the number of streams named for trees is as follows:

Trees

Oak	69

(Live Oak, 28; White Oak, 13; Red Oak, 7; Pin Oak, 8; Post Oak, 5; one each: Willow Oak, Lone Oak, Shinery)

Cedar	57
Elm	56
Cottonwood	52
Willow	29
Walnut	26
Cypress	24
Pecan	20
Hackberry	17
Pine	16
Sycamore	13

Other trees represented in stream names and the numbers of them are: *Gum,* 9; *Mesquite,* 8; *Cherry,* 8; *Peach,* 7; *Mulberry,* 6; *Hickory,* 5; *China,* 5; *Birch,* 5; *Beech,* 4; *Bois d'Arc,* 4; *Ash,* 3; two each—*Chinquapin (Yonker Pin,* one), *Myrtle, Dogwood, Crabapple;* one each—*Alder, Haw, Holly, Juniper, Magnolia, Maple, Palmetto, Paradise* (Ailanthus?), *Pawpaw, Persimmon, Redbud, Retama,* and *Yupon.* Related names are: *Timber,* 3; *Grove,* 3; *Little Timber,* 2; and one each—*Cross Timber, Greenwood, Thickety, Mott, Wood Hollow, Orchard,* and *Isle du Bois,* one of the few French names.

Because of climate, streams named for oak, cypress, pecan, and pine trees abound in East Texas; similarly in drier West Texas cedar, cottonwood, and hackberry appear. Location alone is not, however, a totally reliable index to tree names; for example, some of the twenty-four *Cypress* creeks are located in the bottoms of the Guadalupe River north of San Antonio, and the first settlers there survived the early years by cutting cypress, making shingles, and hauling them to San Antonio to sell.[12]

The many streams bearing the name *Oak* indicate the importance of that tree to pioneers. Oak was useful for housing timbers, fence posts, wagon wheels and coupling poles, and singletrees and doubletrees for plows and vehicles. Cedar, too, was important and when large enough substituted for oak in some uses, such as fence posts and firewood. The story is told that wealthy West Texas ranchers who retired to San Antonio paid dearly for cedar wood to burn, long after natural gas was commonly used. Elm was a hard, strong wood useful for saddle trees and wheel hubs.[13] Cottonwood and willow trees, often the only green in the dun color of much southwestern scenery, gave names to many Texas watercourses. Of the fifty-two called *Cottonwood,* a few are the Spanish *alamo,* and some of the *Willows* are the Spanish *suaz.* Black walnut trees, largely in East Texas, provided hard wood for gunstocks, foundation timbers, and furniture.

The pecan, now the state tree, was valued by the Indians for its nuts long before white men came, as is shown in the Caddo Indian folktale of the old woman who gathered and hoarded all the pecans; eventually Coyote killed her because of her greed, and "ever since then the pecan trees have grown everywhere and belonged to all of the people."[14] In the fall of 1858, when Judge S. C. Cross settled in Hood County in Central Texas, the pecan crop was so plentiful that his children raked up the nuts by the hatful, beat them up, fed them to chickens, and produced the fattest ones in the settlement. The Judge also brought the first hogs into the area, and they grew so fat on pecans and acorns and multiplied so prolifically that they stocked the whole neighborhood and anyone who wished could capture them for his own.

The bois d'arc tree, also called Osage orange, hedge apple, and mock orange, was extensively cultivated once in East and Central Texas, where three counties have *Bois d'Arc* creeks. One historian says:

Early settlers used this wood for fence posts, house blocks, pilings for bridges, and for other purposes. Settlers from Ohio, Illinois, and some other states were familiar with osage hedge fences in their home states; so, soon after their arrival in Texas they began planting the seeds of the osage apple where fences were needed. In an article in the *Texas Almanac* of 1868, former Governor J. W. Throckmorton explained how to plant, grow, and develop an osage hedge fence from seeds or from cuttings. . . . After barbed wire fences came into use the osage hedge was regarded as a nuisance, particularly adjacent to cultivated fields since nothing would grow within fifty to seventy-five feet of it.[15]

Shrubs are represented in stream names as follows: *Brushy*, 49; *Grape*, 9; *Briar*, 9; *Berry*, 4; *Mayhaw*, 3; and one each— *Butternut*, *Catclaw*, *Muscadine*, and *Screwbean*. Plants also gave names to streams: *Cane*, 44; *Grass*, 10; *Cattail* (and *Rush*), 7; *Onion*, 5; *Hay*, 4; *Cactus*, 3; *Moss*, 3; *Cotton*, 3; *Sage*, 2; *Loco*, 2; one each—*Buttercup*, *Corn*, *Cocklebur*, *Goard*, *Goldenrod*, *Lily*, *Melon*, *Nettle*, *Pumpkin*, *Pursley*, *Violet*, *Weed*, and *Wheat*. Hobart Huson of Refugio County says that *Melon Creek* is a corruption of *Malone*, for John Malone.[16] S. W. Ross of Kilgore mentions *Peatown Branch* and *Peavine Creek* in Gregg County. He says that in the 1870's Trip Elder came from Georgia, built a sawmill and store on the bank of a creek; he sold mostly peas at his store because they were plentiful; hence the people got in the habit of saying, "Let's go to Peatown," and the post office became that.[17]

The traveler in some parts of Texas today who sees untended pastures overgrown with prickly pear may feel that the pioneers were remiss in giving only three creeks the name *Cactus*. The changing use of land has caused the prickly pear, like the mesquite, to flourish since prairie fires are no longer common. Another menace is the loco (Spanish, crazy) weed which gave its name to two streams. The gray-green leaves and bright purple flowers arrive early in the spring to tempt grazing animals. When addicted to the weed, animals hunt for it, eat it, and eventually become "locoed," that is, grow thin and unsteady, and even die. A common belief on the Davis Ranch, Wheeler County, was that range horses, caught up and broken to ride, were likely to be dangerous when overheated if they had eaten extensively of loco weed.

III

Settlers were also impressed by the terrain surrounding streams, by the nature of the water they contained, and by their size, and named more than five hundred of them accordingly:

TERRAIN

Prairie	20
Bluff	16
Flat	14
Mountain	11

Crooked, 9; Hill, 8; Valley, 8; Rough, 8; Lost, 8; Fall, 7; Glade, 6; Richland, 5; Island, 4; Shoal, 4; Line, 3

Two each—Knob, Scatter, Broad, Mound, Canyon, Meadow, Ridge, Cutoff

One each—Blackland, Bottom, Branch, Channel, Cove, Delta, Desert, Eddy, Glenwood, Gravelly, Ground Gulley, Hayrick, Highbank, Hollow, Incline, Low, Oasis, Point, Shut-In, Steep, Straight, Table, Wood Island

Spring water, valued above all other types in the pioneer period, accounts for the many *Spring* creeks. A desirable homesite included a spring near enough to prevent ambush by Indians. Springs, of course, gave names to towns as well as creeks, such as *Big Spring* and *Coldspring*. Appreciation of good water is expressed in the many *Clear, Cold, Sweet,* and *Sweetwater* creeks. But many creeks were muddy or full of dangerous quicksand; thus *Mud* or *Muddy* creeks and the

Boggy creeks (including the Spanish *Atascosa Creek*). The three *Stink* creeks were evidently not named by proper Victorians.

NATURE OF WATER

Spring	64
Dry	43
Boggy	27
Clear	26
Mud, Muddy	17
Lake	16

Moss, 6; Deep, 6; Cold (Frio, 1), 5; Waterhole, 4; Running, 4; Pond, 4; Stink, 3; Wells, 2; Rainy, 2

One each—Artesian, Bay, Dead, Glaze, Natural Wells, Roundhole, Sour, Sweet, Sweetwater, Smoky

Color and size account for more than 130 creek names: *Black*, 15; *Blue*, 13; *Red* (*Red Bank*, 4; *Red Paint*, 1), 8; *White*, 6; *Yellow*, 6; *Green*, 4; *Paint*, 3; *Dark* (*Dark Valley, Dark Canyon*), 3; and one *Chocolate Creek*. Some of these, such as *Black*, *White*, and *Green*, may be family names. The three *Paint* creeks were perhaps so called because they supplied clay for Indian war paint, or possibly they had some connection with the spotted or "paint" ponies favored by Indians. Neither guess explains *Turkey Paint Creek*. Size gave names to seventy-five creeks: *Long*, 36; *Big*, 27; *Little*, 11; and *Short*, one.

Since landmarks were important in the early days, a number of streams were named to indicate that they were just that: *Sixmile*, 6; *Threemile*, 5; *Fourmile*, 4; *Fivemile*, 3; *Eightmile*, 3; *Tenmile*, 3; *Twomile*, 2; *Ninemile*, 2; one each—*Half*, *Mile and a Half*, *Twelvemile*, and *Fifteenmile*. Unique in numbering are some tributaries of the Canadian River in the Panhandle where streams are named *First, Second, Third, Fourth*, and *Fifth* creeks. Similar are the branches of historic *Coleto Creek* in far South Texas—*Threemile Coleto, Eight-, Twelve-*, and *Fifteenmile Coleto*. There are also four *Double* creeks, three *Twin* creeks, and one *Nine Point Creek*.

IV

The importance of animals, wild and domesticated, to early Texans is evident in the fact that almost five hundred streams bear their names, including those named for fish, birds, and insects:

ANIMAL KINGDOM

Horses 67
    (Mustang, 35; Wildhorse, 3; Pony, 3; one each—Horsepen, Horse-head, Paint Horse, Horse Thief)
Turkey (Gobbler, 2) 50
Bear (Bearpen, Bearsfoot) 43
Cattle 43
    (Calf, Maverick, Bull Wagon, Bull Hide, Bull)
Panther 38
    (Tiger, 8; Cat, 6; Leopard, 4; Leon, Leoncita)
Deer 32
    (Buck, 13; Doe, 2; Bucksnag, Buckhorn)
Wolf (Coyote, 3) 23
Buffalo (Cibolo, 5) 19
Hog (Shoat, Swine) 12
Beaver 12
Antelope 11

    Polecat, 6; Wildcat, 5; Mule, 5; Coon, 4; Rabbit, 3; Squirrel, 3; Goat, 2; Sheep (Lamb), 2; Dog, 2; Prairie Dog, 1

Fish (Catfish, Trout) 16
Snake (Rattlesnake, 7; Moccasin, 3; Cotton Mouth) 14
Alligator 11
Turtle (Tortugas) 5

    One each—Frog, Mussel, Otter, Oyster

Game birds account for thirty-five names: *Duck,* 10; *Buzzard,* 5; *Eagle,* 4; *Goose,* 3; *Crow (Crowsnest),* 3; two each—*Dove, Owl, Pigeon Roost;* one each, *Partridge, Raven, Falcon,* and *Bird.* The thirteen streams named for insects are: *Bee,* 11, and *Grasshopper* and *Wasp,* one each.

The mustang horse was evidently the most noticeable animal in many areas of Texas in the early days. Early maps bear the

legend "Wild Horses" written in large letters across otherwise
blank spaces. J. Frank Dobie estimates the number of mustangs
at about a million.[18] "Mustangers" who made a business of capturing wild horses usually had to go far out past settled areas
where they drove mustangs into pens built around waterholes,
hence *Horsepen Creek*. In addition to being used for riding and
working, mustangs were sometimes eaten; some colonists who
lost their supplies at sea existed in the winter of 1821-22 on
horsemeat. Jared Groce, planter and builder of the first cotton
gin in the state, kept two hunters busy killing mustangs to feed
the slaves on his plantation in the lower Brazos Valley. Captain
Jack Hays's Rangers were supposed to be able to eat mustang
meat if nothing else was available. The fame of Texas mustangs
spread over the nation during the Mexican War from the
reports of soldiers stationed at Corpus Christi who enjoyed the
sport of chasing wild horses on the prairies to the north.[19] Even
though thirty-five creeks in Texas recall the mustang, probably
others now called *Horse Creek* were also named originally for
the mustang. However, most of the *Horse* creeks are in West
Texas and the Panhandle and therefore may have been named
for ranch horses. At any rate, it is fitting that the horse, the
best insurance against distance, weather, and Indians for early
Texans, should be commemorated in so many Texas stream
names.

Even more plentiful in pioneer days were wild turkeys,
which once were so common along the Red River in Northeast
Texas that settlers ate only the breasts.[20] When they ran out
of corn for bread, they boiled turkey breasts, dried them in an
oven, and pulverized them to make a kind of bread. The tall
grasses of the prairies, the pecan groves of the creek bottoms,
the acorns of the oak forests, and the low-hanging branches of
elm trees made ideal feeding and roosting places for the wild
turkey, as indeed they still do on a much more limited scale,
since, according to authorities, more than half of the wild
turkeys now in the nation are in Texas.[21] Turkeys furnished food

for farmers and ranchers in parts of South Texas until the 1880's.[22] Long after turkeys had been killed out elsewhere, they continued to be plentiful in the breaks along the foot of the High Plains, so much so that the town of *Turkey* was named in 1893 for them.[23] The importance of the wild turkey to settlers is reflected in the fact that fifty streams now bear its name.

Cattle, still part of the image of Texas, contributed almost as many names. Wild cattle, reputedly wilder than deer and fiercer than buffalo, could not be domesticated and were often shot as game. A congressional report of frontier problems in the Texas Republic stated that at the time of the Revolution there were at least three million wild cattle between the Nueces and the Rio Grande.[24] Actually they existed in all parts of the state except the High Plains. Although they were descendants of Spanish cattle brought to the New World long before, settlers called them "wild" or "mustang" cattle, and it was not until after the Civil War that range men began calling them "Texas cattle," which eventually meant Longhorn.[25] The late development of the word doubtless accounts for the absence of streams of that name. Similarly, the ranching industry, of comparatively late development, contributed only nineteen stream names: *Bronco, Corral, Home Ranch, Pasture Draw, Pickett Ranch, Range, Ranch* (2), *Rustler* (2), *Saddle, Saddle Horse, Spade Draw, Stampede, Three Corrals, Windmill.* Cattle brands account for two names, *X T Canyon* and *H O Canyon,* which Barry Scobee of Fort Davis says was named for the brand of Jack Hardwick, who owned a ranch in the canyon about 1890.[26] *Maverick Creek,* the most unusual of these linguistically, comes from the common noun, *maverick,* in turn derived from Samuel A. Maverick, lawyer and signer of the Texas Declaration of Independence.[27] That Texas was cow country is emphasized by the fact that, despite the thousands of sheep and goats owned by the Spanish, only two *Goat* creeks and two *Sheep* creeks recall them. The patient work ox, once a necessity, is remembered in only two names, *Ox Yoke Creek* and *Bull Wagon*

Creek; similarly, the mule gave its name to only five creeks.

Bears were probably as numerous as wild turkey in Texas in the early days, though settlers were far more accustomed to them than they were to other forms of wild life in the West, such as coyotes and horned toads. The bear had already entered into American metaphor ("bear hug," "grouchy as a bear," "bear by the tail"), and had long since been a staple food. One old-time Texan said that he had killed bears that rendered between thirty and forty gallons of fat.[28]

The most feared wild animal of the frontier and the one about which most folktales have clustered[29] was the panther, called "painter" or "mountain lion" by frontiersmen and now called "cougar" by scientists. "Many folk tales repeat the savagery of cougars," says a Texas scientist, "their numerous attacks on man, and their bloodcurdling screams, but authentic unprovoked attacks on man are far less numerous than those of the domesticated bull."[30] Nevertheless, the animal accounts for thirty-eight stream names in Texas, a number which includes other names for the same animal—*Leopard, Tiger, Cat,* and the Spanish *Leon* and *Leoncita.*

The wolf, for centuries a figure in European lore, was never feared so much as the panther. The large gray wolf that fed on the buffalo and largely disappeared with it, the red wolf of East Texas, and the coyote combined to give names to twenty-three streams. Only three of that number are called *Coyote Creek,* probably because pioneers made little or no distinction between these animals. In the lore of the Panhandle the large gray wolf was often called by its Spanish name, *lobo,* but corrupted into *loafer,* and since it was considered a menace to human beings as well as animals, it is surprising that not one stream bears its name.

Of all the game animals found in early Texas, the buffalo made the most dramatic appearance. The awe felt by settlers is expressed in this letter written during the Republic period:

You would scarcely believe me were I to tell you of the vast herds of buffalo which are about here [between the Brazos and Little Brazos rivers in present Brazos County]; I have frequently seen a thousand in a day.... If we desire buffalo meat, we are able to go out, load our horses and return the same day.[31]

When bread was not available, one historian writes, dried buffalo meat was mixed with honey as a substitute; "this combination was not only healthful but had a pleasant taste and had the additional advantage of being plentiful."[32] Another historian quotes an old-timer as saying, "We used the tanned hides, with hair left on, for rugs on the dirt floors of our log cabins, and the heavy mop which hung between the eyes for chair cushions. We also used the hides for cover."[33] The significance of buffalo in Texas is evident in the nineteen *Buffalo* creeks and three towns, *Buffalo, Buffalo Gap,* and *Buffalo Springs.*

Most of the eleven *Alligator* creeks are logically located in Southeast Texas, but the few far inland in Central Texas may be the result of myths rather than the presence of alligators. The extinct wild pigeon is remembered in two *Pigeon Roost* creeks in the woodlands of East Texas where they stopped in migration in such numbers that they broke limbs on trees where they roosted.

V

The same matter-of-fact attitude that caused pioneer namers to use the names of plants and animals for streams also led them to name for events, household items, tools and implements, and even food:

Mill	46
Camp	28
House	11
(Big House, Blockhouse, Brickhouse, Greathouse [2], Tradinghouse, Log House, Rock House, Stillhouse)	
Honey	11

Deadman	9
Hurricane	8
Bones (Jawbone, Backbone, Sparerib, Elbow, 2)	6
Battle	6
Dugout	6
Town	6
Station	5
Flag	5
Bridge	5
Dinner	4
Tanyard	4
Sunday	4
Home	3
Sawmill	3
Village	3
Pole	3

Two each: Chimney, Blanket, Washboard, County Line, Christmas, Government, Six Shooter, Trail, School

One each: Stone Chimney, Cabin, Button, Coffee Mill, Cream Level, Crockery, Door, Irons, Tape, Beef, Celery, Candy, Ham, Jelly, Mush, Barrel, Board, Box, Canoe, Carryall, Casks, Grindstone, Kyak, Leather, Log, Ox Yoke, Pipe, Pump, Bent About, Bee Dee, Beef Hollow, Fossil, Big Trestle, Boom, Carasse, Camp Meeting, Centralia, Clay Pit, Colony, Council, Cyclone, Holiday, Friday, New Years, Dead Horse, Double Horn, Fuzzy, Garden, Gauge, Getaway, Good, Greasy, Hunting Bayou, Hunting Shirt, Independence, Junk Yard, Kite, Lookout, Marine, Meridian, Monkey, Muscle, Needmore, Noodle, Not, P D, Pen, Picnitt, Pilot, Plus, Quarry, Raggedy, Rippy, Scuffle Hollow, Sixto, Sloop, Sour Dough, String Prairie, Swampoodle, Stiff, Tar Box, Tick, Tobacco, Tootle, Touchstone, Turnover, Turnpike, Whiskey, Wilds

A group of stream names that indicate the presence of the military on the Texas frontier are: *Bugler, Canon, Canon Snap, Massacre, Messbox, Major, Fort Ewell,* and possibly *Camp Duffau* and *Camp Rice.* It would be interesting to know what human characteristics or conflicts lie behind these creek names: *Alarm, Big Head, Friendship, Happy, Hardshell, Harmony, Hasty, Pleasant, Poor* (2), *Privilege, Repress, Rowdy, Squabble, Tardy, Thunder Struck, Union,* and *Wanders;* or such a miscellaneous group as this: *Bayou Din, California* (4), *Carolina,*

Cloud, Como, Convict, Doctors, Dixie, Field, Galveston, Ghost, Ice, Imperialist, Irish, Jayhawkers, Kuy, Lodi, New, Mission, Mukewater, Obar, Oil Well, Patroon, Pikes Peak, Pilgrim, Well, Purgatory, Rome, Spindletop, Skull, Tailes, and *Tebo.* The memorable events, situations, or people that gave rise to such names are now so long in the past that recovery of explanations seems impossible. Numerous questionnaires to local people produced only a few stories, but they were interesting ones. According to Clayton W. Williams of Fort Stockton, *Six Shooter Draw,* Pecos County, may be named for the stockman who, upon being notified that it would henceforth be against the law to carry a six-shooter, came riding into town dragging a gun at the end of his rope; since he ranched beyond the draw, he probably said that he dragged the gun all the way from *Six Shooter Draw.*[34] *Scalp Creek,* Menard County, is not, as the name suggests, a result of Indian attacks on people; R. S. Weddle, Menard, writes:

According to the late Fred Ellis, Sr., a couple of cowhands of A. H. Murchison were rounding up strays when they came onto two steers that had been killed with arrows. The skin had been stripped from the head and neck, the choice part for making arrow quivers in the eyes of the Indians. The creek where the scalped steers were found was named for the incident.[35]

Mr. Weddle also has two stories explaining the name of *Los Moras Creek,* Menard County: first, that it is Spanish for the mulberries growing along the banks; and, second, that it is really *Lost Morris* for a Fort McKavett soldier lost in the region on a scouting expedition. *Turnover Creek,* Coryell County, was named when supply wagons of a military force moving west from Fort Gates turned over at the place. A party of Indian fighters camped on a creek in Kendall County; upon breaking camp a Mr. Saner left his pipe behind and had to return for it; the incident gave *Pipe Creek* its name.[36] *Horse Thief Canyon,* Jeff Davis County, was named because horse thieves camped there in 1885, according to Barry Scobee of Fort Davis. *Tanyard Creek,* Red River County, got its name from a tanyard which Rowland T. Bryarly built there about 1840.[37]

VI

When rocky terrain or minerals in the water formed the main feature of a stream, settlers named it for that obvious characteristic. Sand, for instance, was a nuisance: when wet, it could be treacherous quicksand; when dry, it dragged at the wheels of wagons. Salt, a blessing for man and beast in the proper amount and a curse in excess, gave names to many streams.

ROCKS AND MINERALS

Rock, Rocky	68
(Flat Rock, 6; White Rock, 2; Stoney, 2; one each—Red Rock, Pot Rock, Slickrock, Table Rock, Stone Bottom)	
Sand	60
Salt	57
(Saline, 7; Salado, 4; Lick, 4)	
Sulphur	15
Copperas	6
Iron	4
Chalk	3

Two each—Bitter, Gyp, Alum, Quicksand, Crystal, Coal Kiln, Mine
One each—Alkali, Croton, Flint, Gold, Mineral, Silver, Silvermine, Soda, Isinglass

The presence of sulphur in creek water may account for the three *Stink* creeks mentioned elsewhere. The widely practiced nineteenth-century health fad of drinking sulphur water gave rise to several health resorts located at mineral springs in Texas.

VII

Despite the centuries of Spanish dominance of Texas, only about two hundred of the more than four thousand stream names in the state are obviously Spanish. Among reasons are that Texans were naturally hostile toward anything Spanish after the Revolution and that Spanish settlements were actually few in number and confined to those very areas where Spanish names are still found—the Border, the Rio Grande Valley (though some names here are the result of twentieth-century real estate promotion), and around Nacogdoches and El Paso.

Many Spanish names given to streams are confusing, or, more accurately perhaps, a result of confusion: some are archaic words; others are dialectal spellings which are considerably at variance with standard Spanish; still others are misspellings or corruptions of Spanish words by Anglo-Americans and Texas Mexicans. Consequently, Spanish stream names in the following table are given without translation as they are spelled on the Texas State Highway Department county maps, the accuracy of which local residents may well question.

TEXAS STREAMS WITH SPANISH NAMES

Adinosa	Calaveras	Conquista	Julio
Agua Azul	Calero	Corazones	Kayatana
Agua Dulce	Caliche	Cornudas	La Parra
Agua de Piedra	Cantu	Cucharito	Las Arches
Aguja	Capote	Cuevas	Las Tablas
Agula	Carricotes	Cuevero	Los Moras
Alamacita	Carrizo	Daros	Lavaca
Alamo	Cavasso	Dismero	Leon
Alazan	Cayanosa	Dolores	Leona
Alibates	Cerrito	Ecleto	Lie Festa (*sic*)
Amaladersos	Cesario	El Barroso	Limpia
Appurceon	Chacon	El Moro	Los Linguish
Aquilla	Chaparrosa	El Sarco	Los Raices
Arenosa	Charamusca	Escondido	Los Redos
Balcones	Charco Redondo	Espada	Macho
Balluco	Chico	Esperanza	Manas
Banquete	Chicolete	Espio	Maravillas
Barilla	Chiltapin (5)	Fandango	Marcado
Barraceto	Chiquita	Flores	Martenas
Barrego	Chispa	Fresno	Matanosa
Batella	Cibolo	Frio	Medina
Becerra	Cienega	Galina	Medio
Becerro	Cito	Gallina	Mesquitoso
Bofecillos	Clareno	Guayule	Minneosa
Bonita	Coetas	Hondo	Mucorrera
Cabeza	Coleto	Isleta	Muela
Cachate	Coloma	Jabonoso	Mujares
Caiman	Comeios	Jahuey	Navidad

Nombre de Dios	Perdiz	Salado	Tecoyas
Ojo de Agua	Petronita	Sambarieto	Terretas Blancas
Olmos	Picosa	San Casmiro	Todos Santos
Oso	Piedro	San Cirilo	Torneros
Paisano	Pintas	Sandia	Tornillo
Pajarito	Pinto	Sandiguela	Toro
Palmas	Placedo	San Miguel	Torres
Palo Alto	Poesta	San Roque	Tortugas
Palo Blanco	Pontesualis	Sarco	Tovar
Palo Duro	Punte de Agua	Saucita	Tres Palacios
Palo Pinto	Quemado	Sauz Mocho	Tule
Paloma	Quintana	Serasco	Valeno
Papalote	Ranchero	Sierrita de la Cruz	Vatoso
Pedernales	Refugio	Souceda	Velenzuelo
Pedencia	Rejo	Sous	Venado
Pederosa	Resaca	Tajanes	Verde
Pena	Retama	Talpacate	Yo-Lo-Digo
Penitas	Rita Blanca	Tapado	Zapata
Perdido	Sabinal (2)	Tecolote	Zuesco

The Spanish in Texas gave names to streams for the same obvious reasons that Anglo-Americans after them did: terrain, nature of the water, colors, animals, and plants. Señor Mercurio Martinez, native of Zapata County, says that *Arroyo Tigre Chiquito* is a branch of *Arroyo Tigre Grande,* both in the area of a ranch founded by Don Benito Ramirez which he called El Tigre and which now is under Falcon Reservoir. Similarly, Don Anastacio Garcia named his original grant Charco Redondo, and that name became attached to the arroyo. *Arroyo Valeno,* Señor Martinez writes, derives from the surname of Juan and Jesus Vela, brothers from old Guerrero, Tamaulipas, who founded a ranch near the Rio Grande, a portion of which is now under Falcon Reservoir.[38] At the opposite extreme of the state, E. S. Collins, Channing, explains that Spanish livestock owners from Santa Fe grazed animals in the upper Panhandle and named creeks *Rita Blanca* (white), *Punta de Agua* (point of water), *Los Redos* (lost wheel, lost wagon wheel), and *Tascosa* (*atascosa*–boggy).[39] Clayton Williams, Fort Stockton, points out that in addition to *Paisano Creek* in Pecos County there is also a pass in the Davis Mountains by that name. *Cayanosa Draw,* he thinks, is a corruption of *cayanto,* and *Assibuche Draw* a corruption of *acebuche,* a wild olive tree. Miss Eleonore Jandt of Seguin explains that *Cantu Creek,* Guadalupe County, got its name from Jesus Cantu, who was given a special grant of land by the State of Coahuila and Texas; *Geronimo Creek* is not, she adds, named for the famous Apache chief, since as early as 1831 it was called *Tio Geronimo* and then *San Geronimo.*

One significant difference between Spanish and Anglo-American stream names in Texas is that the Spanish occasionally gave religious names, such as *Navidad* and *Nombre de Dios.*

VIII

Indians, particularly the Plains Indians, retarded the Spanish expansion into parts of Texas for more than a hundred years, and for more than fifty years afterward they menaced the Anglo-American frontier. Despite that prominence, hardly more than one hundred stream names in Texas recall Indians. Early Texans were apparently anxious to forget the fierce Comanche and named only four *Comanche* creeks as compared with twelve for the friendlier Kickapoos.

STREAM NAMES ASSOCIATED WITH INDIANS

Indian (Indio, 1)	39
Kickapoo	12
Tonkawa	6
Comanche	4
Keechi	4
Tehuacana	4
Cherokee	3
Shawnee	3
Lipan (Lapan)	3
Karankahua	3
Biloxi (Paluxy)	2

One each—Apache, Anadarko, Bedias, Caddo, Choctaw, Delaware, Ioni, Kiowa, Natchez, Pottawatomie, Quapaw, Seminole, Wichita, Attoyac,

Blackhaw, Coahoma, Concatana, Copano, Elkhart, Hisaw, Itasca, Matate, Naconiche, Pinchachay, Quitaque, Quihi, Swauano, Tallahone, Tandakee, Tantabogue, Teneha, Towash, Toyah, Waxahachie

A very few stream names recall individual Indians: *Jim Ned,* Anadaqua chief;[40] *One Eye* and *One Arm,* Cherokees; *Bowles,* Cherokee chief, killed in Henderson County; *Katemcy,* perhaps Katemoczy, Comanche chief; and *Manahuilla,* an unidentified Indian girl. M. H. Marwil of Henderson says that *Tiawichi Creek* is named for John Tiawichi, an Indian or half-breed, who was drowned in the stream. In addition there are five *Squaw* creeks, two *Teepee* creeks, a *Bow Creek,* and a *Spear Creek.*

Here is a recapitulation:

STREAM NAMES ON TEXAS STATE HIGHWAY DEPT. MAPS, 1957

Family, given, and other names of people	1,429
Trees, plants, and shrubs	654
Terrain, size, color, nature of water	589
Animals, fish, birds, insects	496
Household and work items, events	364
Minerals and rocks	238
Spanish names of all types	197
Names associated with Indians	124
Total	4,091

In conclusion, this study of the names of small streams in Texas shows that pioneers who gave these names were seldom as whimsical as they sometimes were in giving names to places. Also, instead of turning to heroes, politicians, and famous people for names, they took them from their neighbors and community leaders, vegetation, animals, terrain, tools, equipment, and memorable events. Altogether, the types of names chosen indicate that the land itself and the people who lived and worked on it were of first importance to early Texans.

1. See John Q. Anderson, "From Flygap to Whybark: Some Unusual Texas Place Names," *The Golden Log* ("Publications of the Texas Folklore Society," XXXI [1962], pp. 73-98.

2. Names were taken from the large official maps of individual counties published by the Texas State Highway Department (Austin, 1957). No attempt was made to collate these names with those listed in *The Handbook of Texas,* ed. Walter P. Webb (2 vols.; Austin, 1952), which does not include many of them, or with topographical gazetteers. A few names included were obtained from local informants and either are at variance with names on maps or are not on county maps. The style of writing names on maps used is adopted herein, e.g., *Mary's Creek* is written *Marys Creek.*

3. River names are not included. Those with Spanish names are: *Colorado, Concho, Brazos, Bosque, Frio, Guadalupe, Lampasas, Lavaca, Leona, Leon, Llano, Nueces, Pedernales, Rio Grande, Sabinal, San Antonio, San Bernard, San Gabriel, San Jacinto, San Marcos,* and *San Saba. Aransas* is in dispute, whether it is Spanish or Indian. *Red River* has been called *Rio Roho, Rio Roxo, Red River of Natchitoches,* and *Red River of Cadodacho.* The *Trinity* was originally called *La Santisima Trinidad.*

4. Rivers with Indian names are *Angelina, Neches,* and *Wichita,* and probably *Navasota.* The origin of *Pecos* is unknown.

5. *The Journals of Ralph Waldo Emerson,* ed. Edward W. Emerson and Waldo E. Forbes (Boston, 1909-14), VI, 494-95.

6. Choctaw *bayuk,* meaning river, creek, bayou. William A. Read, *Louisiana Place-Names of Indian Origin* (Baton Rouge, 1927), Louisiana State University, Bul. XIX, New Series, No. 2.

7. These categories are not "scientific" according to the rules of toponymy, the emphasis here being historical and folkloristic.

8. A grant from the Organized Research Fund of Texas A. and M. College for parts of the summers of 1960 and 1961 provided opportunity to prepare and mail questionnaires to 193 public libraries and to 190 newspaper editors, postmasters, and individuals, seeking information on place names and stream names.

9. Šeguin *Enterprise,* December 8, 1960; Eleonore Jandt, Seguin, Texas, to J.Q.A.

10. *The Handbook of Texas,* I, 939, hereafter cited as H.B.T.

11. *Ibid.,* I, 495.

12. Guido E. Ransleben, *A Hundred Years of Comfort in Texas, A Centennial History* (San Antonio, 1954)

13. *Forest Trees of Texas: How to Know Them* (Texas Forest Service: Bul. No. 20 [College Station, Texas, 1953]). Eighteen species of oak now grow in Texas.

14. George A. Dorsey, *Traditions of the Caddo* (The Carnegie Institution [Washington, 1905]), p. 53.

15. J. L. Stambaugh, *Collin County* (Austin, 1953), pp. 116-17.

16. Huson to J.Q.A., reply to inquiry, 1960.

17. Ross to J.Q.A., reply to inquiry, 1960.

18. *The Mustangs* (Boston, 1952), p. 108.

19. John Q. Anderson, "Soldier Lore of the War with Mexico," *Western Humanities Review,* XI (Autumn, 1957), 329.

20. Fannie Cora Potter, *History of Montague County* (Austin, n.d.) pp. 18-19.

21. Eugene A. Walker, "Tips on Wild Turkey," *Texas Game and Fish* (Texas Game, Fish and Oyster Commission [Austin, 1950]), states that in 1945 there were between 97,000 and 105,000 wild turkeys in the state. See also Roger M. Latham, *Complete Book of the Wild Turkey* (Harrisburg, Pa., 1956).

22. Mrs. I. C. Madray, *A History of Bee County* (Beeville, Texas, 1939), p. 7.

23. It was first called *Turkey Roost.* Among names submitted for a post office were *Badger, Antelope,* and *Turkey.* The Post Office Department approved *Turkey* because no other town in the nation had that name. Inez Baker, *Yesterday in Hall County, Texas* (Memphis, Texas, 1940).

24. Clarence R. Wharton, *Wharton's History of Fort Bend County* (San Antonio, 1939), p. 39.

25. J. Frank Dobie, *The Longhorns* (Boston, 1941), p. 38.

26. Scobee to J.Q.A., reply to inquiry, 1961.

27. *The Longhorns,* p. 48.

28. Pat B. Clark, *The History of Clarksville and Old Red River County* (Dallas, 1937), pp. 38-39.

29. J. Frank Dobie, "Throwing Sunbonnets to Panthers," a paper presented at the annual meeting of the Texas Folklore Society, Austin, Texas, April, 1954.

30. William B. Davis, *The Mammals of Texas* (Texas Game and Fish Commission [Austin, 1960]), Bul. No. 27, p. 111.

31. Elmer G. Marshall, "The History of Brazos County, Texas" (Master's thesis, University of Texas, 1937), p. 12.

32. Annie Carpenter Love, *History of Navarro County* (Dallas, 1933).

33. Beatrice Grady Gay, *"Into the Setting Sun,"* A History of Coleman County (Privately printed, 1936), p. 179.

34. Williams to J.Q.A., reply to inquiry, 1961.

35. Weddle to J.Q.A., reply to inqury, 1961.

36. Mrs. E. B. McMordie to J.Q.A., reply to inquiry, 1960; and Librarian, Kendall Co., Boerne, to J.Q.A., reply to inquiry, 1961.

37. E. W. Bowers, Clarksville, Texas, to J.Q.A., reply to inquiry, 1961.

38. Martinez to J.Q.A., reply to inquiry, 1961.

39. Collins to J.Q.A., reply to inquiry, 1961.

40. Gay, *op. cit.* A. Morton Smith, *The First 100 Years in Cooke County* (San Antonio, 1955), p. 4, says that Jim Ned was a Delaware chief, as does H.B.T., I, 913.

41. Marwil to J.Q.A., reply to inquiry, 1960.

Appendix

Texas watercourses named for families (small rivers, creeks, draws, branches, bayous, canyons, arroyos)

(Note: Hyphenated names indicate that the stream flows into another county: Milam-Lee. Comma separations indicate more than one county.)

Name & Number	County	Name & Number	County
Adams (4)	Brown, Burnet, Anderson, Orange	Barrett	Jones-Haskell
		Barton (4)	Donley, Parker, Hays-Travis,
Adaway	Rusk		Roberts
Adlong	Harris		
Aherns	Comal	Bartons	Bastrop-Fayette
Aiken	Red River	Barts	Medina
Red Aleck	Kent	Bassett	Bowie
Alexander	Hamilton	Bassford	Galveston
Allans	Austin	Bastrop	Brazoria
Allcorn	Brazos	Bates (2)	Comal, Leon
Allen (6)	Donley, Cherokee, Shelby, Sabine, Kerr, Lee-Milam	Bauerlin	Bandera
		Bauman	Llano
		Baylor (2)	Childress, Fayette
Allens	Milam-Lee	Beacham	Upshur
Alley	Marion	Beals	Howard
Alvin	Presidio	Beans (2)	Cherokee, Jack
Anderson	Bowie	Bearfoot	Montague
Jim Anderson	Young	Beasons	Grimes
Anding	Anderson	Beaumont	Liberty
Anthony	Kaufman	Beck (2)	Anderson, Collin
Arms	Harrison	Beckard	Donley
Armstrong (5)	Cass, Parker, Ellis, Houston, Comanche-Hamilton	Beckum	Harrison
		Bedford	Llano
		Belknap	Montague
Arnold	Collin	Bell (5)	Cherokee-Smith, Burleson, Donley, Live Oak, Parker
Arthur	Presidio		
Ashby	Rusk-Nacogdoches		
Austin	Brazoria	John Bell	Dickens
Avery	Milam	Bennets	Lampasas
Auburn	Smith	Bennett (2)	Mills-Lampasas, Bell-Milam
Baden	Montague	Bergher	Lamar
Bailey (3)	Clay, Collin, Fisher	Bernard	Austin
Baileys	Lampasas	Berryhill	Rusk-Nacogdoches
Bain	Anderson	Berrys	Parker-Comanche
Baker (3)	Cass, Lamar, Somervell	Best	Bee
		Billiams	Tyler
Bakers (2)	Nacogdoches, Hardeman	Bingham (2)	Cooke, Nacogdoches
		Birchman	Cooke
Balance	Newton	Birkhand	Red River
Baldin	Walker	Bishop	Jasper
Ball	Motley	Blacks	Haskell
Ballard	Motley	Bledsoe	Liberty
Ballinger	Austin	Bliss	Leon
Barber	Cherokee	Block	Williamson
Barkman	Bowie	Blocker	Denton
Barnes	Rusk	Blundell	Morris
Barnett	San Saba	Blythe	Bowie
Barnetts	Delta	Bodan	Jasper
Barnhard	Rusk-Nacogdoches	Bolivar	Kaufman
Baron	Gillespie	Boon	Wise

Name & Number	County
Boons (3)	Leon, Fayette, Kinney-Uvalde
Boothe	Bowie
Borden	Fayette
Boregas	Sabine
Borlandy	Brewster
Boughmans	Wharton
Bowden	Somervell
Bowers	Anderson
Bowman	Brazos
Box	Anderson
Boxes	Cherokee
Boyce	Kaufman
Boyd	Anderson
Brack	Newton
Bracken	Houston
Bradford (3)	Irion, Bell, Culberson
Bradtree	Montague
Brady	McCulloch-San Saba
Brauley	Shelby
Brays	Harris
Brewer	Williamson
Brewington	Bandera
Brewster	Cooke
Brinkley	Freestone
Brittain	Shelby
Brizendine	Williamson
Brook	Panola
Brookeen	Ellis-McLennan
Brooks (2)	Fayette, Upshur
Brookshire	Waller-Fort Bend
Brown (3)	Cass, Coryell, Freestone
Browns (4)	Freestone-Leon, Mills-Brown, Lampasas, Cherokee
Browning	Van Zandt
Bry	Williamson
Buckley (2)	Shelby, Val Verde
Buckner (2)	Fayette, Karnes
Bufford	Rusk-Nacogdoches
Buford	King
Bugby	Hutchinson
Bullard (3)	Fannin, Hall, Harrison
Buller	Cherokee
Burgess	Parker
Burk	Bee
Burke (2)	Hopkins, Wood

Name & Number	County
Burleson (2)	Lampasas, Williamson
Burnet	San Saba
Burns	Denton
Burrell	Jefferson
Burris	Jasper
Burton	Red River
Burtons	Lamar
Busch	Anderson
Busley	Orange
Butler (2)	Smith, Harrison
Cade	Newton
Cages	Young
Calloway	Tarrant
Calvert	Red River
Camberon	Jack
Campbell (4)	Briscoe, Robertson, Guadalupe, Menard
Campbells	Gregg
Canant	Anderson
Carlow	Cass
Carmel	Williamson-Milam
Carpenters	Harris
Carpers	Comal-Hays
Carrington	Burleson
Carrol (2)	Donley, Jack
Carron	Cass-Marion
Carson	Hutchinson
Carters	Brazos
Case	Grayson
Casey	Reeves
Cass	Rusk
Cassidy	Walker
Castle	McLennan
Castleman (2)	McLennan, Gonzales
Catney	Bell
Cattlet	Wise
Cauthorn	Schleicher-Sutton
Cazey	Bandera
Cedron	Bosque
Cercey	Leon
Chamberlain	San Saba-Mills
Chambers (3)	Shelby, Rusk, Hill-Ellis
Chamblee	Van Zandt-Henderson
Champion	Mitchell

Name & Number	County	Name & Number	County
Chandler	Williamson-Milam	Copeland	Leon-Madison
Chapman	Menard	Copelle	Sabine-Jasper
Chappell	Comanche-Hamilton	Coppers	Anderson
		Corey	Cass-Marion
Childers	Zavala	Corley	Milam
Childress	McLennan	Cornell	Jeff Davis-Culberson
Choates	Polk		
Church	Colorado	Coryell	Coryell
Cidwell	Parker	Cottle	Gonzales
Clark (2)	Bandera, Bell-Milam	Counts	Parker-Comanche
Clarks (4)	Collin-Denton, Jackson, Lavaca, Harrison	Cowan	Williamson
		Cowsers	Smith-Cherokee
Clay	Washington	Cox (4)	Bosque, Reeves, Scurry, Limestone-Robertson
Clays	Milam		
Clemens	Gonzales	Coxs (2)	Sterling, Jackson
Clemons	Collin	Crabb	Walker
Cleveland	Jack	Craddock	Lamar
Click	Lamar	Cramers	Moore
Clifton	Wilson	Crasco	Colorado
Cobb (4)	Leon, Montague, Ellis-McLennan, Robertson	Crawford	Angelina
		Crockett	Parker-Comanche
		Cross (4)	Somervell, Harrison, Lee, Williamson
Cobbs	Madison		
Cockerell	Stephens-Throckmorton	Crutchers	Red River
		Cryer	Navarro
Coe	Washington	Cryers	Brown-Mills
Coggins	Llano	Culver	Matagorda
Cole	Cass-Marion	Cummins (3)	Colorado, Johnson-Navarro, Lee-Washington
Coleman (2)	Bastrop, Ellis-McLennan		
Coles	Washington	Cunningham	Cass-Marion
Coley	San Jacinto	Curry (2)	Eastland, Kendall
Colley	Cass-Marion		
Collier	Red River	Dabbs	Polk
Colliers	Harrison	Dalby	Bowie-Red River
Collin	Shackleford	Daniel	Gregg
Collins (2)	Houston, Lamar	Daniels (2)	Anderson, Bowie
Conkline	Childress	Darnell	Archer
Conner	Sabine	Daros	Kinney-Uvalde
Conners	Young	Darrs	Bell
Connor	Houston	Darst	Guadalupe
Conway	Hood	Davidson (3)	Dickens, Burleson, Milam-Lee
Cook	Shackleford		
Cooke	Cherokee	Davis (12)	Jasper, Newton, Panola, Stephens-Young, Houston, Van Zandt, Fannin-Lamar, San Saba, Rusk, Archer, Williamson-Milam, Limestone-Robertson
Cooks (2)	Kinney-Uvalde, Smith		
Cooper (3)	Calahan, Gregg, Red River		
Coopers (2)	Van Zandt-Henderson, Cherokee		

Name & Number	County	Name & Number	County
Dawson	Presidio	Eads	Leon
Day	Bowie	Eagans	Kaufman-Henderson
Deaton	Val Verde	Eckhardt	Williamson
Delaney	Anderson	Edmoore	Smith
Dements	Cherokee	Elam	Bandera
Denis	Williamson	Elba	Grayson
Denton (4)	Kaufman-Tarrent Montague-Wise, Gonzales	Elijah	Washington
		Elkins	Reeves
		Ellinger	Fayette
		Ellington	Cass
Dickens	Polk	Elliott (3)	Bowie, Cass, Lampasas
Dickey (2)	Polk, Houston		
Dickeys	Parker	Ellison	Morris
Dickinsons	Galveston	Elmir	Parker-Comanche
Diffy	Kaufman-Henderson	Ely	Anderson
		Ennis	Scurry
Dikes	King	Epps	Schleicher-Kimble
Dillard (3)	Red River, Walker, Upshur-Camp	Ernst	Brewster
		Eubanks	Callahan
Dismero	Nueces	Evans (2)	Moore, Val Verde
Ditmar	Gillespie	Everett (2)	Rusk-Nacogdoches, Jasper
Dixon (3)	Dallas, Leon, Hutchinson		
		Evert	Val Verde
Dockum	Dickens	Ezell (2)	Limestone-Robertson, Kaufman
Dodds	Van Zandt		
Dokegood	Garza		
Dolan	Val Verde	Fain	Mills
Dollarhide	Angelina	Fairchilds	Fort Bend
Donahue (4)	Sabine, Newton, Waller, Williamson-Bell	Farmers	Montague
		Faulkenberry	Limestone
		Fields	Menard
Donalson	Lampasas	Fielders	Val Verde
Doss	Lamar	Fitzhugh	Collin
Downey	Brewster	Flagg	Parker
Doyle	Mitchell	Flanigan	Rusk-Nacogdoches
Dozier (2)	Collingsworth, Cooke	Fleming	Red River
Drakes (2)	Anderson, Tyler	Flemming	Kimble
Drennan	Fannin-Lamar	Floyd	Cass
Drews	Liberty	Ben Fort	Grimes
Dudleys	Haskell	Foss	Fort Bend
Duffau	Comanche-Bosque	Foster	Milam
Dugan	Wilbarger	Fosters	Delta
Dulaney	Fisher	Foyle	Shackleford
Dunbar	Schleicher-Sutton	Franklin	Collin
Duncan	Comanche-Hamilton	Frazier	Cass-Marion
Dunn	Robertson	Frederick	Kendall
Duns	Delta	Freemans	Lampasas
Dutch	Rusk-Nacogdoches	Frizelle	Sabine-Jasper
Duty	Fayette	Frost	Anderson
Dyer	Williamson-Milam	Fuller	Bell
Dyes	Bosque		

Name & Number	County	Name & Number	County
Gageby	Hemphill	Haleys	Harrison
Gamble	Bee	Halifax	Hays
Garcitas	Jackson	Halis	Anderson
Garland	Anderson	Halls (2)	Harris, Brazoria
Garners	Harris	Hamilton	Burnet
Garrett (2)	Wise, Rains	Hardeman	Matagorda
Gary	Bosque	Hanibal	Parker
Gaston	Freestone	Hardin	Concho-McCulloch
Gault	Dallas	Hardin-Russell	Burnet
Gazley	Bastrop	Hardins	Robertson
Gentle	Collin	Hardy	Rusk-Nacogdoches
Gentry	Kimble	Hardys	Lavaca
Geronimo	Guadalupe	Harkell	Val Verde
Gibbons (2)	Nacogdoches, Grimes	Harl	Milam
		Harmons	Walker
Gibson (2)	Bosque, Erath	Harpers	Walker
Giladon	Van Zandt	Harral	Pecos
Gilbert	Wichita	Harrington	Delta
Gilleland	Travis	Harris (5)	Grayson, Menard, Red River-Bowie, McLennan, Smith
Gilley	Rusk-Cherokee		
Gilliland	Angelina		
Gillis	Marion	Harrison	Harrison
Gilmore	Erath	Harrston	Burnet
Givins	Stephens	Hart	Reeves
Glenn (2)	Hudspeth, Brewster	Harveys	Colorado
Glover	Bell	Hawkins	Gregg
Goens	San Saba	Hayden	Ellis
Goldman	Anderson	Haydon	Parker
Goldstens	Scurry-Kent	Hayes	Leon
Gonzales	Stephens	Haynie	Grimes-Walker
Gordon	Lamar	Helser	Comal
Gould	Dawson	Heltons	Gregg
Graham (3)	Gray, Jasper, Angelina	Henderson (4)	Cass-Marion, Jack, Kerr, Marion
Grays	Navarro	Hendon	Cherokee
Greenlee	Presidio	Hendricks	Milam
Greens (3)	Fayette, Harris, Bastrop	Henesy	Leon
		Hennings	Parker-Comanche
Greer	Anderson	Herman (2)	Panola, Mason
Griffin (2)	Leon, Kinney-Uvalde	Herndon	Collin
		Herron	Red River
Griffins	Garza	Hester	Lee
Groesbeck	Childress-Hardeman	Hickey	Burnet
Guthrie	Howard	Hickman (2)	Polk, Newton
		Hicks (2)	Lamar, Bandera
Hady	Fort Bend	Highsaw	Anderson
Hagers	Houston	Hildebrandt	Jefferson
Haggerty	Harrison	Jim Hill	Harrison
Hale	Leon	Hills	Smith-Cherokee
Hales	Houston	Hines	Leon
Haley	Leon	Hinton	San Saba

Name & Number	County	Name & Number	County
Hitson (2)	Stephens, Hudspeth	Jasper	Wise
Hitt	Smith	Jeeter	Newton
Hobbs	Bastrop	Jenkins	Stephens
Hockley	Cooke-Denton	Jimms	Williamson
Hogan	Bosque	Jinks	Williamson
Hogans	Panola	Johnson (6)	Marion, Gregg,
Holbrook (2)	Bowie, Wood		Jasper-Sabine,
Holder	Nolan-Fisher		Kimble, Kerr, Llano
Holeman	Freestone-Limestone	Johnsons	Crockett
Holland	Grimes	Jones (11)	Bowie, Montague,
Holley	Washington		Kaufman-Hender-
Hollis	Leon-Madison		son, Smith, Camp,
Hollowman	Anderson		Leon, Fayette,
Holmsley	Comanche-Hamilton		Brazos, Polk, Fort
Holynok	Williamson-Milam		Bend, Wharton
Hookers	Burleson	Cobb Jones	Franklin
Hooking	Burnet	Jordans (2)	Washington,
Hooks	Bowie		Jasper
Hoosier	Goliad	Journigan	Delta
Hopes	Brazos	Joy (2)	Kimble, Williamson
Hord	Goliad		
Hords	Coleman-Brown	Kaiser	Kendall
Horsley	Van Zandt	Karnack	Harrison
Horton	Gregg	Kaufman	Cass-Marion
Hostella	Walker	Kay	Moore
Housen	Sabine	Keegans	Harris
Howards	Crockett	Kellers	Jackson
Howell	Polk	Kelley (2)	Red River, Cass
Hubbard (2)	Bowie, Harris	Kellisons	Houston
Hudspeth	Cherokee	Kelly (2)	Donley, Concho-
Hughes (2)	Cass-Marion, Panola		McCulloch
Hughs	Lampasas	Kelsey	Upshur
Hull	Harris	Kemp	San Saba
Hunt (2)	Wise, Jack	Kennedy	Polk
Hunter	Cooke	Kent (4)	Culberson, Donley,
Hurds	Robertson		Motley, Edwards-
Hurger	Newton		Real
Hurst	Travis	Kerr (2)	Jackson, Washington
		Keuhns	Lavaca
Iatan	Howard-Mitchell	Keyes	Wood
Ijams	Chambers	Keys	Cherokee
Isaac (2)	Reagan, Comal	Keyser	Mason
Ivys	Austin	Kicester	Wilson
		Kid	Jefferson
Jackson (7)	Cass, Dallas,	Kildoogan	Fisher
	Panola, Bandera,	Kilgore	Goliad
	San Saba, Harris,	Kimball	Tyler
	Washington	Kimbau	Polk
Jacobs (2)	Comal, Karnes	Kinchelo	Lampasas
James	Kimble-Mason	King (3)	Cass, Polk,
Jarrell	Rusk-Nacogdoches		Brown-Mills
Jarvis	Wharton		

Name & Number	County	Name & Number	County
Kingham	Nacogdoches	McCain	Washington
Kings	Kaufman-Henderson	McCall	Blanco
Kinnon	Leon	McCampbell	San Patricio
Kirby	Dallas, Presidio	McClellan	Gray
Kitchens	Marion	McComb	Culberson
Koonce	Van Zandt	McCoy (2)	Dewitt, Red River
Krisp	Kimble	McCullum	Donley-Briscoe
Kruse	Bowie	McDaniell	Anderson
Lacy (2)	Kaufman-Henderson, Sterling	McDonald (2)	Crosby-Garza, Victoria
Joe Lake	Cottle	McDowell (2)	Potter, Stephens
Lambert	Hood	McFadden	Panola
Landers	Cook	McFall	Milam
Landreth	Crane	McFarland	Jackson
Lane	Sabine-Jasper	McGary	Walker
Langford	Red River	McGee	San Jacinto
Langham	Harris	McGoughlin	Henderson
Larrisons	Cherokee	McGraw	Newton
Larue	Henderson	McGrow	Tyler
Law	Rusk-Gregg	McGrue	Shelby
Laxon	Bandera	McInturff	Van Zandt
Ledbetter	Anderson	McKay	Hemphill
Lee (2)	Chambers, Houston	McKee	Terrell
Legg	Nacogdoches	McKenzie (2)	Gaines-Dawson, Kent
Legion	Gillespie-Llano	McKim	Jasper
Leon	Leon-Madison	McKinney	Bowie
Lewellyn	Wood	McLean	Houston
Lewis	Baylor	McManus	Polk
Lillus	Wilbarger	McNames	San Patricio
Lindleys	Montgomery	McNeal	Brazoria
Lindville	Brazoria-Matagorda	McNeil	Gregg
Linn	Freestone-Leon	McTennel	Karnes
Lloyd	Scurry	Machae	Sterling
Loggins	Angelina	Madden	Hudspeth
Longs	Jackson	Maddox	Sabine
Lopez	Irion	Madera	Jeff Davis
Loren	Cooke-Denton	Magill	Llano
Louis	Jasper	Maha	Travis
Love	Bandera	Majors	Ellis
Lovelace	Ellis-McLennan	Mallory	Lamar
Lozier	Terrell	John Mann	Hall
Lucas	Atascosa	Manness	McLennan
Luce	Liberty	Manning	Hamilton
Lynch (2)	Houston, Lampasas	Manske	Williamson
Lynn (2)	Tarrant, Smith	Manson	Cherokee
Lytters	Bastrop	Mansons	Anderson
McAffey	Rusk	Mantell	Kinney-Uvalde
McBee	Van Zandt	Manton	Polk
McBride	Potter	Marley	San Saba

Name & Number	County	Name & Number	County
Marshall (3)	Mason-Llano, Briscoe, Gillespie	Millers (3)	Baylor, Fayette, Goliad
Martin (4)	Moore, Johnson, Mason, Frio-LaSalle	Mills (2)	Anderson, Limestone-Robertson
Martinez (2)	Mason, Shelby	Minden	Rusk-Nacogdoches
Martins (3)	Panola, Dimmitt, Jack-Wise	Mitchel	Anderson
		Mitchell (5)	Briscoe, Franklin, LaSalle, Gonzales, Parker-Comanche
Mason (2)	Harris, Williamson-Milam		
Masons	Bandera	Mixons	Lavaca
Massey	Gregg	Monahans	Midland
Mathis (3)	Brazos, Mills, Cherokee	Montague	Cooke
		Montgomery	Limestone
Maxey	Lamar	Mooar	Scurry
Maxwell	Lamar	Moody (4)	Upshur, Gregg, Mason, Harrison
Mayde	Harris		
Mayfield	Washington-Austin	Moore (3)	Hutchinson, Comanche-Hamilton, Palo Pinto-Jack
Maynard	Menard		
Maysfield	Milam		
Meade	Bowie		
Meakin	Panola	Moores	Newton
Meckel	Schleicher-Sutton	Morgan (3)	Howard-Mitchell, Coryell, Burnet
Meddlin	Upshur		
Medley	Jeff Davis-Presidio	Morgans	Polk
Medlin	Young	Morris	Franklin
Melton (2)	Navarro, Newton	Morriss	Harrison
Mellons	Jasper-Newton	Moses	Galveston
Menard	Polk	Muhle	Baylor
Menger	Kendall	Mullanox	Potter
Menzie	Menard	Mullin	Brown-Mills
Mercer (2)	Coleman-Brown, Comanche-Hamilton	Murchison (3)	Houston, Bee, Kaufman-Henderson
Bert Meriz	Crockett	Murphy (3)	Shackelford, Bee, Anderson
Merrill (2)	Jeff Davis, Presidio		
Merrits	Hopkins	Murray	Gonzales
Meuseback	Gillespie	Murvaul	Panola
Meyers	Terrell	Musquiz	Jeff Davis
Miers	Val Verde	Myer	Grayson
Milam (3)	Denton, Bowie, Williamson		
		Nabors	Mills
		Nail	Panola
Milby	Jackson	Nails	Lee
Milheim	Austin	Nash (2)	Eastland, Guadalupe
Milhiglum	Bell		
Miller (8)	Llano, Blanco, Newton, Colorado, Cherokee, Haskell, Culberson-Reeves, San Jacinto	Neal	Rusk-Nacogdoches
		Jim Neal	Eastland
		Neils	Bosque
		Nelson	Walker
		Newman	King
Quil Miller	Johnson	Newton	Newton

Name & Number	County	Name & Number	County
Neyland	Jasper	Pirtle	Rusk-Nacogdoches
Nicholas	Newton	Pitts	Van Zandt
Nixon	Anderson	Plowman	Bosque
Noble	Lamar	Plummer	Lipscomb
Nolan	Bell	Plummers	Limestone-
Noland	Johnson		Robertson
Noltke	Upton	Pollard	Moore
Nolton	Kinney-Uvalde	Pompea	Tyler
Norton	Victoria	Pompey	Mills-Brown
		Pope	Wood
Oatman	Llano	Pophers	Angelina
Odell	Angelina	Porter	Shelby
Oglesby	Coryell	Porters	Wharton-Jackson
Olivers	Denton	Poteet	Fisher
Oppenheimer	Val Verde	Potter (2)	Kimble, Comal
O'Quinn	Fayette	Powell	Howard
Orman	Hamilton	Prescott	Mills
Osman	Val Verde	Price (3)	Collin, DeWitt,
Otis	Bastrop		Williamson
Owen	Rusk-Nacogdoches	Puckett	Wood
Owens (2)	Limestone-	Pulaski	Wilson
	Robertson,	Pulliam	Edwards-Real
	Crockett	Purtis	Kaufman-Henderson
		Pyle	Brewster
Paces	Polk		
Page	Kinney-Uvalde	Quinlan	Kerr
Panton	Lavaca	Quitman	Hudspeth
Parker (7)	Rusk-Nacogdoches,		
	Medina, Bee, Jasper,	Rabb	Fort Bend
	Ellis-McLennan,	Rabbs	Lee-Washington
	Donley-Briscoe,	Ragsdale (2)	Lavaca, Cherokee
	Rockwall	Rainey (2)	McLennan, Coryell
Patrick	Parker	Rainwater	Wood
Patterson	Lampasas	Randolph	Guadalupe
Patton	Freestone-Limestone	Random	Fort Bend
Payne	Panola	Rankin	Upton
Peacock (2)	Cass, Morris	Ratliff	Colorado
Pemberton	Glasscock	Rattan	Williamson
Pennington (2)	Llano, Bell-Milam	Ray	Harrison
Perkins	Sabine-Jasper	Rays (2)	Smith, Hunt
Perry	Camp	Reagan (2)	Rusk-Nacogdoches,
Peter (2)	Burnet, Houston		Brewster
Peters (3)	Red River, Goliad,	Redgate	Colorado
	San Patricio	Redmond	Liberty
Petit	Madison	Reed (2)	Burleson, Leon
Pevitot	Jefferson	Reeds (2)	Matagorda, DeWitt
Pew	Coryell	Reese (3)	Bell, Newton,
Peytons	Matagorda		Liberty-San Jacinto
Pfeiffer	Kerr	Reeves	Stephens-Young
Pickens	Henderson	Reinhardts	Harris
Picket	Karnes	Reiss	Robertson
Pipers	Colorado	Resley	Parker-Comanche

Name & Number	County	Name & Number	County
Snell	Red River	Tempe	Polk
Snow	Lamar	Theuvines	Tyler
Sorrell	Comal	Thomas (2)	Archer, Cass
Sowells (2)	Parker-Comanche, Comanche-Hamilton	Thompson (4)	Bowie, Harrison, Parker, Walker
Sowes	Williamson	Thompsons	Brazos
Sparks	Burnet	Thornton	
Spencer (3)	Moore, Presidio, Williamson	[Rustlers] Thouching	Hall Tyler
Spries	Bandera	Threadgill	Mason
Stagg	Comanche-Hamilton	Throckmorton	Collin
Stamp	Newton	Thurston	Terrell
Stanard	Bandera	Thut	Gray
Stanley (2)	Angelina, Grayson	Tidwell	Robertson
Stark	Kimble	Timmons	Panola
Starks	Newton	Tinsley	Gonzales
Starrett	Leon	Tomlin	Leon
Steel	Kerr	Tommelson	Washington
Steele (3)	Bosque, Robertson, Limestone-Robertson	Townsend Trimmer	Cooke Bell
		Trotti	Jasper
Stephens	San Jacinto	Truillo	Oldham
Steppe	Brown-Mills	Tuttle	Panola
Sterling	Sterling		
Stevens (2)	Gillespie, Lamar	Underwood	Newton
Stewart	Red River		
Stewarts (2)	Denton, Montgomery	Valentine Vanham	Tom Green-Menard Gonzales
Stills	Anderson	Van Horn	Jeff Davis-Presidio
Stillwell	Brewster	Van Zant	Somervell
Stockard	Henderson	Varner	Brazoria
Stone	Mason	Veale	Young
Stouts	Franklin	Venchoner	Wise
Stovall	Angelina	Vestal	Leon
Stover	Collin	Vince	Houston
Stribling	Blanco	Volkman	Menard
Strickland	Kenney-Uvalde		
Striker	Smith-Rusk	Wadsworth	Matagorda
Strouds	Hood	Wagner	Bowie
Stuarts	Colorado	Waldrop	Kaufman-Henderson
Hulf Stuttlee	Jack-Stephens	Walker (5)	Roberts, Presidio, Ellis-Kaufman, Tarrant, Jefferson
Styes	Brazoria		
Sutherland	Jackson	Walkers	Camp
Sutton (2)	Chambers, Walker	Wallace (7)	Hamilton, Houston, Irion, Bandera, Johnson, San Saba, Val Verde
Swager	Shackelford		
Tankersly	Titus	Waller (2)	Travis, Bee
Tarkington	San Jacinto	Wallis	Wharton
Taylor (5)	Harris, Jefferson, Lampasas, Smith, Shackelford	Walls Walters	Wharton Kendall

Name & Number	County	Name & Number	County
Ward (2)	Bowie, Leon	Wilkins	Cass
Warring	Hamilton	Willford	Stonewall
Warsaw	Kaufman	Williams (8)	Bandera, Harris,
Wasson	Hudspeth		Cooke-Denton, Polk,
Waters	Llano		McLennan, Jasper,
Watson	Throckmorton		Fayette, Kaufman-
Watts	Coleman-Brown		Henderson
Waulege	Lee	Williamson (2)	Gillespie-Blanco,
Wayne	Walker		Travis
Weathersby	Live Oak	Willis	Williamson
Weaver	Bowie	Willoughby	Mills-Brown
Webber	Red River	Wilshire	Smith-Rusk
Webster	Cass	Wilson (12)	Bell, Bosque, Cooke,
Weide	Mason-Llano		Collin, Johnson,
Weirs	Williamson		Karnes, Kerr,
Wesco	Wood-Franklin		Matagorda, Parker,
Whatley	Cass		Sabine, Shelby,
Wheeler (3)	Coleman, Somervell,		Williamson
	Williamson	Winans	Bandera
Whiteley	Houston	Winters	San Jacinto-Liberty
Whites (5)	Chambers, Walker,	Woodbury	Rains
	Grayson-Collin,	Woodfin	Shelby
	Childress, Leon	Wooten	Rusk-Nacogdoches
Whitman	Burnet	Wordswell	Gaines
Whitmans	Fort Bend	Worser	Palo Pinto
Whitmore	Morris	Wright (2)	Jasper, Llano
Whitney	Ellis	Wrights	Walker
Wickson	Brazos		
Wiers	Montgomery	Yeager	Blanco
Wilbarger (2)	San Saba-Mills,	Ygnacio	McMullen
	Travis-Bastrop	Young (3)	Bowie, Guadalupe,
Wilburn (2)	Cooke, Cass-Marion		Red River
Wilderson	Panola	Youngs	Lavaca
Wilds	Rusk-Nacogdoches	Zoro	Val Verde

Texas streams bearing Christian names

Name	County	Name	County
Dan	Angelina	Jocks	Roberts
Eds	Bowie	Jim John	San Saba
French John	Llano	Talking John	Hardeman-Foard
Georges* (2)	Polk, Somervell	Johns* (2)	Cass, Delta
Jack* (2)	Angelina, Bowie	Jonah	Hall-Childress
Jacks* (3)	Hill, Fayette,	Joshua*	Kendall
	Hardin-Tyler	Mack* (2)	Anderson, Walker
Jakes (2)	Red River, Titus	Pats	Roberts
Jerrys	San Saba	Steve	Van Zandt
Big Jim	Reagan	Tom (3)	Comal, King,
Jims	Cass		Motley
		Long Tom	Polk

*May be a family name.

Name & Number	County	Name & Number	County
Angelina	Rusk	Leota	Bell
Aurelia	Sabine	Lilly	Upshur
Bonita	Potter	Betty Logan	Coleman
Caroline	Freestone	Lola	Wise
Cathey	Bell	Lucy	Lampasas
Clare	Newton	Magie	Anderson
Elizabeths	Denton	Mariana	Wilson
Gracie	Gregg	Margaret	Brewster
Harriet	Denton	Marys	Parker
Henrietta	Tarrant	Little Marys	Parker
Huana	Shelby	Polly	Nacogdoches
Jenny	Eastland	Queen	Williamson
Juanita	Matagorda	Rebecca	Comal
Kate	Borden	Rose (2)	Smith, Howard
Lallah	Erath	Ruby	Polk
Laurelia	Polk	Victoria	Montague
Lelia	Donley		

Other

Name	County	Name	County
Pa	King	Mexican (2)	Briscoe, Dickens
Dads	Hemphill	Negro (3)	Dimmitt, Freestone,
Gal	Anderson		Houston
Grannies	Shelby	Nigger (3)	Limestone, Randall,
Sister	Kendall		Travis
White Woman	Lipscomb	Paddy	Leon
Bachelor (2)	Coleman, Kaufman	Rangers	Hays
Dutchman (2)	Gregg, Motley	Swede	Kendall
Lone Man	Hays	Supple Jack	Lavaca

Social Customs in
O. Henry's Texas Stories

E. HUDSON LONG

IN THE SPRING of 1882, William Sidney Porter, a young man from Greensboro, North Carolina, arrived in Texas. His destination was the Dull Ranch of 250,000 acres, extending from La Salle County into the counties of Frio and McMullen. This ranch, where young Will Porter was to live for two years, was managed by the famous Captain Lee Hall, a former Texas Ranger, whose assistants included several seasoned members from his old command. Here Will Porter absorbed the atmosphere of the cattle country so well that years later he put it into short stories with such accuracy that J. Frank Dobie has pronounced them "true to the people and range of the old days as well as fascinating to readers of any day."[1]

In "The Higher Abdication" O. Henry has described the home of a successful rancher: "The ranch-house was composed of four large rooms, with plastered adobe walls, and a two-room wooden ell. A twenty-feet-wide 'gallery' circumvented the structure." Set in a grove of "live-oaks and water-elms near a lake," the house seemed "more of the South than of the West" because of the "massive pendants of the melancholy gray moss" that hung from the trees (178).[2]

Another ranch house—this time on a sheep ranch located 110 miles southeast of San Antonio—is described amidst "a lordly grove of magnificent live-oaks. . . . The house, of red brick, one story, ran low and long beneath the trees." There was an "arched passageway, picturesque with flowering cactus and hanging red earthen jars" dividing the house through the middle, while "A 'gallery,' low and broad, encircled the building" (1244). Near the house were "transplanted grass and shrubs," and vines climbed about the "gallery." To the rear was a small lake; farther back "stood the shacks of the Mexican workers, the corrals, wool sheds and shearing pens."

The guest room in a ranch house not far from Corpus Christi was naturally located on the east side. O. Henry depicts it thus:

> The floor was bare and clean. White curtains waved in the gulf breeze through the open windows. A big willow rocker, two straight chairs, a long table covered with newspapers, pipes, tobacco, spurs, and cartridges stood in the centre. Some well-mounted heads of deer and one of an enormous black javeli projected from the walls. A wide, cool cot-bed stood in a corner. Nueces County people regarded this guest chamber as fit for a prince (158).

With his description of another such room O. Henry reminds us that the climate was semitropical, and that the "bare appearance and the scantiness of their furniture" was a part of "well-conceived efforts to conform to it" (1245).

Rocking chairs were looked upon as the ultimate in ranch-house furnishing. The Mired Mule Ranch was fixed "up fine with rocking chairs and window curtains" (144). In "A Poor Rule" the suitors for the hand of Miss Ileen Hinkle sat in the "willow rocking-chairs" next to "the lucky one that sustained the trim figure of Miss Hinkle" (808). In "The Last of the Troubadours" when night came ". . . Sam and old man Ellison dragged their chairs out under the hackberry trees," a custom which seems to have been general (814). But Sam, as O. Henry informs us, preferred a cot, for ". . . he never sat up when he could lie down; and never stood when he could sit" (814).

In "Hearts and Crosses" there was a "water-jar hanging on the gallery" (114). In "Hygeia at the Solito" there was cool water to drink in the "red jar hanging on the gallery" (158). When the Cisco Kid returned to his beautiful Mexican sweet-

heart in "The Caballero's Way" she told him, "There is cool
water in the jar for you" (207). And in "The Hiding of Black
Bill" the lone bandit who had held up the "Katy" drank water
from "a red jar hanging up" at the sheep ranch he had selected
as a hideout (699). Sam Galloway of "The Last of the Troubadours" reclined at ease while "the Kiowa brought cool water
from the red jar hanging under the brush shelter" (815). At
another ranch a young lady fresh from the social life of New
York City found herself with the ever present "hanging red
earthen jars" (1244).

O. Henry noted the traditional hospitality of the region,
saying humorously, "Hospitality in the prairie country is not
limited. Even if your enemy pass your way you must feed
him before you shoot him. You must empty your larder into
him before you empty your lead" (434).

In the person of Curtis Raidler O. Henry has described a
typical dispenser of Texas hospitality:

> Six feet two in height, miles broad, and no deeper than a crystal brook,
> he represented the union of the West and South. Few accurate pictures
> of his kind have been made, for art galleries are so small and the muto-
> scope is as yet unknown in Texas. After all, the only possible medium of
> portrayal of Raidler's kind would be the fresco—something high and
> simple and cool and unframed (156).

Back of the cattleman's hospitality was a kindness and
generosity that O. Henry admired, and he explains, "A creature
was ill and helpless; he had the power to render aid—these were
the only postulates required for the cattleman to act. They
formed his system of logic and the most of his creed" (157).
When his hospitality was unfairly abused, however, or he felt
betrayed, the response was quick and definite. Curtis Raidler,
thinking himself tricked, stated, "I can stand a rattlesnake, but
I hate a liar" (161).

The frontier, as we know, imposed social democracy, the
West continued to insist upon it, and Texas inherited the

tradition. There was no place for snobbery. Major Tom King-man in "Friends in San Rosario" had been "mule-driver, cow-boy, ranger, soldier, sheriff, prospector and cattleman. Now, when he was bank president, his old comrades from the prairies, of the saddle, tent, and trail, found no change in him" (454).

Great value was placed upon friendship. This same Major Kingman recalled,

In those days it was expected of a man to stick to his friend, and he didn't ask any credit for it. Probably next day you'd need him to get at your back and help stand off a band of Apaches, or put a tourniquet on your leg above a rattlesnake bite and ride for whisky. So, after all, it was give and take, and if you didn't stand square with your pardner, why, you might be shy one when you needed him (456-57).

True friendships were not hastily or easily formed. Though a stranger was received cordially, he was observed "shrewdly and with suspended judgment." O. Henry underlines Major Kingman's comment by saying, "Picking a comrade on the border is done with ten times the care and discretion with which a girl chooses a sweetheart. On your 'side-kicker's' nerve, loyalty, aim, and coolness your own life may depend many times" (860).

There was a social affability in general that the Texan practiced. Bud Kingsbury from the Panhandle, taking a trip to New York, was unhappy over its absence: "I began to wish that I'd gone to Abilene or Waco for my *paseado;* for the mayor of them places will drink with you, and the first citizen you meet will tell you his middle name and ask you to take a chance in a raffle for a music box" (845).

Close friends, however, did not feel the need for small talk or the necessity of conversation; Baldy Woods and Webb Yeager of "Hearts and Crosses" rode for miles in silence, the only sound being "the soft drum of the ponies' hoofs on the matted mesquite grass, and the rattle of the chaparral against their wooden stirrups" (111).

When a newcomer to the cattle camps had finally won his spurs, and was ready to be accepted by the cowboys as their "stirrup-brother, foot to foot," an initiation followed, such as happened to Curly in "The Higher Abdication":

> Half a dozen six-shooters began to pop—awful yells rent the air—Long Collins galloped wildly across Curly's bed, dragging the saddle after him. That was merely their way of gently awaking their victim. Then they hazed him for an hour, carefully and ridiculously, after the code of the cow camps. Whenever he uttered protest they held him stretched over a roll of blankets and thrashed him woefully with a pair of leather leggins (187).

The latter part of the initiation also occurs in "The Marquis and Miss Sally" when one of the boys tells the character nick-named the Marquis, "It's all in fun. Take it good-natured and they'll let you off light. They're only goin' to stretch you over the log and tan you eight or ten times with the leggin's. 'Twon't hurt much" (987).

On the other hand, the punchers had their own method of showing disapproval, and with which they punished an offen-der: "For three days they did not speak to him, except to reply to his own questions or remarks. And they spoke with absolute and unfailing politeness" (187). They played tricks on one another, uttered "friendly curses and obloquy," but for the offender there was only politeness, which stung.

The cowboys relieved the tedium of the camps by indulging in practical jokes. When Judge Dave Hackett, candidate for re-election, appeared at a Diamond Cross camp, wearing "a frock coat and a high silk hat," the fun began. The boys, utter-ing yells of terror, fled into the darkness, pretending to be afraid of the hat, which they hung in a tree. Immediately "the crash of a dozen six-shooters split the air, and the hat fell to the ground riddled with bullets" (988). The punchers returned with "exaggerated caution," carefully forming "a solemn, wide circle about the hat, gazing at it in manifest alarm, and seized every few moments by little stampedes of panicky flight."

Pretending to fear the hat as a "varmint...the venomous
Kypootum...the chief of the hairy tribe...the dreaded High-
gollacum fantod from the forest," they took the "only one way
to destroy its life," which was to have the hat "solemnly sat
upon" by Old Taller, weighing 240 pounds, "crushing it as flat
as a pancake." The Judge, viewing the proceedings with "wide-
open eyes" and rising anger, remembered the sixty votes on
the Diamond Cross in time to see the point of the joke. Thank-
ing the boys for "this gallant rescue" he pretended that the hat
was a "cruel monster" that had sprung upon him, concluding,
"To you I shall consider that I owe my life, and also, I hope,
re-election to the office for which I am again candidate" (989).

Most cowboys were shy around women, an exception to the
rule being Judson Odom of the Triangle-O Ranch. Jud confided:
"I never was shy about women. I never could understand why
some men who can break a mustang before breakfast and shave
in the dark, get all left-handed and full of perspiration and
excuses when they see a bolt of calico draped around what
belongs in it" (138). The cowboy had no florist, but like Jud
Odom he might visit his favorite girl with "a fine bunch of
blue verbenas that I cut out of a herd of wild flowers ..." (143).

Women were generally treated with gallantry. Even the
murderous Cisco Kid was "*muy caballero,* as the Mexicans
express it, where the ladies were concerned," which caused a
great many women to doubt the stories "circulated about
Mr. Kid." They dismissed his "deeds of infamy" by saying
"maybe he had been driven to it, and that he knew how to treat
a lady, anyhow" (208).

A cowboy, quick to defend a lady's honor, almost shot his
sheepman rival because of ignorance of vocabulary; when the
sheepman tells him, "...you've got the wrong idea....My
object is purely a gastronomical one," the cowboy reached for
his gun, saying "Any coyote...that would boast of dishon-
orable—" (140). Fortunately the sheepman managed to explain
that he was referring to eating pancakes.

Not that the ladies of the ranch country were in need of protection. Some of them might be the type to "sit on the gallery ... and weave rush mats," but others were like the heroine of "The Princess and the Puma," who "while riding her pony at a gallop could put five out of six bullets through a tomato-can swinging at the end of a string" (233).

Apparently young women on the ranches sometimes slipped out alone at night to meet the men they were in love with. Naturally their parents remained ignorant, but there was an independence and candor about the action that O. Henry found admirable. Webb Yeager in "Hearts and Crosses" tells us:

> That heart-and-cross sign was her scheme. Whenever she wanted to see me in particular she managed to put that mark on somethin' at the ranch that she knew I'd see. And I never laid eyes on it but what I burnt wind for the ranch the same night. I used to see her in that coma mott back of the little horse-corral (111).

Because their parents disapproved of their courtship and intended marriage, Yenna Curtis of "The Higher Abdication" rode eight miles at night to meet Ranse Truesdell. They met under a big ratama tree halfway between the ranch houses. O. Henry pictures it romantically: "The yellow ratama blossoms showered fragrance that would have undone the roses of France. The moon made the earth a great concave bowl with a crystal sky for a lid" (183).

O. Henry's ranch characters spent much time out of doors, exhibiting the same appreciation of nature as their creator. "It is a bold chronicler," says O. Henry, "who will undertake the description of a Texas night in the early spring" (223). The air "heady with ozone" and perfumed by "leagues of wild flowerets," the sky "a turquoise cover" in which the moon appeared "a great, round, mellow searchlight," the sounds of "the clear torrent of the mocking-birds' notes" and the whip-poorwills that "twittered in the long grass" contributed to the glory of an evening when "it would not have been preposterous for one to tiptoe and essay to touch the stars, they hung so bright and imminent" (223).

Horseback riding furnished entertainment, exciting, sometimes "glorious." And O. Henry recalled, "Think of the gallops over those leagues of prairies, with the wind tugging at the roots of your hair..." (1240). Sometimes the rides were at night. A young lady, romantically inclined toward her ranch foreman, confided, "Best of all were the rapturous horseback rides with Teddy, when the moon gave light over the windswept leagues, chaperoned by the wheeling night-hawk and the startled owl" (1247). And especially pleasant were courting rides in "a feather-weight buck-board, behind a pair of wild, cream-colored Spanish ponies...," leaving the road to strike across "a world carpeted with an endless reach of curly mesquite grass." The ride becomes vivid:

> The wheels made no sound. The tireless ponies bounded ahead at an unbroken gallop. The temperate wind, made fragrant by thousands of acres of blue and yellow wild flowers, roared gloriously in their ears. The motion was aërial, ecstatic, with a thrilling sense of perpetuity in its effect (1243).

At Pimienta Crossing a cowboy was outraged because a girl he fancied had "gone riding with Jackson Bird, the sheep man from over at Mired Mule Cañada" (139). The rancher felt that the sheep-raiser was a threat to his way of life, a natural enmity that is recorded by O. Henry. There was old Cal Adams, the sheep-raiser in "The Missing Chord," who was a failure in his occupation. "Old Cal," we are told, "was so obscure in his chosen profession that he wasn't even hated by the cowmen. And when a sheepman," says O. Henry, "don't get eminent enough to acquire the hostility of the cattlemen, he is mighty apt to die unwept and considerably unsung" (224).

There was nothing unusual about settling matters with a gun. Sam Galloway did this in "The Last of the Troubadours," though with ironic results. Thinking he was doing his host a

favor, Sam had goaded a threatening cattleman into drawing
first. With fingers made nimble from playing the guitar Sam
proved the superior gunman; and with eager witnesses to
testify, he suffered no inconvenience.

Another such incident involved Luke Standifer, who "had
served the commonwealth as Indian fighter, soldier, ranger,
and legislator" (488). Standifer, unable to aid the daughter
of an old friend in any other way, shot her worthless and brutal
husband. He enraged his antagonist, a noted desperado, into
drawing first, thereby treating the bystanders to "the most
beautiful exhibition of lightning gun-pulling ever witnessed
in the Southwest" (496). O. Henry concludes the incident with
the information that the only "inconvenience" for Standifer was
a "necessary formal hearing," since all witnesses saw his oppon-
ent draw first.

There was a general leniency toward all shooting. As
O. Henry puts it in "The Reformation of Calliope," "In Quicksand some indulgence was accorded the natural ebullition of
human nature. Providing that the lives of the more useful
citizens were not recklessly squandered, or too much property
needlessly laid waste, the community sentiment was against
a too strict enforcement of the law" (261). Especially was
opinion lenient in the matter of shooting Mexicans. Calliope
Catesby, well liquored and bent on a shooting spree, included
in his opening sortie a "new gilt weathercock," a "yellow dog,"
and a "Mexican who was crossing the street from the Blue Front
grocery, carrying in his hand a bottle of kerosene." The unfortunate Mexican was "stimulated to a sudden and admirable burst
of speed, still grasping the neck of the shattered bottle"
(260-61).

Of the Cisco Kid O. Henry wrote, "It had been one of the
Kid's pastimes to shoot Mexicans 'to see them kick' " (203). The
Kid, outlaw that he was, sometimes engaged in other recrea-
tions: "He moodily shot up a saloon in a small cow village on
Quintana Creek, killed the town marshal (plugging him neatly

in the centre of his tin badge), and then rode away, morose and unsatisfied. No true artist is uplifted by shooting an aged man carrying an old-style .38 bulldog" (204).

In "Law and Order" Bud Oakley, a deputy to Sheriff Luke Summers, says:

> If a respectable citizen shot a Mexican or held up a train and cleaned out the safe in the express car, and Luke ever got hold of him, he'd give the guilty party such a reprimand and a cussin' out that he'd probable never do it again. But once let somebody steal a horse (unless it was a Spanish pony), or cut a wire fence, or otherwise impair the peace and indignity of Mojada County, Luke and me would be on 'em with habeas corpuses and smokeless powder and all the modern inventions of equity and etiquette (918).

As the ranches were often remote from centers of population, many functions were perforce held there. In "Madame Bo-Peep of the Ranches" the heroine speaks of her wedding celebration: " 'And I was thinking,' said Octavia softly, 'of a wedding gallop with my manager among the flocks of sheep and back to a wedding breakfast with Mrs. MacIntyre on the gallery, with, maybe, a sprig of orange blossom fastened to the red jar above the table' " (1252).

On occasion, a ranch wedding might be followed by the traditional honeymoon journey, as was the case in "The Pimienta Pancakes" when a disappointed suitor suddenly learns that the girl he wanted had just married, "and gone to Waco and Niagara Falls on a wedding tour" (143).

O. Henry has described a Christmas celebration on the ranch of Madison Lane: "Christmas Eve fell as balmy as April. Perhaps there was a hint of far-away frostiness in the air, but it tingled like seltzer, perfumed faintly with late prairie blossoms and the mesquite grass" (1208). That night the entire house was "brightly lit" to welcome the guests who were arriving "in buckboards and on horseback." There was a Christmas tree, of course, and even an improvised Santa Claus for the children. "The evening went along pleasantly. The guests enjoyed

and praised Rosita's excellent supper, and afterward the men
scattered in groups about the rooms or on the broad 'gallery,'
smoking and chatting" (1208).

Music sometimes found its way to the cattle country. Miss
Willella Learight "sang some, and exasperated the piano quite
a lot with quotations from the operas" (141). And the piano
was not unknown on the sheep ranches. Rush Kinney in "The
Missing Chord" tells a young woman, "I shouldn't like anything
better than to ride home of an evening and listen to a few
waltzes and jigs, with somebody about your size sitting on the
piano-stool and rounding up the notes" (225). At the Rancho
de las Sombras, O. Henry says, "Often the Mexicans would
come up from their shacks with their guitars and sing the
weirdest of heartbreaking songs" (1247-48). And, of course,
Sam Galloway, the last troubadour, went from ranch to ranch,
singing and playing the guitar.

Funerals in remote places were conducted from the ranch
houses, where the custom seems to have included hymn-singing.
Judson Odom warned his rival, ". . . don't go and mistake sentiments for syrup, or there'll be singing at your ranch, and you
won't hear it" (141).

A holiday celebration in a border town might include on the
American side of the river: "a cattlemen's convention, a bull
fight, and an old settlers' barbecue and picnic" (165). In "Art
and the Bronco" we are told that the San Saba country enjoyed
a "well-known superiority in steer-roping contests" (405). In
"One Dollar's Worth" Littlefield, the young district attorney,
and his sweetheart shot plover from a buckboard, drawn by
horses that "stand fire so nicely" (1194). And we are told, "The
plover-shooting was fine that afternoon" (1196). Prizefighting
furnishes the introduction for "Hygeia at the Solito" (154).
"An Afternoon Miracle" includes a carnival show with a snake
charmer (169).

Perhaps in quest of amusement the ranchman ventured to
the city. O. Henry tells us:

Consider that at that time San Antone was the hub of the wheel of Fortune, and the names of its spokes were Cattle, Wool, Faro, Running Horses, and Ozone. In those times cattlemen played at crack-loo on the side-walks with double-eagles, and gentlemen backed their conception of the fortuitous card with stacks limited in height only by the interference of gravity (168).

And in "A Call Loan" O. Henry depicts the early millionaires of the Lone Star State:

In those days the cattlemen were the anointed. They were the grandees of the grass, kings of the kine, lords of the lea, barons of beef and bone. They might have ridden in golden chariots had their tastes so inclined. The cattleman was caught in a stampede of dollars. It seemed to him that he had more money than was decent. But when he had bought a watch with precious stones set in the case so large that they hurt his ribs, and a California saddle with silver nails and Angora skin *suaderos,* and ordered everybody up to the bar for whisky—what else was there for him to spend money for? (229)

Of course, the ordinary cowboy sought diversions of a less expensive but more rambunctious sort. Buck Caperton in "The Lonesome Road" recounted how he and Perry Rountree "roamed around considerable, stirring up the echoes and making 'em attend to business," and Buck stated, "Why, when me and Perry wanted to have some fun in a town it was a picnic for the census takers. They just counted the marshal's posse that it took to subdue us, and there was your population" (545).

In "Art and the Bronco" the cowboys were preparing to celebrate. They "must ride wildly through the town, creating uproar and excitement. Liquor must be partaken of, the suburbs shot up, and the glory of the San Saba country vociferously proclaimed. A part of the programme had been carried out in the saloons on the way up" (407). The punchers had their own expression for other nocturnal entertainment, such as Phonograph Davis' remark, "I've viewed the elephant with the Mayor of Fort Worth, and I've listened to the owl with the gen'ral passenger agent of the Katy, and they can keep up with the percession from where you laid the chunk" (987).

The cowboy liked whiskey, and he imbibed freely. When Jeff Peters and Andy Tucker, O. Henry's notorious confidence men, cornered the whiskey market by buying all the saloons in a little flood-isolated town in "Texas on the bank of the Rio Grande," the firm of "Peters, Satan, and Tucker" enjoyed a "beautiful and simple swindle." The price of a drink sky-rocketed to one dollar, and Jeff Peters insured law and order by bribing the town marshal and his deputies with free drinks. "There was about 1,500 grown-up adults in Bird City that had arrived at years of indiscretion; and the majority of 'em required from three to twenty drinks a day to make life endurable" (269).

In "Hearts and Crosses" Baldy Woods, in consultation with his boss, "poured out a third drink that was larger by a finger than the first and second" (109). In the story "Law and Order" Bud Oakley expressed the general sentiment of the cowboys toward prohibition, referring to a character he had ignored, ". . . I'll bet a quart of sheep dip that he's some double-dyed son of a popgun out rounding up prohibition votes" (915).

Smoking was a part of the ranchman's everyday life. Baldy Woods and Webb Yeager, riding together until their routes diverged, "reined up for a parting cigarette" (111). When Ripley Givens of "The Princess and the Puma" was provided the luxury of black coffee and cigarettes O. Henry added, "What ranchero could desire more?" (234). Indeed, tobacco was more than a diversion; it ranked as a necessity, no more to be neglected than food and drink. Its absence could cause anger:

"The boys was smokin' cut plug and dried mesquite leaves mixed when I left," sighed Mustang Taylor, horse wrangler of the Three Elm camp. "They'll be lookin' for me back by nine. They'll be settin' up, with their papers ready to roll a whiff of the real thing before bedtime. And I've got to tell 'em that this pink-eyed, sheep-headed, sulphur-footed, shirt-waisted son of a calico broncho, Sam Revell, hasn't got no tobacco on hand" (177).

Sometimes, though seldom, a man failed to master the art of rolling a cigarette; such was Deputy-Marshal Buck Caperton: "cigarettes rolled with sweet corn husk were as honey to Buck's palate," but "though he could finger the trigger of a forty-five with skill and suddenness, he never could learn to roll a cigarette" (544).

The cowboys sometimes gathered at the only store in the vicinity, "arranged themselves comfortably on the steps," and ordered canned fruit: ". . . bust me open a can of green-gage plums, Sam," said one, while another ordered, "Open me some yellow clings." The storekeeper "chopped open with a hatchet the tops of the cans of fruit" (178). Then tin spoons were passed around, and the cowboys were soon scraping tin against tin as they ate from the cans. In a country where fresh fruit was unknown the canned variety became a treat.

In 1884 Will Porter left the ranch country for Austin, where he remained until 1895, when he began alternating his time between Austin and San Antonio. Later in mid-fall of that year he moved to Houston, residing there until the summer of 1896. His impressions of town life were as vivid as those of the ranches, and he later recalled some of the customs he had noticed.

People in the towns often sat on porches or went into yards for comfort. In "The Moment of Victory" Myra Allison was "sitting in a rocking chair on the porch, sewing" (763). In "The Indian Summer of Dry Valley Johnson" old Dry Valley "sprawled all day on a canvas cot under a live oak tree at his back door" (238). For protection against the sun a lady might carry a "parasol . . . of white silk" with fringe of lace (170). At home her bed might be decorated with "pillow-shams" (400).

O. Henry tells us also of the German people living "away up among the little mountains on the Pedernales River, in a little town called Fredericksburg." These settlers had brought the social customs of the old country with them. "Of evenings they sit at little tables along the sidewalk and drink beer and play pinochle and scat" (253).

In San Augustine the social set enjoyed "two ice-cream suppers" a week and "four germans" (756), the latter sponsored by a club. In Austin, we learn from "Georgia's Ruling," people enjoyed "summer opera" (1221), and for the sports lover there was the baseball team (1223). O. Henry mentions baseball again in "Buried Treasure" (732). The men of a small town are depicted playing checkers in "The Lonesome Road." In San Antonio bashful Tansey of "The Enchanted Kiss," captivated by his landlady's daughter, sometimes played a "blushing, delirious game of cribbage with her in the parlor" (478). Young men in San Antonio are shown spending the entire evening "playing billiards" (478).

Texans have always played dominoes, so naturally we find a character called Ed, who "forgathered [with his friend] in the back room of Snyder's saloon every afternoon after work, and played dominoes" to console himself for the loss of a beautiful girl, who, he lamented, "had a spirit and charm that could have enabled her to pluck rubies like raspberries from the crown of Belgium or any other sporty kingdom" if she had sought a more sophisticated environment (732). In Ed's unnamed "Texas prairie town" there were "Friday night debating societies—by way of culture" (732). In Austin O. Henry mentions people holding "strawberry feasts" (400).

Willy Robbins, who became a hero of the Spanish-American war, "... played the triangle in our serenading and quartet crowd that used to ring the welkin three nights a week somewhere in town" (756). This was in San Augustine, where Willy was also a member of the "militia company," and San Augustine had an "athletic association," which broadened the activities of the younger set. Dances were a frequent form of entertainment, but this same unfortunate Willy "danced like he had hind hobbles on" (756).

Ben Granger in "The Moment of Victory" tells us of an

"ice-cream sociable" that was held at Mrs. Colonel Spraggins':
"We fellows had a big room upstairs opened up for us to put
our hats and things in, and to comb our hair and put on the
clean collars we brought along inside the sweat-bands of our
hats—in short, a room to fix up in just like they have everywhere
at high-toned doings" (756). And in those days of detachable
cuffs for dress shirts a man carried a "cuff-fastener" in his pocket
(214).

The parlor of the Hinkle family in "A Poor Rule" contained
"willow rocking-chairs, and home-knit tidies, and albums, and
conch shells in a row. And a little upright piano in one corner"
(803-4). At the piano sat the daughter Ileen, complimented by
O. Henry as "a fruit-stand blonde—strawberries, peaches, cher-
ries" (802). A character in "Buried Treasure" includes in his
idea of a happy home, a "piano with an automatic player in
the sitting-room" (733-34).

In the story of Dry Valley Johnson's Indian summer, "Dry
Valley was to call for the girl one afternoon at six for a walk,"
O. Henry adding, "An afternoon walk in Santa Rosa was a
feature of social life that called for the pink of one's wardrobe"
(241). Buggy rides were another special function. "Dry Valley
bought a buggy with yellow wheels and a fine trotter in San
Antonio. Every day he drove out with Panchita" (241). In "Fog
in Santone" the man from Toledo, Ohio, suddenly remembered,
"Got an engagement for a hack ride out to San Pedro Springs
at eleven" (994).

In "The Sphinx Apple" we find the old custom, inherited
from the South, of sending love notes by messenger. Bildad
Rose, the stage driver, says of a lonely old man, "I reckon
Redruth waits about nine year expecting her to send him a
note by a nigger asking him to forgive her" (219).

Church is seldom mentioned by O. Henry, but Dry Valley
Johnson took his girl "to parties and dances, and to church"
(241). In "Bexar Scrip No. 2692" one contribution to the social
standing of the dishonest Mr. Sharp was that "he went to

church regularly" (1056). In "The Red Roses of Tonia,"
O. Henry says:

> Now, if one supposes that Easter, the Goddess of Spring, cares any
> more for the after-church parade on Fifth Avenue than she does for her
> loyal outfit of subjects that assemble at the meeting-house at Cactus,
> Tex., a mistake has been made. The wives and daughters of the ranchmen
> of the Frio country put forth Easter blossoms of new hats and gowns as
> faithfully as is done anywhere, and the Southwest is, for one day, a
> mingling of prickly pear, Paris, and paradise (1632-33).

O. Henry has poked fun at Austin society in his description
of a debut in "Tictocq." The debutante wears "a china silk,
cut princesse, with diamond ornaments, and a couple of towels
inserted in the back to conceal prominence of shoulder blades"
(1017). When she banteringly chides a young man as recreant
he replies:

> "Oh, come off.... I've been having a devil of a time fitting pants
> on a lot of bow-legged jays from the cotton-patch. Got knobs on their
> legs, some of 'em big as gourds, and all expect a fit. Did you ever try to
> measure a bow-legged—I mean—can't you imagine what a jam-swizzled
> time I had getting pants to fit 'em?" (1018)

Nevertheless, society was news, and the society columnists
had their followers, one being Miss Katie Peek, whose enchant-
ing kiss O. Henry acclaimed as "violets! electricity! caramels!
champagne!" Katie in "an elaborate, pale blue wrapper, cut to
fit, ... her little, bare feet ... thrust into house-shoes rimmed
with swan's down . . . was attacking the society news of the
latest Sunday paper" (486).

O. Henry found snobs in Austin, as we find them elsewhere;
of one he wrote, "The bluest blood flowed in her veins. Her
grandfather had sawed wood for the Hornsbys and an aunt on
her mother's side had married a man who had been kicked by
General Lee's mule" (1046).

The representative from Soapstone County looking for room
and board in "Aristocracy Versus Hash" became disgusted with

"people of fine descent," such as "a cousin of General Mahone of Virginia [who] wanted four dollars an hour for a back room with a pink motto and a Burnet granite bed in it," and "an aunt of Davy Crockett [who] asked eight dollars a day for a room furnished in imitation of the Alamo, with prunes for breakfast and one hour's conversation with her for dinner." In desperation he sought a "... back-woodsy, piebald gang, who never heard of finger bowls or Ward McAllister, but who can get up a mess of hot corn-bread and Irish stew at regular market quotations" (1043).

In San Antonio one might find the equivalent of a nightclub, such as was detected by Walter Goodall, who heard "a noise of wind and string instruments" (995). Inside, Goodall entered a "kind of antechamber, plentifully set with palms and cactuses and oleanders," where people sat drinking at "little marble-topped tables." There was a stairway with an attendant to be paid, before, as O. Henry continues, "Goodall goes upstairs and sees there two galleries extending along the sides of a concert hall. . . . These galleries are divided into boxes or stalls, which bestow with the aid of hanging lace curtains a certain privacy upon their occupants" (995). Considerately, O. Henry soon provides Goodall with an attractive feminine companion who exhibits "an Eve-like comeliness."

In the Mexican quarter of San Antonio at night two O. Henry characters hear "a guitar's tinkle, and the demoralizing voice of some señorita singing" what seems to have been a Mexican version of the blues (994). Once "the historic Alamo Plaza, in the heart of the city" had been the scene of "fun and frolic." O. Henry recalls, "Drawn by the coquettish *señoritas,* the music of the weird Spanish minstrels, and the strange piquant Mexican dishes served at a hundred competing tables, crowds thronged the Alamo Plaza all night." There one might eat "*chili-con-carne,* a dish evolved by the genius of Mexico,[3] composed of delicate meats minced with aromatic herbs and the poignant *chili colorado*—a compound full of singular savor and a fiery zest," while one sat at a table "covered with gaudy oil-cloth" (483).

In "The Higher Abdication" reference is made to the custom of eating at the free-lunch counter, present at every saloon, which might offer food ranging from "pig and cabbage" (175) at the cheaper establishments to delicacies at the bar of the Menger. In Austin, during a session of the legislature, "Senators Kinney and Mullens came to an understanding in the matter of irrigation and art while partaking of long drinks in the café of the Empire Hotel" (402). But liquor of a more sophisticated sort was also available in the cities. Tansey, longing for a certain unattainable girl and the "sweetness of her delectable lips," headed for a San Antonio saloon to drink "absinthe—beyond doubt the drink most adequate to his mood" (479).

Townspeople in a festive mood, or in a spirit of celebration, did the best that they could with what was at hand. The San Augustine Rifles, returning from victory over Spain, were honored with "speeches and chili-concarne at the Palace Hotel." A local young lady read a poem, followed by a "salute of nine guns" (762).

Interior decorating was also limited by the resources of the region. The office of a small-town bank president is described: "On the wall was the mounted head of a Texas steer with horns five feet from tip to tip. Opposite hung the major's old cavalry saber that he had carried at Shiloh and Fort Pillow" (455).

Many years later William Sidney Porter, writing under the pseudonym of O. Henry, was to recall the people, incidents, and customs of his Texas days for the purposes of fiction. This was in New York when his books reached a national reading public. O. Henry's memory served so well that Walter Prescott Webb has said, "His stories may be classed as among the best of the region and of their kind."[4]

1. John William Rogers and J. Frank Dobie, *Finding Literature on the Texas Plains* (Dallas: Southwest Press, 1931), p. 51.

2. The page numbers after each quotation from O. Henry refer to *The Complete Works of O. Henry* (2 vols.; Garden City, New York: Doubleday & Co., 1953).

3. O. Henry was aware that chili originated with the Mexicans in San Antonio, not in Old Mexico.

4. Walter Prescott Webb, *The Great Plains* (New York: Ginn & Co., 1931), p. 464.

The Cowboy in the British West Indies

ROGER D. ABRAHAMS

CHRISTMAS ON NEVIS, British West Indies, is the time of greatest festivity on that island. Many institutions survive that stem from England and point out the close cultural (as well as political) relationship which many of the smaller British West Indian islands have with the mother country. Wassailing, which goes under the name of "serenading," is still practiced. Arising at 11:00 P.M. on Christmas Eve, the singers make the rounds of the more wealthy residents of the island, caroling and begging "a penny to buy ... Christmas bread," or ordering the master or mistress to "pass the glass and bottle here."

Similarly, "Buzzard" troupes go about during all the nights of the Christmas season giving little improvised plays, usually based on some local happening, but flavored with traditional toasts such as

> Hark, hark the dog do bark
> Beggers are going to town.
> Some in rags and some in tags
> And some in velvet gown.[1]

or

> Christmas is coming, the geese are getting fat.
> Please to put a penny in the old man's hat.
> If you haven't got a penny, a half penny will do.
> If you haven't got a half penny, well God bless you.[2]

168

At the end of their performance, the "Buzzard" troupe may present this demand:

> Master and Mistress, if there is anything to offer
> Offer it in a saucer.
> If it's even a little drugsy water [unclean drink]
> It break wind [revives energy] from dandylion [he-man] chest.

or they boast:

> We are the buzzard boys
> We buzzard for a piece of bread.
> If anyone try to cut us down [i.e., if another buzzard
>   group comes along to challenge them]
> We buzzard until we dead.

As with many other aspects of the Christmas celebration on this island, these buzzard pieces seem to go back to the mumming tradition which until recently was so widespread in England. Though the St. George play, characteristic of the mumming, has not left any definable trace on Nevis folklife, other similar plays have existed for at least the last hundred years, and to some extent are still being played. (Many of the players have recently migrated to England, weakening the tradition considerably.) Perhaps the most common are *David and Goliath* and *Giant Despair,* the latter a four-hour dramatic rendition of parts of *Pilgrim's Progress.*

The dramatic performances are in the same pattern of alternation of scene and musical interlude as is found in the buzzard. Generally the scenes take between thirty seconds and two minutes and the music lasts two or three minutes. In the longer plays, the music is usually provided by the "big drum" band— one fife, one trap drum, and one bass drum, all homemade. In some communities this is varied by "string bands" (two or three guitars, a *cuatro* or four-stringed small guitar, a fife, a *giro* or tin-can noisemaker, and a *baha* or bass bamboo pipe) or a "tambourine band" (guitar, *cuatro,* trap drum, *baha,* large tambourine played like a drum, and fife). In the buzzard, the musical interlude is generally sung by the players.

Until about 1910-15 the plays were the major entertainments on the island at Christmas. Since then, such groups as the buzzards have sprung up, and the effects of many other cultures have asserted themselves in other institutions. The gaudiness and excitement of Carnival (Mardi Gras) has infected concepts of parading and costuming. New performing groups have sprung up utilizing bizarre and garish costume. "Saguas," for instance, wear cutaway coats, high hats, and colored shoes; the "Maka-Zhombies" wear multihued clothes and walk around on stilts. Some groups wear bull horns and "play the bull," trying to corner and mock-gore an onlooker until he gives them a penny.

The influence of American culture is predominant in two other types of groups, the "Cowboys" and the "Indians." The idea for both of these stems from popular cultural media that have been exported to the island from the States for a number of years, predominantly the movies and the comic books. Both groups organize their activities on the same pattern as the longer plays, with the alternation of music and dialogue, but derive their costuming, movements, and dialogue from the newer influences. The Indians talk in a kind of extremely fast gibberish, with lines usually ending "King George said I be an *Indian*," or "President Roosevelt make me an *Indian!*"

Of all the Christmas groups, the most popular and widespread seem to be the Cowboys. Nearly every community seems to have at least one group who regularly dress as cowboys and go about giving short dialogues based on their conception of what a cowboy should say and how he should say it. Here is a dialogue that is fairly typical:

> A: Hello, cowboy.
> B: Say, I could remember once I raid a train.
>   The cashier run like heck through the rain.
>   I call at him, he wouldn't stop

> I took out my forty-five and loosen his bloody elbow-cap.
> I went and stretch him out
> It was blood and bullet through his mout'.
> What do you think about that guy?
> C: Do you fellows realize who I am?
> OTHERS: We don't care.
> C: Well I'm the curly wolf of the high mesa,
> With some cactus t'orns in my hair.
> And don't rub me the wrong way
> For I am boss of you boys until doomsday.[3]

This would then be followed by a song, usually a commercial Western tune, such as "Midnight on the Prairie" or "I'm Back in the Saddle Again" (Riding the midnight train!). Some of the songs are traditional though, as with the others, they probably were transmitted through the movies or via a commercial recording. Often they are texts which take elements from a number of sources.

> I met her on the mountain top
> And I left her standing alone.
> I find myself on the midnight train
> I shot a poor sheriff down.
>
> All those cowboys bring me guilty
> For murder in the first degree.
> They tied me up with a ball and chain
> And they take me to the penitentiary,
>
> 'Cause I ain't got nobody
> Nobody cares for me.
> I'm so sad and lonely
> Darling, why don't you come and take
> a chance with me.

Sometimes the song and speech are intermingled:

Hello boys. My name is Esperanzo de Mia. I'm chief in charge of the flying vaqueros. Let me tell you all of something I have done. . . . Let me tell you something, fellows. I walked down the lanes of my old Kentucky home, I met a poor cowboy.

(sung)

> As I walked down the streets of Laredo one morning,
> As I walked down the streets of Laredo one day,
> I met a poor cowboy all wrapped in white linen,
> Wrapped up in white linen as cold as clay.

(spoken)

> I can see by his outfit that he was a cowboy.
> The words he used when I slowly passed by.
> Said, "Come and sit down beside me and hear my sad story,
> I got shot in my breast and I'm going to die."

This was the end of the story as far as this scene was concerned, but the same informant later sang the whole song as he knows it, adding the following stanzas:

> Go send a letter to old grey-haired mother,
> Carry the same to my sister so dear.
> For not even a word that I could have mentioned
> When the crowd gathered 'round me my story to hear.
>
> Go beat the drum slowly and blow the fife loudly,
> And bear the dead march as we carry him along.
> Away to the cattle house and then to the cemetery,
> He's gone to his maker, a cowboy, he's dead.[4]

Another traditional cowboy song which appeared in both sung and spoken form is "The Buffalo Skinners." One of the speeches which I collected was:

> The summer season is ended.
> The driver I couldn't pay.
> My outfit got extravagant
> I am dead damn broke I say.
> So load up band of cowboy
> And merrily we would go.
> That's why we leave their bones to dry
> On the hills of New Mexico.

Another player came up with the song, in fragmentary form:

Right here our pleasures ended,
Trouble just begin.
The first headstone that hits us
Gosh, how those cattle run.
They run into t'orns and cactus
They had but little show
Gosh, how those redskins watch
From the hills of Idaho.

And now we're past old Burger's Creek
And homeward we are bound.
No more in this damn country
Would ever we be found.
Go back to wives and sweethearts
And tell others not to go
To that God-forsaken country
Called New Mexico.[5]

Sometimes one player will step out and give a speech.

I'm Fred Rigdon, star from Idaho, who wears a brace of black
buttons, forty-five degrees, slugging against my lean hips, natural as if
I were born with them. My draw is more fast than fast.

I'm Bing Crosby from the golden city. And the world in my corner
and the doom. For four days I was waiting behind the cloud for someone
to come and break me down, and can't have no one did it. If you want
to get me, you come right over here now. I'm the only star in town, and
no man could be boss of me here. If you're not of the same opinion I
could change your mind. Tomorrow morning you meet me at Lorna
Doom and the fastest gunman tells it.

Often these same kinds of boasting speeches are found in the
middle of longer dialogues:

A: Say, Hello, stranger. Who are you? Where are you heading now?
B: Say, stranger, put your hands up.
A: Say, mister, when my hands go up, you'll be going down.
B: Say, see that cloud over there. Seems like rain is heading this way.
Try not to break or make a hair, mister. Once I go away and the town
was robbed, and robbed by you, and what cause?
A: Break me down? Break me down? You'll find some holes in your
face you'll have to use a microscope just to see them. I'm the guy they

call Oklahoma Kid, and the world in my corner and doom. And anyone try to cut 'cross me, I'll saddle them, saddle my horse, ride them away over Mexico range.

B: I'm the only cowboy in town, when the boss is out on a four days vacation, I leave in charge, say, "You don't allow no gamblers and strangers more than one day or two days inside." Any man coming down can see I'm boss around here. I'm the only man could be boss of them, too.

The dialogues are not always boasts, however. Here is one comic scene:

BARMAN: Hello, cowboys.
COWBOY: Say, what kind of drinks do you have in stock, barman?
BARMAN: Oh, I have cream soda.
COWBOY: Yeah.
BARMAN: Irish potatoes.
COWBOY: Yeah.
BARMAN: Chocolate, pineapple and marshmallow soda.
COWBOY: Yeah.
BARMAN: As close as you dare, delicious guava berry. What you don't see, ask for.
COWBOY: Well, get me a delicious guava berry.
BARMAN: Well, sure.
COWBOY: *(Drinks with proper sound effects and chokes)* God damn it, barman, where did you get the drinks, God damn it, to hell?
BARMAN: What next?
COWBOY: What about the Deadman's Punch?
BARMAN: Sure we have Deadman's Punch. Open your hatch boy. *(Goes to pour drink down cowboy's throat)*
COWBOY: No, barman, what if you t'row it in my nose? My mouth ain't open as yet. Come on. *(He drinks and again chokes. Sets the glass down)* Barman, that's a very good drink. Well, I'll see you sometimes.
BARMAN: Now how 'bout the change.
COWBOY: What?
BARMAN: The cash.
COWBOY: The cash?
BARMAN: You'll meet me on the range and you'll get that. *(Cocks finger like a pistol)* Bullets.
COWBOY: *(Giving him money)* Thanks, much.

It has often been said that the cowboy has been the gift of the United States to the world. The Western song, with its cousin the country song, has traveled all over the world via phonograph records. The people of Nevis have carried this one step farther and fashioned one aspect of their traditional Christmas folk drama to include this lusty breed.

1. For a history of this rhyme, see Peter and Iona Opie, *The Oxford Dictionary of Nursery Rhymes* (Oxford, 1951), pp. 152-53.

2. This is a common rhyme in both England and the United States, though the money referred to is strange in the latter. My father taught it to us in Philadelphia in the late 1930's. For English reportings, see Peter and Iona Opie, *Lore and Language of Schoolchildren* (Oxford, 1959), p. 52.

3. The tone of these speeches resembles many of the "toasts" (long narrative poems) found among the American Negro. This is probably due to the effect of the cowboy "boast" on the folklore of both groups rather than to any other relationship.

4. Laws's *Native American Balladry* (B 1) (Philadelphia, 1951) gives a full discussion of this complex song.

5 See Laws for this song as well.

Adam's Rib

GEORGE D. HENDRICKS

THE FACT IS that men and women are different. They were made different. Folklore makes much of this difference. It emphasizes the contention more than the happiness arising from this difference. And it is pretty obvious that the great body of this folklore emanates from men rather than women.

Often the male folk-analyst, in explaining woman's shortcomings, traces her origin to some lower animal. A salty country doctor named Joseph H. Peck, for example, writes an article for *True Magazine* (May, 1961) entitled "Life with Women and How to Survive It."

Adam was made of the dust from the ground, but the chronicler neglects to say how long it took to develop him. He was the last apple of the family tree and in no way resembled his distant ancestors. I am inclined to believe that the original rootstock was the wolf, or some other canine animal. Man's habits and social behavior more closely resemble the canine than any other member of the zoo. . . .

Eve was not a true woman because she was constructed entirely from masculine materials. It is not likely that she would ever have been able to bear a daughter as her basic ingredients were purely masculine. . . . [Cain, Abel, and Seth had to get their mates from the land of Nod.]

We are justified in believing that the girls over in Nod were also the end results of some of Nature's experiments, which probably began with lions and tigers. . . .

Women have been compared to cats ever since men could use words, and for the best of reasons: they act like them.

Semonides of Amorgos, Greek iambic poet of the seventh

century B.C., wrote that various kinds of women evolved from different animals:

> When God made woman, He made her mind different from man's.
> He made her of a bristly sow. Everything about her is disorderly, defiled with dirt; and she herself grows fat sitting on the dunghills in clothes as filthy as herself. So much for one kind of woman. . . .
> Another kind He made of a bitch, a busybody like her mother. This one wants to hear all and know all and is always peering and prying about and barking even when she sees nobody. No man can stop her threats, not even if he knocks her teeth out with a stone. . . .[1]

Other women Semonides considers being made from cats, mares, vixens, and apes. Only those made from bees are good women:

> The kind made of a bee is another story. Happy is the man who gets her. She is without blame, and life flourishes because of her. Pre-eminent among women, she is loving and loved and the mother of fair and honorable children. Divine grace pervades her. She never sits among the women when they tell stories about fornication. Such a wife is the best and wisest that Zeus bestows on a man.[2]

Stith Thompson's motif A1224.3 is a Scandinavian legend that woman was created from a dog's tail. And tale type 137.12 is a German folktale that bad women are a combination of nine different animals. In his book *The Crooked Rib*, Francis Lee Utley unearthed an anonymously published work, *The Scholehouse of Women*, probably written in the 1540's by Edward Gosynhill:

> A woman once argued with the author [Gosynhill] that women were superior to men because they were made of man's rib, while man was of earth only. He answered that a rib is crooked, stiff, sturdy, and evil to rule. Put two ribs in a bag and they will clatter like a woman. In reality God made woman out of a dog's rib, since the dog ate Adam's rib, which He had intended for the purpose. This is why women bark and bawl like a cur.[3]

Somebody named Sharp found in a Persian poet's writings a

combination of both good and bad flora and fauna in woman: "In the beginning, said a Persian poet—Allah took a rose, a lily, a dove, a serpent, a little honey, a Dead Sea apple, and a handful of clay. When he looked at the amalgam—it was a woman."[4]

The disgruntled male folk-analyst sometimes associates the origin of the female sex with the devil himself. Woman, the serpent, and the devil have certain specific relationships. Stith Thompson's motif A1371.1 concerns a European folktale in which the devil in the form of a serpent is fighting a woman. St. Peter cuts off their heads and exchanges them. This explains woman's perfidy. Oscar Von Wertheimer, in an article on "The History of the Devil" (*Living Age*, April 14, 1925), cites various ancient lores which maintain that the devil and women are associates in crime, that women are possessed of the devil, that woman "was made from a crooked rib, and hence has a natural inclination to corrupt ways." And according to Maximilian Rudwin, "A curious Jewish tradition teaches that the devil and woman had a common origin in Adam's rib. Old Nick is believed by certain rabbis to have come out of the hole left by the removal of the rib from Adam before it was closed."[5] But probably the most ingenious of all tales linking the creation of the devil, woman, and serpent is the following translation of an old French *pourquoi* tale collected by James R. Foster:

When God created woman he took a rib from Adam's side. This rib he laid upon the grass while he sewed up the wound. The serpent slipped up and stole it, and as in those days he had four good legs, he made off very fast. God sent Michael after him. The Archangel soon caught hold of him and thought he had him fast, but the serpent pulled away violently and, leaving his legs in Michael's hands, slithered off into the underbrush.

The Archangel was very sorry the snake got away and told the Eternal Father how it happened. The Creator was angry because of the loss of Adam's rib. After a moment or two of reflection, he took up the serpent's legs, breathed on them and in this way created Mother Eve. And that is why woman is so perfidious. Since that day no serpent has ever had any legs.[6]

Certainly the conception of the first woman being created from the first man's rib is age old. It probably preceded the formulation of the Old Testament. Samuel Noah Kramer attributes its origin to a kind of freak play on words from the mythology of ancient Sumer:

> For why a rib? Why did the Hebrew storyteller find it more fitting to choose a rib rather than any of the other parts of the body for the fashioning of the woman whose name, Eve, according to the Biblical notion, means approximately "she who makes live"? The reason becomes quite clear if we assume a Sumerian literary background, such as that represented by our Dilmun poem, underlying the Biblical paradise tale. For in our Sumerian poem one of Enki's sick members is the rib. Now the Sumerian word for "rib" is *ti* (pronounced "tee"). The goddess created for the healing of Enki's rib therefore was called in Sumerian Nin-ti, "the lady of the rib." But the very same Sumerian word *ti* also means "to make live." The name Nin-ti may thus mean "the lady who makes live," as well as "the lady of the rib." In Sumerian literature, therefore, "the lady of the rib" came to be identified with "the lady who makes live" through what may be termed a play of words. It was this, one of the most ancient of literary puns, which was carried over and perpetuated in the Biblical paradise story, although here, of course, it loses its validity, since the Hebrew word for "rib" and that for "who makes live" have nothing in common.[7]

Kramer's logical deduction does not conflict with the findings of Sir James G. Frazer, who devotes a good portion of Volume I of his *Folklore in the Old Testament* to this subject. He explains the biblical Genesis story of creation as a merging of two separate and originally independent documents. The first (as in Gen. 1) derives from what is termed the Priestly Document, composed by priestly writers during the Babylonian captivity. The other (as in Gen. 2) comes from the Jehovistic Document, written three hundred years earlier (probably 900 B.C.). It is the latter which displays the original author's deep contempt for woman for having caused the sorrows of the human race by her credulous folly and unbridled appetite. It was he who could very well have borrowed the motif from Sumerian lore.

Frazer then traces the motif of the rib-creation throughout

the world of primitive cultures—such as those of the early Egyptians, Greeks, Australians, Maoris of New Zealand, Tahitians, Polynesians, Bedel Tartars of Siberia, Hopi Indians, and Eskimos. It is odd that some of these peoples infuse female human origins with the feline species, just as does our good Dr. Peck, whom I have quoted earlier. Frazer deduces that these worldwide counterparts of the rib-creation motif are the results of early Christian missionary teachings, with local native adaptations.

Certainly biblical teachings, from Eve on down, have been harsh on women, if taken literally. Deuteronomy forbids women to wear men's clothes (22:5). I Corinthians (11:5-15) says they must wear their hair long. II Timothy (3:6) says they are silly and easily led into error. Numbers (31:15,16) says they are active in instigating iniquity. And Proverbs (21:19) says, "It is better to dwell in the wilderness, than with a contentious and angry woman." I Timothy (2:11) says, "Let a woman learn in silence with all submissiveness."

Most succinct and to the point is the following translation of a fable from the Talmud, which is a collection of Jewish civil and canonical laws not included in the Pentateuch:

THE MAKING OF EVE

When God decided to create Eve, He considered from what part of Adam's body he should fashion her.

He said, "I will not fashion her from his head lest she be too vain. I will not fashion her from his eyes lest she be eager to see all things. I will not fashion her from his ears lest she be a gossip. I will not fashion her from his heart lest she be envious. I will not fashion her from his hands lest she grasp things that do not belong to her. I will not fashion her from his feet lest she be a gadabout."

"I will fashion her from a hidden part of his body, a part which will be covered even though he stand naked."

And as each nerve and tissue he created, God said, "Be thou a modest wife, an exemplary woman."

Nevertheless, God's plans were thwarted. Woman is proud; she is eager to see all and know all; she has nine measures of talk; she is jealous; she craves for things that are not hers; and she is a gadabout.[8]

In "Adam's Diary" Mark Twain shows Adam's displeasure at Eve's nine measures of talk and her vanity:

> I have never heard the human voice before, and here upon the solemn hush of these dreaming solitudes it offends my ear. . . .
> The new creature says its name is Eve. I have no objections. . . . She told me she was made out of a rib taken from my body. This is at least doubtful, as I have not missed any rib. . . . She fell in the pond yesterday when she was looking at herself in it, which she is always doing. . . .[9]

Mark Twain has his Adam, after a period of ten years with Eve, come to his senses and reverse his viewpoint:

> At first I thought Eve talked too much, but now I should be sorry to have that voice fall silent and pass out of my life. Blessed be the chestnut that brought us near together and taught me to know the goodness of her heart and the sweetness of her spirit.[10]

Relax is a magazine designed for male consumption and devoted to photographs of unclad female anatomy and bawdy stories supposedly based upon fact, folklore, fiction, and fantasy. The editors of its first issue, May, 1957, include the following legend about the first man and woman, the authenticity of which is doubtful because Polynesia has no horses or gazelles. I am including it, however, because it fits the pattern of parodies of woman's loquacity; and, though it may be tainted by a journalistic touch, it probably comes ultimately from a genuine grassroots folklore:

> An ancient Polynesian legend symbolizes the eternal battle of the sexes. Tatwahstri, the Polynesian god, created man. When he saw that man was lonely and sad, Tatwahstri gave him a companion—a woman. Man and woman, alone in their Garden of Eden, lived out their love story.
> One day the man went to speak with the god, who lived in a palace hidden among the boulders of an ancient volcano.
> "Lord," said the man, "I was lonely and craved company. Thou, oh generous one, didst give me a woman. And I was happy at first. But the woman is as haughty as a peacock, yet banal and empty like a basket without fruit. She speaks incessantly and says nothing. She is as headstrong as an untamed horse which for lack of bridle does not know where

to go. She is silly, pompous, immature. I was alone and life was sad, but now my life is intolerable. Lord, take her away and leave me with my loneliness."

And the god complied with the man's wishes.

Several days later the mortal returned. "Lord!" he cried, "I have committed a grave error. I was not happy with the woman but without her I am even more unhappy. I miss her foolish chatter, I keep remembering her gazelle-like grace, her bird-of-paradise gestures, her dazzling beauty. Lord, I cannot live without her. Give her back to me."

And the god gave her back to him.

Several days later the man was back, terribly distressed. "Lord," he sobbed, "I did not know what I was saying. It is a thousand times better to live alone but free. The woman is a tyrant and she wishes to make me her slave. She is arrogant, impatient, insufferably demanding. Lord, punish me, but take her away."

And the god answered, "Keep her! That is your punishment."

But surely there is more than one way to look at the symbol of Adam's rib. Somebody named Henry wrote,

Woman was taken out of man—not out of his head, to rule over him; nor out of his feet, to be trampled under by him; but out of his side, to be equal to him—under his arm, that he might protect her, and near his heart that he might love her.[11]

This passage is almost identical, both in wording and in sentiment, with an old southern ballad collected by George Pullen Jackson and included in the Lomax collection.[12] Compatible with this interpretation is the Chinese legend of creation, as related by Helena Kuo:

When we Chinese women marry, we want to believe that we have moulded our lives into another life. We feel it is an act of creation. We believe that "woman is made of water and man of clay." The meaning of this is that the clay of man cracks unless it is permeated by water—a discovery made by the Creator when he made man of clay and saved him from crumbling into nothingness by adding water.[13]

And though Simone de Beauvoir may not be quite so submissive as Miss Kuo, she intimates practically the same thing in her discussion of The Second Sex:

Eve was not fashioned at the same time as the man; she was not fabricated from a different substance, nor of the same clay as was used to model Adam: she was taken from the flank of the first male. Not even her birth was independent; God did not spontaneously choose to create her as an end in herself and in order to be worshipped directly by her in return for it. She was destined by Him for man; it was to rescue Adam from loneliness that He gave her to him, in her mate was her origin and her purpose; she was his complement on the order of the inessential. Thus she appeared in the guise of privileged prey. She was nature elevated to transparency of consciousness; she was a conscious being, but naturally submissive. And therein lies the wondrous hope that man has often put in woman: he hopes to fulfill himself as a being by carnally possessing a thing, but at the same time confirming his sense of freedom through the docility of a free person. No man would consent to be a woman, but every man wants woman to exist.[14]

These three passages present the woman as of more pliable substance than her lordly mate. She is the romantic feminine, nonaggressive component of the conjugal partnership. She is Adam's delicate rib made still more fragile, passive, and desirable in her metamorphosis. She is as delightfully tender as melting snow, but like François Villon's snows of yesteryear, she is gone forever.

How could a mere rib stand vertically by itself unsupported? In his book *Adam's Rib,* psychiatrist Martin G. Vorhaus tells us we are all bisexual in just about everything except our genitalia themselves. Men vary in demeanor from the masculine bully to the effeminate coward. And though the range in women's behavior is wide, there are very few mere Adam's ribs running around loose. Men and women are as they are because things are as they are.

Nowadays the pressure is upon the young woman to get her man. If she has enough masculinity in her, she will go hunting. Her archetype is one of our favorite caricatures in modern fiction, movies, and cartoons. How often this occurs, Dr. Vorhaus cites in a typical conversation between two buddies:

"When did you propose to her?"
"Come to think of it, I never did."
"You mean she proposed to you?"

"Of course not, she's not like that."

"Well, how did you *know*?"

"I don't know, it sort of happened. We first got around to assuming, to taking it for granted, that some time—when we could afford it—that we would get married."

Each reader will remember how true this is of his own experience. . . .

The deciding issue for the more passive male is the awakening interest of an active woman in his existence, his availability and his desirability. This is not the man whose face is slapped; he doesn't want to risk a rebuff so he waits for a "green light." Sometimes he waits and waits and the exasperated young woman wonders why he doesn't recognize a green light when it flashes on.[15]

Times have changed. Denton, Texas, now has a men's flower gardening club, and I personally have lectured to four all-female groups. I also participated in a hot PTA election last year. Women are becoming family chauffeurs, with schedules to meet commitments at certain times and places on the dot in snow, sleet, rain, or fog. Woman is taking over the family household budget with a vote often outweighing her mate's. Dr. Vorhaus summarizes the finality of woman's becoming masculine:

At long last, she can appear publicly in masculine clothes, not only for sports but even in her casual daily togs—and this, with almost universal approval! She smokes on the street without censure; she drinks at a bar without condemnation. One by one the sports barriers have fallen and made way for her. Only polo is still holding out as anachronistically as the all-male-executive flight between Chicago and New York. In these and other ways her life has broadened, enriched by the fulfillments of her masculine component.[16]

This all makes us wonder whatever became of Adam's rib. Doubtless there were social tensions that caused the original Jehovistic author to view his contemporary women with contempt as far back as 900 B.C. Twentieth-century subways don't promote amenities between the sexes. Recently, according to an AP release, a New York transit company placed placards in its coaches with pictures of knights offering ladies their seats, bowing gracefully—accompanied by a slogan, "Be a knight for a day." Results were less than satisfactory. A chorus of male objections resulted:

"This city has a higher concentration of uncouth female hooligans per square foot of land area than any other city in the world. It would contribute vast improvement to their manners if the old-fashioned ducking stool were brought back into use."

"Gallantry and courtesy will return when women start looking and acting like women again—when they stop cutting their hair as short as a man's, when they stop wearing dresses that destroy all their appeal."

"Women asked for equal rights and they got 'em."[17]

A multitude of female opinions were equally vehement:

"Men—phooey."

"It is laughable to think of a man giving up his seat to anyone. The majority of them in this city are too rude to begin with. Aside from that, after pushing, kneeing and pinching his way through the subway door during a rush hour, he couldn't move if he wanted to. About a month ago I was knocked to the floor and rather than help me up, men walked over me to get into the train. Give up a seat? Who are they kidding?"[18]

Social pressure is a powerful impetus, whether it stirs a modern woman to get her man or a modern man to get a subway seat. The trouble with women, however, is that there is something about them (with all their faults) that is irresistible. George J. Trimble was a frontier marshal and miner who died at the age of a hundred and four in Merced, California, on Wednesday, November 8, 1961. Mr. Trimble, shortly before dying, said he had dedicated his life to three things: whiskey, women, and independence. At the age of ninety-seven he was arrested in a Merced tavern for hitting an eighty-three-year-old man with a cane. He said the man had made offensive remarks to a seventy-two-year-old woman. The woman must have been an elemental daughter of Eve, the kind of woman who would provoke one man to offensive language but at the same time would be alluring enough to entice another to her rescue.

Whether she is an unclad Eve, a hoopskirted Victorian, or

someone in slacks, woman is provokingly appealing. An Italian, Doctor Paolo Rosatti (D.A.—Doctor of Aesthetes), has discovered why women like Sophia Loren and Gina Lollobrigida are so irresistible:

> Go into any Italian kitchen, and you will see why Italian women have the loveliest, healthiest eyes in the world.
> There you will find an enchanting angel slicing onion. Exquisite tears will be rolling from her eyes like the precious diamonds they are.
> It is the tears that make the eyes colorful, strong, irresistible, and utterly feminine.[19]

It is true; feminine tears will tear a man apart quicker than anything else. Doc Peets was the sage of the frontier cowtown named Wolfville, in Alfred Henry Lewis' immortal 1897 book by the same name. Doc Peets's philosophy on women is short and to the point: "There's nothin' ketches me like a female of my species in distress."[20]

And that, exactly, was the downfall of Adam.

1. Charles Neider, *Man Against Woman* (Boston, 1957), pp. 79-82.
2. *Ibid.*
3. Francis Lee Utley, *The Crooked Rib* (Columbus, 1944), p. 256. Professor Utley states that this tale is widespread in Europe from Russia to Flanders, as in Oskar Dahnhardt, *Natursagen* (Leipzig and Berlin, 1907-12), I, 114-23.
4. *Women Pro and Con* (Mount Vernon, N. Y.: Peter Pauper Press, 1958), p. 28.
5. Maximilian Rudwin, *The Devil in Legends and Literature* (Chicago, 1931), p. 1.
6. James R. Foster, *Great Folktales of Wit and Humor* (New York, 1955), p. 5.
7. Samuel Noah Kramer, "Mythology of Sumer and Akkad," in *Mythologies of the Ancient World* (New York, 1961), pp. 102-3. In Sumerian mythology Dilmun corresponds to Eden and Nin-ti to Eve, but Enki is a water-god. There may be no clear-cut parallel with Adam, as six different kinds of men were first created; but Enki is said to have created a man of clay, as a kind of experiment.
8. Manuel Komroff (ed.), *The Great Fables of All Nations* (New York, 1935), pp. 117-18.
9. From Clifton Fadiman's edition of Mark Twain's "Adam's Diary" and "Eve's Diary," in *This Week Magazine*, October 11, 1959.
10. *Ibid.*
11. *Women Pro and Con*, p. 59.

12. John A. and Alan Lomax, *American Ballads and Folk Songs* (New York, 1934), pp. 567-68. The title is "Wedlock." Originally it appeared in George Pullen Jackson, *White Spirituals of the Southern Uplands.*

13. Helena Kuo, "American Women Are Different," *American Mercury,* June, 1942.

14. Simone de Beauvoir, *The Second Sex,* trans. H. M. Parshley (New York, 1961), p. 131.

15. Martin G. Vorhaus, *Adam's Rib* (New York, 1959), pp. 79-80.

16. *Ibid.,* p. 159.

17. Francis Stilley, "Courtesy Drive Stalls as Shoving Continues," AP Release, *Fort Worth Star-Telegram,* April 7, 1961.

18. *Ibid.*

19. WNS release, "Irresistible Eyes Due to Onions," *Dallas Morning News,* November 19, 1961.

20. Alfred Henry Lewis, *Wolfville* (New York, 1897), p. 29.

"The Texas Rangers" in Aberdeenshire

KENNETH S. GOLDSTEIN

THE OVERWHELMING BULK of ballads and songs reported from oral tradition in America during the past half-century has come to us from the British Isles. This Anglo-Scots-Irish tradition, following the several waves of emigration to this country from the "old country" since the seventeenth century, is too well known to American ballad and folksong scholars to necessitate documentation here. The reverse movement of folksongs—*from* America *to* the Old World—has received all too little attention.

To American folklorists and field workers, this matter may not seem particularly important. We suffer from a kind of naïve ethnocentricity-in-reverse, in which we have become so accustomed to accepting the almost entirely one-way traffic to our shores of Anglo-Saxon stock and traditions, that we never think of the possibility of *our* native folk traditions crossing the ocean to find even limited acceptance in the Old World. This, plus the general insularity of our collectors, seen in the fact that so few American field workers have ever shown the slightest interest in overseas collecting, may explain this seeming disinterest.

However, even armchair folklorists should have come face to face with this issue simply as a result of their reading British and Irish collections of folksongs and ballads. Some few of these collections point up the "back home" movement of folksong, and even suggest the manner in which this movement has taken place. As examples we may cite the collection of some occupational songs of American origin, undoubtedly brought to Britain by returning emigrants. This must certainly have been the case with "Miner's Life Is Like a Sailor's," reported from Wales by A. L. Lloyd,[1] and "The Lumbering Boys" ("The Jam on Gerry's Rocks"), collected in Aberdeenshire by Gavin Greig.[2] A few of our songs may have passed into British tradition as a result of performances by American minstrel singers and vaudevillians who played the British music halls during the last century. Some of these songs found their way into print through the broadside and songster presses, and fed into the oral traditions of British countrymen. Alfred Williams found at least four of these "minstrel" pieces, "Old Dan Tucker," "The Blue-Tail Fly," "Bob Ridley," and "Johnny Bowker," in the mouths of his Upper Thames neighbors during the opening year of World War I.[3]

And, too, any American folklorist who has shown even the slightest interest in shanties must be aware of the large number of American shipboard worksongs which passed into usage aboard British and European sailing vessels.[4] Less obvious is the fact that sailors, either British or American, brought American songs and ballads with them when visiting British and Irish ports, and helped to start these on their way into the oral repertories of the natives. For examples of this mode of oral circulation one need only turn to the fascinating but little-known collection of sea songs and ballads made in southeastern Ireland during the late 1930's and early 1940's by Joseph Ranson.[5] Included are excellent versions of "The Stately Southerner," "Paul Jones' Victory," "The Cumberland's Crew," "The Loss of the Albion," and "The Titanic."

Still, the list is a small one indeed if we rely on published collections for evidence of the transoceanic transmission of American folksongs. One suspects that in some cases such songs were simply of too little interest to British collectors to warrant their inclusion in their published works. And, too, we can be sure that certain American songs, especially those of an out-

spokenly ribald and bawdy nature, never saw the inside of
the book printer's workshop; the hedgerow schoolmasters and
ministers who comprised a large part of the British collecting
fraternity certainly sheared their collections of such "mon-
strosities"—witness, for example, their infantile antics in
bowdlerizing and recomposing even the least offensive of such
materials found in their own traditions.[6]

These were some of the salient points which I kept in mind
when I began my field work in the Buchan District of Aberdeenshire, Scotland, in the fall of 1959.[7] To be sure, my main
reason for collecting in Aberdeenshire was *not* to discover the
degree to which American folksongs existed in the repertories
of Scots traditional singers—but this was *one* of several matters
which I intended looking into in the course of my field work.

Almost immediately I discovered that a rather large number
of American songs were known by my informants. Some knew
the origin of these songs; others could not have cared less. The
songs varied greatly in type and origin. American hillbilly and
country songs were fairly popular and sung by both old and
young singers. Despite the fact that these songs could be traced
to recordings released in Britain during the 1930's and 1940's,
I make reference to them because they had passed into oral
circulation in the space of one or two decades. Most of my
informants had these songs orally from other singers who probably had them first or second hand from recordings. The songs
had already undergone the various changes implicit in a mainly
oral tradition. The most popular songs in this group were the
"blue yodels" of Jimmie Rodgers. More than one of my informants tickled my sense of proportion by following their performance of some superb and rarely collected seventeenth-century
ballad with a yodeling rendition of one of the numerous
creations of "The Singing Brakeman."[8] If they were not yet
folksongs, they were well on their way.

The next largest group of American folksongs known by my
Buchan informants were songs learned from American service-

men during World Wars I and II. These included some older traditional songs, a fair number of American soldiers' songs, some bawdy and obscene songs, and some few sentimental pieces of stage origin.

A third group of songs included various minstrel show and vaudeville pieces which passed into local circulation during the latter half of the nineteenth century, when American entertainers visited the music halls of Aberdeen and lesser northeastern Scottish cities and towns.

But of most interest to me were those few American folksongs which appeared to have been brought to Scotland by either immigrants, visitors, or returning emigrants. A fragmentary version of "The Streets of Laredo" to an unusual tune excited my interest in these songs. A magnificent performance of "The Jam on Gerry's Rocks," sung to me by a local shepherd fifty years after Gavin Greig had first reported the song in Scottish tradition, fired my interest still further. But the moment of glory was when my finest informant, Lucy Stewart of Fetterangus, Aberdeenshire, first sang to me "The Gallant Ranger," a superb version, both textually and musically, of "The Texas Rangers."[9]

The Gallant Ranger
(Sung by Lucy Stewart, Fetterangus, Aberdeenshire; collected by Kenneth S. Goldstein, January, 1960)

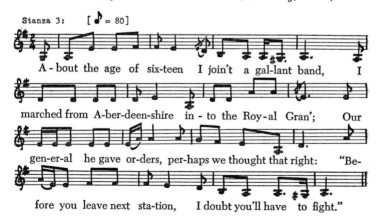

Stanza 3: [♪ = 80]

A-bout the age of six-teen I join't a gal-lant band, I marched from A-ber-deen-shire in-to the Roy-al Gran'; Our gen-er-al he gave or-ders, per-haps we thought that right: "Be-fore you leave next sta-tion, I doubt you'll have to fight."

1. Come a' ye gallant rangers and listen now tae me,
   I'll tell ye's a' a story that happened unto me;
   My name it's nothing extrae an' that I need nae tell;
   My mind wis bawnt on ranging, a-rovin' fare-'e-well.

2. O, up spoke my aul' mother, this word she said tae me:
   "My boy, they are all strangers, I doubt* you better stay,
   I thought that you were childish and you inclined to roam,
   I'll tell ye by experience—you better stay at home."

3. About the age of sixteen I join't a gallant band,
   I marched from Aberdeenshire into the Royal Gran';
   Our general he gave orders, perhaps we thought that right:
   "Before you leave next station, I doubt you'll have to fight."

4. I saw the Indians comin', I knew their savage yell;
   My patience at that moment no mortyal tongue could tell;
   I saw their glitterin' lances, their bullets round me fell;
   My mind wis bawnt on ranging, a-rovin' fare-'e-well.

5. We fought for full nine hours before the fight wis o'er;
   The sight of dead and woundit I nivir saw before;
   Five thousan' gallant rangers that ivir left the West
   Lay buriet by their comrades, and peace shall be their rest.

6. Perhaps ye've got a father, likewise a mother, too;
   Perhaps ye've got a sister to weep an' murn for you;
   An' if that be your siteeation, an' you incline to roam,
   I'll tell ye by experience—you better stay at home.

7. Come a' ye's gallant rangers aroun' me here this night,
   Whativir you do for a livin', for God's sake nivir fight,
   Your enemy is quite careless, they shoot right in the crew—
   They're boun' tae hit somebody an' perhaps it might be you.
                    (*Music transcribed by Norman Cazden*)
   I doubt — I'm sure (or, no doubt — idiomatic)

Lucy Stewart, aged fifty-nine, was the major tradition-bearer in a family whose store of folklore seemed almost unlimited. From this family I collected over 200 ballads and songs, some 65 tales and legends, 185 riddles, more than 300 children's games and rhymes, innumerable superstitions and beliefs, examples of witchcraft, devil lore, weather lore, dream warnings, fortune telling—indeed, the full gamut of folklore tradi-

tions existed in this one marvelous family. From Lucy alone
I collected over 175 ballads and songs, more than half of these
in full textual versions. And even in those songs in which she
was unable to remember more than a few verses, her tunes
were always so well shaped that her stock of melodies was in
itself a treasure trove. The rich musical tradition of the family
was of such high order that Lucy rarely repeated a tune—only
six duplications of tunes existed in her entire repertory. Though
she was the only member of the family who was unable to read
music or play any instrument, as often as not any question
concerning music which arose in the family would be settled
with Lucy's aid. This despite the fact that every member
of the family was known by friends and neighbors throughout
the Buchan District as a fine musician or singer—all except
Lucy, that is.

Lucy's tradition was a wholly private family matter. In the
very village in which she lived no one outside the Stewart
family even knew that she sang. She was extremely reticent
about singing in the presence of persons not related to her, and
it took me more than two months to pry loose from her the first
song. From then on her songs flowed in a seemingly endless
stream.

"The Gallant Ranger" was one of the first songs which Lucy
sang for me. Needless to say, I was extremely surprised to hear,
in the heart of Scotland's most tradition-bound county, a native
American ballad which I considered a product typical of the
western frontiersmen and plainsmen of the last century. Before
I had a chance to ask where the song had come from, she
informed me that she had learned it at her mother's knees when
she was about ten years old (around 1911). When I asked her
what the song was about, she informed me that it referred
to the great mutiny of the Bengali sepoys in India in 1858!
"Many's a Scotch sodger wis sent tae fecht 'ere," she solemnly
told me. To Lucy this was no foreign song; it was as much a
part of Scottish history as was the Battle of Harlaw. Indeed,

during those few minutes in which I heard her sing the ballad and then explain its meaning (to her) in terms of British history, I wondered if perhaps "The Texas Rangers" might not simply be an American rescension of a British original. Logic reasserted itself rather quickly after the magic of that moment; there were too many internal clues in her text for it to have been anything but one of those few examples of the trans-Atlantic migration of native American song.

Several months later, I brought my tapes to the School of Scottish Studies at the University of Edinburgh, to have copies made for their archives. I mentioned my find to Hamish Henderson, a research fellow at the school, and Scotland's leading collector of Lowland Scots folk traditions.[10] After a few minutes of searching through the archive shelves, he placed a reel of tape on the nearest empty tape deck. He then played for me the second version of "The Texas Rangers" which I was to hear sung some five thousand miles from its probable place of action.

THE TEXAS RANGERS

(Sung by Geordie Robertson, Aberdeen;
collected by Hamish Henderson, 1954)

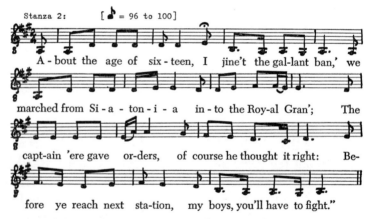

1. Come a' ye Texas Rangers, whaur e'er 'at ye be,
   I'll tell tae you a story 'at happen't unto me;
   My name it's nothing extrae, bit' at I'll nivir tell;

My min' wis bent on rangin', a-rovin' fare-ye-well.

2. About the age of sixteen, I jine't the gallant ban',
   We marched from Siatonia into the Royal Gran';
   The captain 'ere gave orders, of course he thought it right:
   "Before ye reach next station, my boys, you'll have to fight."

3. I saw the Indians comin', I heard 'em give their yell;
   My feelings at that moment no mortyal tongue can tell;
   I saw their glitterin' lances, their arrers roon' me fell;
   Ma heart it sank within me, ma courage almost fell.

4. I thought on my dear mother when [in] tears she said to me:
   "To you they are all strangers, my boy, you'll better stay."
   But I thought 'at she wis childish, or else she didn't know
   My mind wis bent on rangin', a-rovin' for to go.

5. We fought for full nine hours before the coorse wis o'er;
   The like of dead an' woundit I nivir saw before;
   Five hundred gallant Rangers that ivir saw the West
   Lay buriet by their comrades, sweet peace wid be their rest.

6. Perhaps ye hiv a brother, likewise a sister, too—
   Perhaps ye hiv a mother tae fret an' murn for you.
   If that be's yer sitooation, an' you incline to roam,
   Let me tell ye by experience—you'll better stay at home.

7. Now, come a' ye jolly fellas, that's round me here tonight,
   Whativir ye do for a livin', for my sake nivir fight,
   For the enemy they're quite careless, they shoot right in the crew,
   An' they're boun' tae hit somebody an' perhaps it may be you.
   (Music transcribed by Norman Cazden)

Mr. Henderson collected the ballad in Aberdeen in 1954, from Geordie Robertson, then aged eighty-two. Mr. Robertson indicated that he had learned the song some ten years earlier, in Aberdeen, from a Charles Robb, a farm servant from New Deer, in the heart of the Buchan District. Not only were Geordie's text and tune closely related to Lucy's fine version; they had come from an agricultural worker located only a few miles from where she had lived most of her life. Mr. Henderson had tried to locate Charles Robb at the time, but was unable to do so, and so could not help me in trying to trace the song any closer to its possible source in Scotland.

An examination of the two versions revealed certain obvious points. The two texts, as well as their tunes, were so closely related to each other that probably both had come originally from some single source. Aside from some minor verbal differences, the two variants differed only in the order of verses and in the obvious localization of the ballad story by its mention of Aberdeenshire in Lucy's text. Both texts contained the unusual last verse, which I have since found to be unrecorded in any of the numerous texts reported in America.[11]

The finding of these two variants of "The Texas Rangers" in Aberdeenshire raises several questions. How and when had the ballad come to Scotland? Why had Scottish singers chosen to include this foreign ballad in their repertories? Where had the unique last verse come from? When, why, and by whom had the ballad been localized and generalized, changing its subject from the *Texas* Ranger to the *Gallant* Ranger? I was unable to locate anyone in Scotland who could help me to answer these questions with any authority in fact. Time and death had erased all certainty. I can only speculate on the answers to these questions.

"The Texas Rangers" ballad probably came to Scotland as part of the song baggage of some Buchan native who had visited or emigrated to America during the second half of the nineteenth century, only to return to his native heath some years later. With him he brought "The Texas Rangers," perhaps part of a larger repertory of songs borrowed from his American friends.[12]

Why should a Scottish traditional singer care to add to his repertory a ballad about American Indians and rangers? Lucy Stewart answered my query with: "A gude tale tell't well, an' a bonnie tune . . . an' ye've a rare song. An' fa widna sing it? It disna matter if it's a Scotch song or no. . . . A' folk hiv a hairt an' a heid tae ken—an' tae sing—a gude yin." Fifty years earlier, on the occasion of his finding a version of "The Jam on Gerry's Rocks" in Buchan, Scotland's greatest collector,

Gavin Greig, wrote: "Although we may be unfamiliar with the circumstances and setting of the tragedy, we can all feel the appeal which the sad event makes to our universal nature—an appeal which is heightened by the straightforward and unpretentious character of the narration."[13] The text is different but the sense is identical.

One can only guess about the source of the last verse. I suspect it was an original verse in one of the earliest forms of the ballad, which disappeared in American tradition by the time the song was first published[14] and has never been recovered in America since that time. I feel fairly certain that it was not a Scottish addition to an existent text, for it is so much in keeping with the language and feeling of the rest of the ballad.

The localization and generalization of the ballad text certainly took place before Lucy learned the song from her mother. Old Betsy Stewart passed on both the song and its historical setting (relating it to the Indian Mutiny), suggesting that as early as 1911 the song was known in the form in which Lucy sang it to me. It would appear that some singer in the chain of its tradition had made the change with the express purpose of making it more meaningful to his potential listeners. Geordie Robertson's text appears to have descended in a straight line from the original Scottish singer, with Lucy's text representing a branch in the diverging tree of its tradition, perhaps dating from the turn of the century or earlier.

1. A. L. Lloyd, *Come All Ye Bold Miners: Ballads and Songs of the Coalfields* (London, 1952), pp. 104-5.

2. Gavin Greig, *Folk-Song of the North-East* (Peterhead, 1909-14), Article CXXXII.

3. Alfred Williams, *Folk-Songs of the Upper Thames* (London, 1923). The minstrel pieces referred to here appear on pp. 142-43, 178, 224-25, and 304.

4. See, for example, numerous British and European shanties of American origin in Stan Hugill, *Shanties from the Seven Seas* (London, 1961).

5. Joseph Ranson, *Songs of the Wexford Coast* (Enniscorthy, 1948).

6. For examples of the slightly ribald songs collected by some of England's leading collectors, but relegated by them to the obscurity of unpublished manuscripts or bowdlerized for publication, see James Reeves (ed.), *The Idiom of*

the People: English Traditional Verse from the Mss of Cecil Sharp (London, 1958), and *The Everlasting Circle: English Traditional Verse from the Mss of S. Baring-Gould, H.E.D. Hammond & George B. Gardiner* (London, 1960).

7. My field work in Scotland was made possible by a Fulbright research grant and a grant-in-aid from the Anthropology Department of the University of Pennsylvania.

8. For an indication of the effect which Jimmie Rodgers has had on *American* folksong, see John Greenway, "Jimmie Rodgers — A Folksong Catalyst," *Journal of American Folklore*, LXX (1957), 231-34.

9. For bibliographical data concerning "The Texas Rangers" ballad, see Malcolm G. Laws, Jr., *Native American Balladry: A Descriptive Study and a Bibliographical Syllabus* (Philadelphia, 1950), pp. 122-23 (Laws A8).

10. I owe thanks to Hamish Henderson for my first meeting with the Stewart family.

11. Dr. Austin Fife has checked his extensive files on western frontier and cowboy songs, and informs me that none of the texts published in America contain the last verse found in the two Scottish variants of "The Texas Rangers."

12. Other possibilities exist. Several of my older Aberdeenshire informants remembered seeing Buffalo Bill's Wild West show when it performed in northeastern Scotland in the first decade of this century. It is certainly possible that some cowboy in the troupe taught it to a Buchan native who in turn started it on its way into Scottish tradition.

13. Greig, *op. cit.*, Article CXXXII.

14. The earliest known publication of this ballad was in Francis D. Allan, *Allan's Lone Star Ballads: A Collection of Southern Songs, Made During Confederate Times* (Galveston, 1874), p. 38, under the title "The Texas Soldier Boy." Dr. Austin Fife reports a text published in the *Texas Stockman and Farmer*, XXIII (November 18, 1903), p. 5, with the assertion by the contributor that he had seen it in print in the late 1850's; Dr. Fife has been unable to substantiate the claim.

Folksong and Folksong Scholarship: Changing Approaches and Attitudes

Introductory Remarks

ROGER D. ABRAHAMS

THE FIRST FOUR PAPERS in this symposium were delivered as a panel, read at the seventy-third annual meeting of the American Folklore Society, held at Austin, Texas, on December 28, 1961. It was the conception of the program committee: Frances Gillmore, chairman, John Q. Anderson, and myself. Always trying to stir controversy, the committee attempted to assemble a series of speakers whose views were widely divergent. What we got was not only this, but a group of papers which were individually consistent and severely outspoken. Further, there was a kind of unanimity in the tone of the papers, in that each in its own way called for a method of attack on problems of folksong investigation which was empirical and analytic.

When the idea of the panel was first crystallized, we had some qualms lest the whole discussion might prove superfluous, as Dr. Wilgus' comprehensive study, *Anglo-American Folksong Scholarship Since 1898* (New Brunswick, N. J., 1959), had so recently covered what seemed to be the same ground. Our worries were soon allayed, for what we had failed to take into account was that those engaged in this discussion were concerned more with what studies should be in the future, and thus were arguing as special pleaders rather than in the objective manner of Wilgus' original discussion.

The titles of the areas to be covered were made by the committee, and only served as a point of departure for each participant. The choice of the labels of literary, anthropological, and comparative was natural, as three of the speakers, judging by their past performances, fit clearly into these categories. Wilgus presented a greater problem as far as such classification was concerned. Almost any term that we discussed in regard to his approach seemed to cast a bad light either on his work or on that of the others. If we used "eclectic," that might indicate to the viewer that his approach was merely a hodge-podge of others. On the other hand, "reasonable" seemed to imply that the others were unreasonable. Thus we hit on "rationalistic," forgetting for the moment that this had a special philosophic meaning. In the end, we were never really sorry that this term was used, as it not only provided the point of departure for his excellent paper, but also furnished much cause for humor and speculation as to what the proper name of his approach would be. He decided that he would not have been at all insulted by "eclectic," and that that was really the most apt term. Dr. Richard M. Dorson suggested in addition that Wilgus is among the ranks of the "hard-minded" and that therefore "pragmatic" would describe his approach just as well.

Basically the names of the other papers were equally schematic. The comparative approach derives directly, as Richmond points out, from a literary method, perhaps best described as the "source and analogue" or literary history approach. Similarly, the literary and aesthetic approach is really generic and historical.

The fifth paper was not a part of this symposium, but is included because it deals with matters not touched on in the others, folk music scholarship, and yet shares with the others an approach which is objective, descriptive, exploratory, and empirical. It stems from Mr. Foss's Master's thesis, written in 1961.

Finally, these papers are important as a group not only for individual and substantive matters, but because of the clarity with which each approach is illustrated, and more importantly because they all sound a call for folklore to enter a new era, an era of strict professionalism, involving a reconsideration of old methods of analysis and an examination of possible new ones. It is a call that all folklorists must heed.

I. On a Peak in Massachusetts:
The Literary and Aesthetic Approach

TRISTRAM P. COFFIN

EVEN WITH THE GUNS of John Greenway primed at my very flank, I wish to begin by stressing the fact that scholars still have something to say about the ballad as a literary form. Books like Albert Lord's *The Singer of Tales*,[1] articles like MacEdward Leach's "The Singer or the Song,"[2] and unpublished hypotheses like those Kenneth Goldstein holds concerning the literate Scottish folk are fresh winds indeed in the foggy world of poetic origins and the ballad. But beyond such pioneering studies are all the things that are yet to be said about the influence of the broadside versifiers on eighteenth- and nineteenth-century prosody—that material which Albert Friedman has surveyed in *The Ballad Revival*,[3] which Vivian de Sola Pinto and Allan E. Rodway have discussed so brilliantly in the introduction to *The Common Muse*,[4] and on which G. Malcolm Laws is about to publish. Nor is there yet a definitive study of Negro spirituals, sentimental song, sea shanties, or musical hall influences. And, as you will soon be hearing from W. E. Richmond and D. K. Wilgus, comparative balladry, classification, and commercial development of folksong themes are virgin tracts. I can think of a dozen books on the ballad as a literary and aesthetic form that desperately seek for their author.

However, as America's ballad scholars look forward at unmapped areas, it might be a mistake to assume that the territory which Gummere, Gerould, and Pound fought over has been thoroughly or even competently mapped. It hasn't. And as one travels these regions class after class, study after study, sometimes he is surprised to find himself on what appears to be "a peak in Darien." Now, I would like to describe for you a vista concerning the ballad and its literary past that I came upon in Wilbraham, Massachusetts, a couple of years ago.

At the end of his serial on "Springfield Mountain" in the *Bulletin of the Folk Song Society of the Northeast*,[5] Phillips Barry presents the hypothesis that the original Myrick version of the ballad was not written before "the second quarter of the last century" or nearly sixty-five years after the event. G. Malcolm Laws, Jr.,[6] among other scholars, has found this statement hard to believe—and, actually, in light of the text of the Myrick "Springfield Mountain" itself, Barry's thesis is preposterous. The Myrick texts of "Springfield Mountain" are all clearly derived from a narrative obituary poem, undoubtedly written about 1761, when the unfortunate youth went out to mow. They include all the clichés and jargon common to the narrative obituary medium, and it would be nonsensical to think that a lapse of two or three generations, rather than the usual two or three days, occurred between the event and the composition of the original poem. If there is doubt in anyone's mind that the Myrick "Springfield Mountain" is a funeral poem, the comparison below should dispel it. The first text is Barry's from a Wilbraham, Massachusetts, manuscript; the second is a narrative obituary composition typical of many printed in American newspapers of the last two hundred years.

Lines written on the Death of Timothy Merrick who was bit by a Rattlesnake in the year 1761.

On Springfield Mountain there did dwell
a likely youth 'twas known full well
Left't Merrick's only Son
A likely youth near twenty one

One Friday Morning he did go
down to the Meadow for to mow
Hee mowed around and he did feel
a poisoning Serpent at his heel

When he received this deadly wound
he dropped his Scythe upon the ground
and straight for Home was his intent
calling aloud Still as he went

't was all around his voice was heard
but unto him no friend appeared
they thought he did Some workman call
but Timothy alone must fall

At length his careful Father went
to Seek his Son in discontent
and there his only Son he found
Dead as a Stone lay on the ground

't was the Seventh of August year 61
This fatal accident was done
may this a warning be to all
to be prepared when God shall call

Who knows but that his blessed feet
are treading the Celestial Street
the brightest Angels bowing round
Jehovah and his golden crown[7]

In loving remembrance of Russell Sidney Biddle who was taken from our midst on Saturday night, Sept. 24, by a special C. D. & M. car going south at eleven o'clock. . . .

Born March 2, 1890, died September 24, 1910.

Darling Russell, he has left us,
   Left us, yes, forevermore:
But we hope to meet our loved one
   On that bright and happy shore.

Darling Russell, how we miss you,
   How we miss your smiling face,
We miss your tender smile,
   We miss you every place.

All is dark within our dwelling,
   Lonely are our hearts today,
For the one we loved so dearly
   Has forever passed away.

We've laid his form beneath the sod
  In a sacred spot we love,
His spirit's gone to be with God
  In that bright home above.

The thought of parting gives us pain,
  Ere when we hope to meet again,
But when we think that death is nigh,
  'Tis hard to say the last good-bye.

Such was the fate of one we knew
  Of one we loved and youthful, too,
Of one whose race so soon was run—
  The Widow Biddle's middle son.

He left his home that eve before,
  And little thought he'd come no more,
Till he a corpse should be brought back,
  All mangled by the street car track.

That night he went to Delaware
  And everything to him seemed fair,
His darling sweetheart by his side
  How dear he loved her, she was to be his bride.

Then they returned, 'twas getting late,
  He saw her home, his fair young mate,
He said good-night, and kissed her dear,
  Little dreaming of what a tragedy near.

The night was dark and the hour was late,
  He sat down on the track to wait.
We do not know the exact time
  The car came rushing down the line.

He had been working very hard that day,
  With his brothers bailing hay,
He must have been very tired and weak,
  For very soon he fell asleep.

The car came rushing down the line,
  The motorman saw him, but not in time,
Then quick as a lightning flash, not long,
  Which hurled him into the great beyond.

In stranger's hands his limbs replaced,
  They washed the blood from his pale, dead face,
They smoothed a curl from his fair young brow,
  No mother there to do that now.

On Saturday night they brought him home,
　On Monday bore him to the tomb;
His mangled body laid away
　To sweetly rest until the judgment day.

Now rest, brave boy, your work is done,
　Your race upon this earth is run,
Although your young life was not long,
　We hope to meet you in the great beyond.

Even though written many years apart, these texts are clearly
from the same literary genre, have the same outlook, use the
same language patterns and meter. That the Barry version of
"Springfield Mountain" is somewhat abbreviated and lacks the
sentimental prologue probably indicates that the manuscript,
which is dated "Wilbraham April 30th 1849," was transcribed
after the poem had been in circulation, surely as a song, for
some time. Poems of this sort were commonly sung to the music
of "Old Hundred" at American funerals[9]—and the Myrick
"Springfield Mountain" fits "Old Hundred" perfectly.

It might be worthwhile to prove Barry's dating of the ballad
incorrect and leave things at that. However, Barry's disregard
of narrative obituary tradition is typical of ballad scholars in
general. It becomes of paramount importance, therefore, to
look well beyond "Springfield Mountain" at the whole matter
of the relationship of the obituary tradition to balladry.

The tradition of the funeral elegy has, of course, been long
established in English-speaking countries, both as a purely
laudatory and as a narrative poetic form. Heaven alone knows
where the custom began. Chinese lyrics, material in the Rig
Veda, in Homer, in the Bible, all indicate that the funeral
elegy, whether narrative or not, goes back as far as we can trace
our civilization. There is some evidence that the custom of com-
posing formal elegiac material may have come to Britain with
the Romans. This much is certain, that by the sixteenth century
and through the eighteenth century it was common enough to
recite or sing elegies at funerals, that elegies were composed

specifically for funeral rites, and that these pieces were affixed to the hearse or thrown into the grave.[10] Both in the Colonies and in Britain, obituary poems were often printed on broadsheets and distributed among the mourners. In more recent times, favorite hymns have replaced such elegies at funerals; but poetic elegiac composition is by no means unknown to the twentieth-century world, and it is still a simple matter to find memorial verse, some of it narrative, in local newspapers.

Perhaps the most significant facet of this tradition is the fact that funeral verse was popular with the broadside printers, who evidently found as steady a business in death as does the mortician. A great many of the broadside elegies stress the same sort of lurid and dramatic details that commercially successful sheets might include and seem to be composed with an eye to the market as well as to the mourner.

Everyone knows that the deaths of criminals, the deaths of prominent persons, and bloody crimes have inspired thousands of broadsheets. It is also general knowledge that some of these, such as the ones on "George of Oxford" or on "The Oxford Girl," have fused with, affected, and changed many of our older ballads. It seems to me equally clear that the tradition of narrative obituary composition also influenced traditional songs and fed out to the folk many verses that were to become traditional favorites. It is my suspicion, although I find it hard to support in a scholarly fashion, that a high percentage of our British ballad texts owe their origin to narrative obituary verse, and that among our native American ballads this tradition is the source of more texts than any other.

All love crime, execution, and disaster ballads follow narrative obituary patterns and are close to being, if indeed they are not, funeral elegies. As one leafs through the Child collection[11] or scans the bibliographical surveys of Malcolm Laws,[12] he is amazed to see how many of the songs could have originated as narrative obituary poetry of one sort or another. We know, naturally, that many of these songs are the products of broadside writers and newspaper versifiers; however, these very broadside writers and newspaper poets are the persons who took over the task of writing obituary poetry in the cities. "Springfield Mountain" is in no way unique. Everywhere there are songs just like it.[13] Such songs differ from the ones that have survived longer in oral tradition in style, in the presence of greater amounts of sentimentality and moralism, and in length— but not in basic nature. There can be little doubt that ballads such as "The Jam at Gerry's Rocks," "Young Charlotte," "John Hardy," "Casey Jones," "Jesse James," and "Pearl Bryan" originated as offshoots of the habit broadside printers and local poets had of writing up newsworthy events at the time of a funeral. *My point is not only that the tradition of narrative obituary verse has fed ballads to the folk for generations, but also that normal ballad composition is but a "broadening" of the tradition of writing narrative obituary poetry about routine lives and people.*

Perhaps it is too much to suggest that the characteristic forms of the Western European ballad developed as the forces of oral tradition worked on narrative obituary poetry—although I admit the idea fascinates me; but it is not too much to suggest that once the British form for the ballad was established it drew largely on the reservoir of narrative obituary verse for its inspiration and subject matter. Tragedy is the stock-in-trade of the balladeer, and surely singers were not ignoring the songs and verse that were coming to them death after death. Folk communities nearly always have a local poet or singer whose job it is to preserve the traditions of the group. If an obituary poem captured something typical enough or spectacular enough so that this singer or his listeners cared to preserve it, it could be set to dozens of melodies. "Old Hundred" was not the only tune available. The steps from this sort of thing to the writing of obituary poems about more scandalous or prominent persons and events, to writing or distributing obituary poems through broadside outlets, to the development of the entire present

Anglo-American ballad tradition are intriguingly direct and simple.

One becomes convinced that it would not be a careless hypothesis to suggest that the epic lai and romantic lai tradition known to the wandering poets of the Middle Ages bred with the tradition of narrative obituary verse to give birth to the ballads of the Western European peoples. The chart below is perhaps too simple, but it may well be closer to the truth than any hypothesis available in print to date.

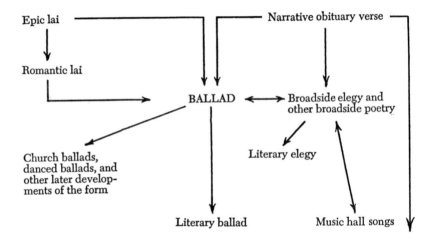

Such a chart demands little explanation. It is obvious that narrative obituary poetry survives in our world in three forms: in elegiac funeral verse, in narrative folksongs, and in the elegiac efforts of literary figures. It is equally obvious that there has been a steady interchange between broadside poetry, music hall compositions, and folk ballads. It may be disputable that the romance and epic lai influenced the ballads as directly as I have indicated, and it may be disputable that the church ballads and danced ballads are chronological developments of the ballad form. For that matter, there is room for much discussion concerning the effect of narrative obituary traditions on the varying ballad types found across Europe. These are matters on which there has been and is to be a mass of bickering and inconclusive scholarship. Only a tremendous amount of hard work and a bit of revelation can clear them up. Here, I have merely suggested the patterns that I consider the most likely. I am confident that the main concept, that the epic-romantic lai and the narrative obituary poem bred to form the ballad, holds up.

But no matter how one feels about my hypothesis, he must be insensitive if he feels no excitement in it. The documentation, the proof of the idea, demands all sorts of studies on the ballad and the romance, all sorts of investigations of the basic similarities of European narrative song types, more histories like John W. Draper's *The Funeral Elegy and the Rise of English Romanticism* which would chronicle the village elegy, its nature, distribution, and relationship to folklore. That books like these wait to be written, that peaks with vistas such as the one from Springfield Mountain still rise in the land of Gummere, Gerould, and Pound is testimony enough that the "literary-aesthetes" have much to rationalize their existence, much to keep them in the stacks.

II. Folksong as an Anthropological Province: The Anthropological Approach

JOHN GREENWAY

WHEN BIG BILL BROONZY was asked, "What are the blues good for?" it was his custom to say that they were like a knife. You could keep it on a shelf and look at it, you could cut bread with it, you could clean your fingernails with it, you could shave with it, you could pare your toenails with it, you could even cut a man's throat with it. So anthropology. The knickknackers are the most numerous practitioners in our discipline, men who have devoted their lives to the study of such things as the typology of footgear among the Hodmadods of Monomatapa, who can assemble statistical analyses of the preference of

savages for saddle oxfords or sneakers, but who have no further
interest in podal exegesis. Cut-and-slash men are fewer; the
names of Hermann Gauch and Hans Gunther stand out,
although there are others more subtly efficient in this specialty.
Every use and user of anthropology is accommodated in our
expanding universe. As the *Fellow Newsletter* acknowledged in
September, 1960, "Our profession is becoming more and more
like a giant spiral nebula, and those of us on one edge seem to
have little in common with our colleagues on the opposite side,
several light years away." There is indeed room for all in the
discipline, but some are less well domiciled than others. The
study of folksong is 'way out, in the Plutonian cold, breaking
away from the gravitational pull of English literature, but not
yet established in an anthropological orbit. There are no solar
systems revolving around a Malinowski or Radcliffe-Brown
for it to settle into, and, with Boas gone, primitive literature too
is flying away from our cosmos. Current anthropology texts give
ten times as much space to potsherd analysis as they do to
literature, though it may be suspected that literature is at least
as important among some of the earth's peoples as broken
pottery. No anthropological author would be able to hold his
head up if he confused a Lino Gray sherd with a La Plata
Black-on-White, yet a distinguished fellow of the American
Anthropological Association in his recent textbook repeats
Schoolcraft's century-old error of calling Hiawatha an Indian
culture hero; another speaks of poetry as separate from song as
a primitive universal. The few general works that even briefly
consider literature apart from myth dispose of it contemptu-
ously as "folklore."

We must first of all clarify this derisive adjective "folk." It
is no more logical to speak of literature among preliterate
peoples as "folklore" than it is to speak of their culinary ware
as "folk pottery." If the word "folk" is to have any semantic
significance at all, it should be restricted to the identification
of a homogeneous unsophisticated group living in but isolated

from a surrounding sophisticated society by such factors as topography, geography, religion, race, economics, and dialect. As it should not be applied to primitive peoples, so also should it not be loosely expanded into a generic term for the essence of a nationality. There is no "American folk," but a variety of American folks, few of whom share anything but unsophistication and isolation. The Koryak enclave in Freehold, New Jersey, has little more in common with the Cornish miners of Colorado than membership in the human race.

Furthermore, the "folk processes" which books have been describing for the last century as fundamental characteristics of the English ballad are a misconception. What happens to ballads and lyric traditional song as they move among the folk is precisely the same thing that happens to everything else in our culture, pottery as well as poetry, that is subject to the molding effects of diffusion, except that the folk manifestation of a literary form is not subject to the calcifying force of print. The difference is not qualitative—as Utley maintained in a recent article, confusing the results of a process with its basis —but quantitative. Not only diffusion, but all the other processes of culture change elicited by anthropological investigation are detectable in poetry and pottery. What Flinders Petrie saw happening to Egyptian vases we can see happening to coffee cups.

Every part of a culture is a microcosm of the whole; whatever principles are valid for any segment of a culture are valid for all parts, for the characteristic *Gestalt* of a culture pervades its every aspect. Hewes, in analyzing what Uranga suggested was the dominant character trait of the Mexican people—a sense of insufficiency—was able to detect it in such widely diverse Iberoamerican phenomena as the *Jorgenegretismo* of Mexican movies; the national homicide rate; the social propensity for "amification"; superdiminutives in speech; micromania in art; the "morbid eagerness" of medical students; necrolatry in confectionary skulls on the Day of the Dead, reporting of gruesome traffic accidents, and veneration of sanguinary *santos*—and obviously the "taurine martyrdom" of the *corrida*.

No element is independent of its culture. Chess is as good an epitome of the civilization in which it is played as its players' marriage customs—even better, since it comprises material as well as immaterial factors. There is no reason for excluding chess from the domain of anthropology except the psychological set of seeing it merely as a game or at most an art.

Similarly a psychological set has kept the study of folksong out of its proper place in anthropology. Since Bishop Percy three centuries ago saved that famous old manuscript from its destiny as a maid's supply of spills and picked out of it some songs that—with judicious emendation—pleased his fancy, folksong has been in the hands of the aesthetes. Some seven hundred ballad collections, many of them analytical, have been published in English during the last fifty years; scarcely one detects any significance other than artistic in its material. All of them are maddeningly repetitious, for the number of worthwhile pieces among the ballads is discouragingly small; "Sir Patrick Spens" is as indispensable to the ballad connoisseur as a spine to a chiropractor. The overwhelming bulk of the folk's efforts in this genre is execrable, as anyone who knows the folk might expect. The anthropologist studies people and their works for what light they throw on the processes of culture; happily he has not the obligation to make moral and artistic evaluations of them. But the literary critic is driven by his romantic bias to believe that men not otherwise engaged in tearing around the countryside in white sheets taken with them from their daughters' beds and planting burning crosses on integrationists' lawns, swoon into sublime trances in which they create out of the pristine beauty of their souls hauntingly poetic songs full of "lily white hands" and "red roan steeds" while the tears blind their bloodshot ee.

The exclusively literary orientation is not only a fatuous

point of approach to an important body of material; it is wasteful. Tens of thousands of songs, narrative and lyrical, have been extirpated by the wilful neglect or suppression of literary collectors who were not able to edit them into propriety. Child and his followers knew the broadside ballad "The Unfortunate Rake" well enough, but in an age when the world's leading playwright thought venereal disease could be communicated by a meerschaum pipe, nicer people than Ibsen had no wish to contaminate themselves with a song on the subject. The ballad had to salivate itself of its depraved condition before it could enter respectable collections. The "Rake," in spite of its affliction, was hardier than most of its fellows, and so lives on—no thanks to the Great Panjandrum and his smaller suc- cedent panjandra. Of course other artistic fellows were going about England at the same time smashing old churches into examples of good Victorian art, but architectural sanity carried them off the scene long before our time.

It is especially unfortunate that the evaluative approach still dominates the study of folksong; for of all the folk arts and crafts, song is the most valuable for anthropological analysis, since it is the most nearly function-free trait in general possession of this otherwise inarticulate society. A chair is function-bound to the purpose of holding the human body in a sitting position; pottery is function-bound to the purpose of holding liquids. You can proliferate legs on the former and handles on the latter, and paint both with designs drawn from all of nature, but their utility limits their developmental possi- bilities. Yet both chair and pot and thousands of other artifacts are assiduously studied by anthropologists to trace cultural evolution, while song is left to the aesthetes—song, which has no real function except to communicate the immaterial culture of its singers: attitudes, emotions, prejudices, biases, ideals, vices, virtues, and, occasionally, art.

It is true, and we are grateful for it, that the aesthetes in expropriating the literature of the illiterate have left us the literature of the preliterate, but they have so well implanted in our minds their own literary prejudices that few anthropologists feel confident of dealing with the genre even among primitives. Richard Chase, corrupted by an impious age which produces works like *The Bible Designed to be Read as Living Literature,* hammered home with italics the dictum that *myth is literature and therefore a matter of aesthetic experience and the imagination* (1949:vi), although every other writer for 2,500 years thought myth had something to do with religion. And Paul Radin obediently responded, finding seven times seven kinds of ambiguity in the Winnebago Trickster myth, positing an aboriginal T. S. Eliot among the Winnebago in the distant dreamtime who found "ordinary words and terms ... indeed completely inadequate. Only symbols, only metaphors, can convey the meaning properly" (1956:138). "What were the remote ancestors of the Winnebago trying to convey to us . . . ?" (1948:9) This, from the Winnebago, of whom Marryat said in his *Diary in America* nearly a century and a quarter ago, they "are considered the dirtiest race of Indians, and with the worst qualities; they were formerly designated by the French *puans,* a term sufficiently explanatory"! If we may dare to invoke a poet's opinion, it is surely true, as Robert Frost once told an amateur prober of ambiguities, "a reader doesn't interpret the poem; the poem interprets the reader."

With the precedent set by Radin and other mystics it is little wonder that, as Thompson lamented ten years ago, "we have been hearing reports of a considerable withdrawal of American anthropologists from the American Folklore Society" (1955:587). This paper is a plea for their return. There is nothing to fear. If anyone wants to interpret "Stopping by Woods on a Snowy Evening" as a poem about a man stopping by woods on a snowy evening, Frost has assured us, "Well, then, that's what I meant by it."

An inescapable syllogism negates the litterateur's exclusive claim to this material. All art is a part of culture; literature is art; therefore literature is a part of culture. And it should be studied by the universal laws of culture. As an artifact of the mind, folksong is an exciting and profitable area of study. All the anthropological processes are there, working free, unhampered by the restrictions of function—diffusion, polygenetic invention, environmental determinism, acculturation, integration, cultural inertia, culture lag, transculturation, metataxis. Goldstein's phonographic study of the ballad mentioned earlier, "The Unfortunate Rake," illustrates all of these processes. Appearing first at the end of the eighteenth century in Ireland, this song about a young man dying of a social disease spread by oral transmission to England, where it lodged for a while as "St. James' Hospital" (a strange place for the venereal Rake to be, for St. James' Hospital was a convent of "14 sisters, maidens, that were leperous, living chastely and honestly in divine service"). Coming to America with other social refugees, it entered three folk societies and was molded by their culture. In the southern Appalachians and other areas where the double standard obtained, it changed sex and turned into a lament for a girl gone to the bad, as in the Virginian "One Morning in May." Among the southern Negroes it reverted to its original reprobation as "St. James' Infirmary." Working the western trails out to the cowboys, it acquired the typical sentimentality of this lonely profession as "The Streets of Laredo." In still another line of development the "Bad Girl's Lament" variant regained unmistakable Irish elements, possibly by transculturation, and turned up in the most unlikely place of all for the Rake in view of the fatal affliction, the Virgin Islands. Meanwhile Australia was settled by lower-class English and Irish emigrants who also knew the "Rake." But in Australia, to borrow a term from the social anthropologists, the Rake's relatives are affinal—the product of his exogamous connection with another proletarian eighteenth-century song, "The Tarpaulin Jacket"—with the typical form being "The Dying Stockman." "The Dying Stockman," incidentally, demonstrates environmental determination, since it equates polygenetically with similar American interment songs on the cattle range; in fact, there is scarcely a frontier theme in American folksong that does not have its parallel in Australia—one could not find a better example of environmental determinism in all ethnology. The Rake at the end of his long career even takes on social protest employment as "The Ballad of Sherman Wu" and economic protest as "The Ballad of Bloody Thursday," finishing metatactically in playful parodies like U.C.L.A.'s "The Professor's Lament."

Literary folklorists recognized the affinity of "The Streets of Laredo" and "St. James' Infirmary," but they did so by applying anthropological observations, just as literature analysts did earlier in recognizing such poetic motifs as the *ubi sunt, timor mortis,* and *carpe diem* categories. Recognition is only the beginning of the job; we need to know precisely why "The Maid Freed from the Gallows" changed so drastically among the Negro folk in the version "The Gallis Pole," and why prisoners at the Angola State Farm sing "Old Rattler" so differently from the North Carolina hillbillies. Alan Lomax has offered an intriguing psychological explanation for differing vocal styles between the white and Negro American folk (1959), but this is only part of an answer for part of the folksong complex for part of the folk. Very much more needs to be done, and it cannot be done so long as we see folksong only as literary art. Beauty is in the ear as well as the eye of the beholder; and to our ears very little of what the folk and preliterate peoples enjoy is attractive. We cannot afford to limit our examination of folk and primitive lore to what we consider good; too much would be lost.

The anthropologist who will take up the work of analyzing folksong for its value as a key to the culture that produced it can expect to grub among the refuse like an archeologist in a midden heap, but the true piece of literature that he will occasionally find will be all the more valuable for the plainness of its setting. Bill Harney listened to some of the most unpoetic talk on earth in his lifetime among the aborigines of northern Australia, many of whom have lost their own language without acquiring that of the whites; but even in this most improbable place he heard a blackfellow express in broken English a lyric on agnosticism that could enter any literature's golden treasury:

> The god-men say when die that Jesus came
> To save our sins and let us know
> The right from wrong and in His name
> To die and into heaven go—
> > Might be, might be, I don't know.
>
> The god-men say when die go sky
> Through Pearly Gates where river flow.
> The god-men say when die we fly,
> Just like eaglehawk and crow—
> > Might be, might be; I don't know.

"The God-Men" is a beautiful thing, but it is one of life's little bonuses; we cannot afford to wait for them.

III. The Comparative Approach: Its Aims, Techniques, and Limitations

W. EDSON RICHMOND

SOME THIRTY YEARS AGO, in a volume which should have served as a model for subsequent ballad studies, Professor Archer Taylor noted that "the comparative study of the English and Scottish popular ballad, although greatly facilitated by the standard collection of Francis James Child, lingers in the doldrums."[1] Indeed, when Professor Taylor wrote in 1931 it was not only comparative ballad study that lingered in the doldrums, for ballad study in general was becalmed. Some scholars spread their sails before the winds of idle speculation about ultimate origins, only to be taken aback by a gale of fact; others took to the boats of additional texts but nearly foundered. Moreover, a sudden tempest scattered the fleet of

scholarship in the next thirty years, and almost every scholar
sailed off in a different direction from the others and searched
for a different port. Thus Professor Taylor's continuing remarks
were lost sight of:

> Obviously we must know the history and relations of the existing
> texts before we can profitably indulge in speculations about ultimate
> origins. . . . It is wiser to stay nearer at home and determine, as well
> as may be, the life history of a single ballad; to seek the information
> to be derived from a study of the texts themselves, instead of visiting
> Malaysia. When we have fuller knowledge of the history of at least
> a score of important ballads, when we know how a ballad behaves on
> the lips of the folk, then we shall have a sufficient stock of information
> for the ethnologist to take journeys afield.[2]

Despite the wisdom of these words, however, and despite
the very fine example set by Professor Taylor's *"Edward"* and
"Sven i Rosengaard," which is, in effect, the proof of the pud-
ding, the past thirty years have shown little evidence that ballad
scholars have learned much about ballads. Their eyes have been
turned outward rather than inward, and each has pursued his
individual course nearly blind to, and frequently contemptuous
of, the work of his colleagues. And the comparative method,
an established discipline amidst chaos, has been virtually
ignored. The score of studies for which Professor Taylor called
has not appeared; indeed, in the English language less than a
dozen important studies have been published, and this number
is not significantly increased when other languages and language areas are taken into account.[3]

Yet the techniques, and probably the aims, of the comparative method in ballad scholarship have been refined from the
techniques and aims of literary scholarship. Ideally, though the
ideal appears to be unattainable, the comparative method seeks
to explain how the variant textual forms of a given ballad came
into being and proceeds from the basic assumption that there
was once an ur-text, a basic form, whence all known texts have
descended. It does not, however, concern itself with origins

except incidentally, for to the comparativist it matters little whether *das Volk* or a highly sophisticated individual *dichtet.* Nor is the method concerned with the function which a ballad plays, or has played, in a community. To the comparativist it is the song rather than the singer that has importance; he is a student of literature, not of society.

As a student of literature, the comparativist is, of course, interested in the aesthetic value of the material which he studies, but in his position as a comparativist he is not concerned primarily with aesthetics. Nor is this retreat from aesthetics a result of his realization that all values are relative, that what is appreciated by one segment of society is scorned by another. It results, rather, from the fact that value judgments have no more place in his scheme of things than do sociological judgments. He is concerned with textual relationships and can neither fairly nor safely eliminate any text, whether aesthetically good or bad, from consideration.

As a student of folksong, the product of people, the comparativist is, of course, interested in the function which this product performs in any given society, but here again this is not his primary concern. The fact that a song may be sung as a protest, as a way of spreading news, or simply as entertainment has little or no relevance to his main problem of establishing the history of the textual variations in a song and showing textual relationships. Thus he does not deny that the aesthetics and the functions of ballads are worthy of study, that to study both aesthetics and function can contribute to our knowledge of the ballad and ballad singers; but for him neither aesthetics nor function has any special significance. He is interested in texts as texts, as specimens in the historical development of a song.

The comparativist, in other words, is a student of the history of individual ballads. Given an indefinite number of texts of a particular narrative folksong, he attempts (1) to establish lines of development, (2) to show how each text is related to every other text, and (3) to suggest what the major and early form or forms of any particular ballad must have been. In doing so, he sometimes finds it possible (1) to indicate relationships between two or more distinct songs, (2) to suggest certain probable relationships between various bodies of song, and (3) to comment on the relationships between ballads and history. As a further by-product, it is sometimes possible for him to draw from his investigations at least tentative conclusions about the manner and nature of the dissemination of oral literature.

These are not modest aims and only infrequently can they be perfectly achieved, but they are, at least, limited and definite aims. They imply that oral literature is worth studying for its own sake, as much so as is sophisticated literature, and they imply also that, being products of human reason, ballads have developed along certain well-defined lines subject to analysis and description.

Indeed, the aims of the comparative ballad scholar are by no means new or original; as was pointed out earlier, they are developed from and closely allied to the aims of the literary historian who deals with periods in which there is considerable textual variation. And just as the aims of the comparative ballad scholar have been developed from the aims of the literary historian, the techniques of the comparativist have been developed from those of the literary historian, though with considerable modification.

Like the historian of literature, the comparative ballad scholar relies heavily upon the basic principles of textual collation. But the nature of oral transmission and dissemination is such that he has had to modify the techniques of the literary scholar in accordance with the peculiarities of verbal tradition. The general pattern for the necessary modifications was introduced by Julius Krohn when, as long ago as 1897, he published his *Suomalaisen Kirjallisuuden Historia*.[4] In this book the foundations were laid for what came to be known as the historic-geographic or the Finnish method of folklore research. It is perhaps significant that although the historic-geographic technique was most clearly described by Kaarle Krohn,[5] the son of the creator of the technique and himself a student of the folktale whose use of German rather than Finnish helped to bring the technique to the eyes of the rest of the world, the historic-geographic method was originally intended to show the relationship between the *Kalevala* and its oral sources. In other words, despite the use to which the historic-geographic method has been put by students of the folktale, it was originally developed as a tool for the student of folksong. Three-quarters of a century of folksong scholarship have, of course, wrought some modifications in the technique, but its basic principles remain unchanged and are still the most reliable tool for the comparativist.

The historic-geographic method as it applies to ballads can be simply described, even though in any given instance its application may be quite complex. It consists of four principal steps: (1) all possible texts of a ballad are collected; (2) the collected texts are grouped according to the geographic area whence they came and arranged chronologically within each area; (3) the individual texts are analyzed and broken down into the motifs which they include; and (4) by a comparison of the grouped and analyzed texts, by a collation if you will, the life history of a ballad, and thus the probable relationship of each text to every other, is reconstructed.

But the application of this general technique to a particular ballad presents many problems. No catalogue or index of ballads devoted to more than fugitive titles or to more than materials collected in a well-defined linguistic area is easily available.[6] As a result, the collection of all known texts of a given song is always difficult, perhaps impossible. This situation is offset, however, by the fact that the material collected eventually reaches a stage of diminishing returns, a stage where additional texts contribute little to the accumulated information. How soon this stage is reached depends upon the popularity of the ballad being studied.

The problems do not end, however, even when enough texts are collected to establish the pattern of a ballad beyond a reasonable doubt. Geographic groupings occasion little difficulty, for they are closely allied to language; but the dating of texts is another matter. Obviously, the text of a ballad is at least as old as the date of its publication, as the manuscript in which it is inscribed, or as the date of its collection from oral tradition. But one can never be certain of how much older it is than its immediate source except insofar as he receives clues from collateral and internal information. The comparative process itself, however, is of considerable assistance in fixing an approximate date for any given text, especially when taken in conjunction with known dates relating to the ballad.

With the third step in the process, another sort of problem arises. Neither a type- nor a motif-index of ballads has yet been compiled. As a result, the motif analysis of ballads is still largely a subjective matter dependent for the most part upon the approach taken by the individual scholar. Unlike the folktale in which one episode flows easily into the next, ballads are by definition stanzaic in their structure and tend to be episodic in the development of narrative details. There is thus a temptation to see motifs in terms of stanzas rather than in terms of narrative elements. As a consequence, ballads are frequently broken into minute details rather than into the larger motifs themselves, and motif variables are considered to be independent motifs. This leads to unnecessary confusion. If, however, a ballad is broken into motifs in the same way in which a folktale can be, a pattern, or series of patterns, begins to emerge; and this, in turn, leads to the possible reconstruction of the life history of the ballad.

Motif analysis is complicated, however, by an additional ballad characteristic: the commonplace stanza. Whether or not the Parry-Lord hypothesis of formulaic composition is applicable to ballads as we usually think of them, there can be no reasonable doubt that when ballad singing was a living art (instead of a survival), ballad singers carried in mental stock a number of stanzas useful to describe or accentuate ordinary events, to extend a song to please an enthusiastic audience, and even to round off an unsatisfactory narrative. Until a relatively complete catalogue of commonplaces is compiled, precise distinctions between motifs which belong to a particular ballad and motifs which belong to the stock of commonplaces will be difficult to establish. The distinction between the two types of motifs is important, since commonplaces which are fairly constant in a particular ballad appear to attract to that ballad motifs and stanzas from other ballads in which the same commonplace also frequently appears.

Nevertheless, in spite of the problems created by the difficulty of precisely dating materials and by the lack of such conveniences as ballad concordances, catalogues, and type- and motif-indexes, the historic-geographic method remains the comparativist's most useful and reliable tool. Moreover, the ballad scholar enjoys one advantage not given to the student of the folktale: the poetic nature of the ballad acts as a conservative force; thus the demands of rhyme, meter, and probably even music tend to restrain variation in phrase, in the way a thing is said, and the relationship between ballad texts is often more easily seen because of this than is the relationship between texts of a folktale.

Whether or not the original text of a ballad can ever be precisely reconstructed by the historic-geographic method is a moot point. Certainly any text so reconstructed should be accepted only with reservations and subject to modifications whenever additional texts are discovered. On the other hand, it is usually possible to reconstruct reasonably accurate local archetypes which, if based upon a sufficient number of texts, are seldom subject to any considerable modification; and, on the basis of a comparison of such archetypes, a reasonable description of an ur-text can be developed in terms of the motifs which it once included. Thus, though his ideal of textual reconstruction may eternally evade the efforts of the comparativist, a judicious gathering, grouping, and comparison of texts makes it possible for him to draw sensible conclusions about the life history of a ballad.

As has been noted before, the work of reconstructing the life history of a ballad would be much simpler were a concordance of ballads based upon subject matter in the manner of Ernst von der Recke's little-known concordance of Scandinavian ballads[7] made generally available and were existing type- and motif-indexes expanded to include ballad materials generally.[8] But even before this sort of work is begun, comparativists—and other ballad scholars—would facilitate communication if they could and would agree upon some specific terminology.

A plea for some kind of uniformity in terminology was made as early as 1928 by Reed Smith, who, attributing his definition to Child as understood by George Lyman Kittredge, says that "version means 'a copy with distinguishing characteristics in plot, style, age, atmosphere, or the like,' and a single version is often represented by several variants."[9] But the terms continued to be used so loosely during the next two decades that it was necessary for Tristram P. Coffin to restate essentially the same position as that held by Reed Smith, though in slightly different terms, in *The British Traditional Ballad in North America*. However, Professor Coffin equated the phrase "story variation" with *version* and "textual variation" with *variant*.[10]

This, however, did not settle the matter, and, in 1959, after summarizing the information given above, D. K. Wilgus suggested that "Coffin's use of the term *story types* to indicate what might be called *versions* seems to stem not only from the confused usage, but from the fact that one of his story types might include several of Child's versions."[11]

Whether or not a strong distinction made between the terms

version and *variant* "has the defect of making the process of tradition rather too simple"[12] is a moot point. No one today argues that folksingers themselves are aware of or care about such distinctions or that terminology such as this describes a traditional process. But when one is working with texts (and perhaps with music as well), one frequently finds that they fall into related groups and that if one is concerned with geographical distribution and textual evolution it is necessary to distinguish between the major and the minor relationships. For the precise indication of such distinctions a uniform system of terminology is of great value.

Ideally, as has been suggested earlier, a particular ballad can be equated with a folktale type, that is, a narrative composed of a series of motifs in such a way that it can be recognized as itself no matter where it is found. To the extent that the concept of a folktale type implies a kind of Platonic form, so also does this concept of a ballad—but no more so. With this as a point of departure, it is then possible to say that a version tells essentially the same story as the ideal type or ballad but varies it in such a way (for example, by the addition or omission of particular motifs) that the narrative itself takes a slightly different turn even though its basic form is plainly recognizable. A variant, on the other hand, consists of minor modifications (verbal shifts, elimination of nonessential stanzas, addition of commonplace materials, and the like) which do not affect the narrative line. A hypothetical ballad might be diagrammed thus:

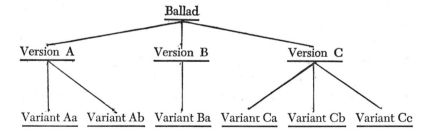

Except in those cases where ballads can be shown to have descended from known, specific poems or songs, it is impossible to say that a particular song is a ballad in this sense rather than a version or even a variant of a ballad. Moreover, the process of oral tradition is so complex that it may produce versions of versions, versions of variants, and variants of variants. Despite such complexity, however, when two or more texts of a particular song are found, textual comparison will often serve to indicate whether they are distinct versions which have been developed from an earlier form or forms of the ballad or whether they are merely variants closely related to and dependent upon each other.

The use of the terms *ballad, version,* and *variant* in this manner is primarily a matter of scholarly and editorial convenience. It enables one to arrange collected texts in related groups and frequently aids the comparativist in showing patterns of evolution. It does not, however, explain the psychology of oral tradition, and it is not intended to do so; it is, rather, simply the application of particular words to various levels of textual development: *ballad* refers to the basic story type, *version* to a shift in the narrative pattern of a ballad, and *variant* to a textual shift. By the use of such terminology the comparativist's description of the life history of a ballad is made considerably simpler to understand.

In a broader sense, however, comparativists are interested in more than reconstructing the life history of a ballad; they are interested as well in the relationships which exist between various bodies of balladry, i.e., between ballads found in the various linguistic and geographic areas of the world, and, to a somewhat lesser degree, in the relationships which can be found to exist between ballads and such things as folktales and legends, epics and romances, and even history.

No one knows for certain how many ballads are part of the international body of song and how many are local and insular. An examination of the notes found in the major national collections suggests that neither political nor linguistic boundaries have greatly hindered the dissemination of ballads, that a very large proportion of the ballads found in any one area can be found in others as well. Yet, when individual ballads are closely analyzed in accordance with historic-geographic principles, it is frequently found that the similarities exist more in the minds of the editors than in the texts themselves. Before any definite conclusions can be drawn, many more studies must be made of individual songs.

Similarly, broad statements about the relationship of ballads to folktales and legends, to epics and romances, and to history are frequently to be found in the major ballad collections. But here again the statements are largely impressionistic and subjective. Without knowing the life history of a particular ballad, no one can say for certain whether it derived from, was the source of, or is simply parallel to similar material in other form.

Such are some of the major problems with which the comparativist attempts to cope. If the proper study of mankind be man, the proper study of ballads is ballads. It is obviously foolish to indulge in speculation about ultimate origins and about the relationship of ballads to singers until we know all that it is possible to know about the relationship of the texts of a particular ballad to every other text and perhaps until we know whether or not a specific relationship can be found between various ballads. Indeed, perhaps the most vexing problem in ballad study today is the amount of unsupported, speculative writing that has been indulged in by many who have written to prove hypotheses of which they were unduly fond, by many who love ballads not wisely but too well.

IV. The Rationalistic Approach

D. K. WILGUS

LET ME BEGIN by pointing out that in commenting on this topic I do not believe I am dealing with an "approach" to folksong which is necessarily a contrast or alternative to those already discussed. Of course, to speak of a *rational* approach to the study of folklore is not only natural, but almost unnecessary. The study of folklore is, with some qualifications, the application of reason to the unreasonable. Some approaches to folklore may be more reasonable than others. But the *rational* is not necessarily the *rationalistic*. And the counterpart of the rationalistic is not necessarily the aesthetic, the comparative, or the anthropological; it is rather the romantic. In these terms, one can discern a rationalistic approach to the study of folksong, although I may not agree with it or even consider it rational.

The rationalistic approach to folksong stretches at least from Joseph Ritson to G. Malcolm Laws, Jr. We might call it the commonsense or hardheaded approach. It looks for the simple rather than the complex. It is interested in documented facts, not suggestions or conjectures. It looks for its evidence in the known present and judges the past to have been of essentially the same pattern. In renouncing the attachment to mysterious processes, however, the rationalistic position tends to create universals of its own. And here indeed is the problem —the development of universalist and absolutist positions.

Is it possible to imagine a Ritson without a Percy? If I concede Albert B. Friedman's conclusion that Ritson was actually "more backward and less imaginative than Percy in trying to cope with the phenomenon of tradition,"[1] I do not have to concede the rightness of Percy's imagination. If I deplore T. F. Henderson's myopic view of tradition, I cannot accept the nebulous view of his "folkist" opponents.[2] If I consider the communal position a romantic fabrication, I cannot accept Louise Pound's conclusion that a ballad has no communal nature unless it is improvised jointly by folk minds in a state of vivid sensation.[3] I do not think I am raising dead issues, for the folk-versus-art dichotomy is still with us and is one of the absolutist tendencies which aid folksong scholarship largely by stirring up so much dust that someone pours living water on it.

Let me illustrate from the criticism of Laws, whose recent work I have found stimulating and useful. In studying balladry in America, Laws has reached a somewhat extreme conclusion, yet one he is able to document, at least from recent tradition. Laws's research has led to the conclusion that drastic revisions in ballad texts are not the "evolutionary result of many contributions from folk singers" or "the mysterious processes of folk transmission," and that a wide distribution of almost identical variants indicates the availability of the variant in many sources—print or phonograph recordings. Though Laws does not deny the "possibility" that revisions of ballads may have reached printers from "a folk composer or even directly from tradition," he emphasizes the role of ballad printers who "ransacked the old broadside sheets for anything that was usable" and adapted the material for their public.[4] The problem of Laws's conclusions is not their immediate validity, but the concepts that lie behind them and the implications placed on them. Laws's discussion of broadside purveyors, folk composers, and tradition seems to imply a mutual exclusion. I am not at all sure of his meaning of *tradition.* Consider one case which seems to fit his basic outline, although it is largely that of the composition and dissemination of a native American ballad.

According to the "mystic" principles of folksong composition and dissemination with which Laws takes issue, "The Death of Floyd Collins" should have sprung up about 1925 in the vicinity of Horse Cave, Kentucky, and have spread and changed in the performances of a succession of folksingers in time and space. In point of fact, the idea of the song was conceived in the mind of Polk C. Brockman, a record distributor and talent scout, as he sat in the Aragon Hotel in Jacksonville, Florida. As always, he was interested in what he thought might sell. Recalling the recording success of what were called "tragedies," he decided that the recent Floyd Collins affair, which had attracted nationwide publicity, would be a natural subject. So he communicated with one of his stable of performers in Atlanta, the Rev. Andrew Jenkins. Jenkins sat down at his piano and composed the song. His stepdaughter took it down, arranged the music, and mailed to Brockman the composition essentially, though of course not exactly, as we find it in folksong collections throughout the United States. Brockman gave the song for recording to another Atlanta artist, Fiddlin' John Carson, who set it to one of his own apparently limited number of tunes (Okeh 40363). Jenkins himself recorded the song later (Okeh 40393), but the chief purveyor was a converted light-opera singer, Marion Try Slaughter, more recognizable under his best-known pseudonym of Vernon Dalhart. Brockman, who had paid twenty-five dollars for the song, sold it to Frank Walker of Columbia Records, who assigned it to Dalhart for recording. There are local variants and adaptations —the most striking of which (collected by Bruce Buckley in southern Ohio) is unpublished—but "The Death of Floyd Collins" as now recovered is generally the Dalhart rendition. We have an example which seems to bolster Laws's conclusions. The song was contracted for and paid for. It was distributed in myriad copies. Dalhart's performances, counting remakes and reissues, appeared on nineteen different recording labels, four times on one of them, three times on two of them, and twice on two others.[5] And at least six other artists recorded the song prior to 1950.[6]

The example does in truth support a conclusion that in the last quarter-century (and probably previously) forms of American vulgar ballads have been disseminated by a broadside process to folksingers, who have generally repeated what they have learned—at least as far as text and basic tune are concerned. But rather than being concerned with what is untraditional in this account, we might conclude that it adds to our knowledge of the traditional process and of the folk composer. Polk C. Brockman was a part of the traditional process perhaps only in the widest sense. But to conceive of him, on the other hand, as a cunning concocter of material which destroyed the tastes of the American folk is unrealistic. Brockman, like other recording scouts and executives of the 1920's, had almost no realization of what he was actually doing. The music merchants simply realized—and slowly—that there was a taste among the American people for material and performances not being satisfied by existing commercial music. Brockman didn't particularly like or dislike the material—Negro and white—which he uncovered and purveyed. He knew that it existed, and he developed a rather shrewd opinion of what would sell, although he—like other music merchants then and now—was often wrong. He sought out folk performers and folk composers, although they soon began to seek him out. He tried them out on the folk audience—at least the folk who consumed recordings. He kept the talent which succeeded and rejected what failed, though he does not know to this day the reasons for the success of certain performers and certain material. And one of his most successful tools was Andrew Jenkins.

An extended biography of Andrew Jenkins may soon be prepared. He is worth a full portrait, and a few sentences can hardly do him justice as a man or even a folk composer. He was born in Jenkinsburg, Georgia, in 1885, and lived out his seventy-one years in northern Georgia. Blind—or nearly blind—from the age of three weeks, he played in youth the French harp, banjo, guitar, and mandolin, and developed in later life —also without formal instruction—proficiency on the trumpet, saxophone, violin, clarinet, and other instruments. He obviously absorbed the traditional, minstrel, and popular songs that floated his way. He grew up amid the sacred song tradition of the Southern Baptist church. Receiving sanctification in 1909 or 1910 during the great Holiness revival, he became a preacher and turned his song to religious purposes. After the death of his first wife, he began supporting himself in 1918 by selling newspapers on the streets of Atlanta, continuing his work as a revivalist. In 1919 he married again—into a musical family. The three stepchildren joined him as the Jenkins family of religious entertainers. When radio came to Atlanta in 1922, Jenkins moved almost immediately into studio entertainment —public, but certainly not professional. And in 1923 he was caught up by the recording industry as performer and composer. In his lifetime of preaching and faith-healing, he composed over 800 songs, about 550 sacred and the rest secular. Was he a folk composer? In terms of his sources, his forms, and the acceptance of his material, I don't think we can deny him the title. He sold his tragedy songs to Brockman, but he was certainly not a professional songwriter—and the professional or amateur status of the folk composer is a matter for determination, not a criterion of judgment. He was of the folk, he wrote for the folk, and he used traditional forms. He gave to the American folk such ballads as "Kinnie Wagner," "Wreck of the Royal Palm," "Little Marian Parker," "The Fate of Edward Hickman," and "Billie the Kid." He contributed revisions of "The Dream of the Miner's Child" and "The Miner's Doom." And—like other folk composers—he has been credited with "The Dying Cowboy," "The Blind Child," and others.[7]

Exclusion of Andrew Jenkins from a concept of tradition can result only from the senseless prolongation of the absolutist dichotomy of folk and art. The dispelling of the mystery surrounding the traditional process should not result in the renunciation of the process. I do not imply that conditions in seventeenth-century London, or eighteenth-century Boston, or nineteenth-century New York were identical with those in twentieth-century Atlanta. But we must not assume a nontraditional character of a process we are still investigating.

Tradition is not a universal absolute, any more than is a folksinger. At most we can speak only of an average folksinger within a given tradition. The Parry-Lord thesis of oral composition[8] is, in my judgment, valid and proved for the tradition of Slavic epic songs, and probably for other areas as well. The application of the thesis to Anglo-American folksongs is dubious, at least in the extreme and absolutist fashion attempted by James H. Jones.[9] But the application is hardly more absolutist than Laws's extension of his conclusions to the Child ballads on the ground that "there is no good reason to assume that the basic causes and results of variation have altered significantly over the centuries."[10] There is not a folk tradition; there are a number of folk traditions, even within the United States. Conclusions concerning vulgar balladry may not apply so aptly to the blues themselves and to lyrics and worksongs. I cannot agree with Albert Lord, if he implies that the process of memorization and recapitulation typical of Anglo-American white folksingers necessarily implies degeneration for their tradition, as it does for the tradition of oral epic in Yugoslavia. Nor would I maintain that the tradition which he has outlined so well may not be helpful in understanding some of the variation in older ballad tradition. I do maintain that the traditional ballad is one thing, the oral epic another; that there are analogies and differences between the two traditions. And I maintain that absolutist concepts, whether rationalistic or romantic, needlessly restrict the field of folksong scholarship.

I chose previously to dwell so intently on commercial aspects of folk tradition—or on commercialized folk tradition—because respectable academic scholarship is today at least ambivalent toward these problems, and just about any idea that is new. I do not charge that academic scholarship is actively hostile to new ideas and new techniques. Our meetings and journals are receptive to new concepts and new materials. But the new ideas and materials must come to us, and in a quite respectable guise as well. During the greatest Anglo-American folksong revival, the members of the academic tradition of folksong study are talking largely to themselves. The campuses of metropolitan universities abound with folksong interest of one sort or another—but the students are one place and the scholars another. They distrust each other almost instinctively. There are many reasons for this anomaly, including timidity, pseudo-respectability, laudable distrust of vague and uninformed enthusiasm. But the academics must come to terms with the new revival—that is, they must learn to use it, and must learn from some of its members as well.

When I speak of academic folksong scholarship, I mean no disrespect. For by academic scholarship in this context I mean simply the dispassionate, objective, and historical investigation of the phenomena of folksong as a self-contained study. It is not the only source of knowledge, but it is the only finally valid tradition. Like all scholarship, it tends to look backward, but it can be at times ridiculous. At the moment it is engaged in a sort of salvage operation, re-examining and correcting and improving the work of our predecessors without venturing too far from their pastures. I shall not try to detail the productions of academic scholarship within the past decade—syllabi, histories of scholarship, collections of Child ballads vastly improved in annotation and consideration of music, and meaningful histories of individual ballads, particularly older ones. I would myself defend their importance and necessity. But the production and the publication of these works are at least tangentially related to a widespread interest in folksong which the academic tradition does not understand and distrusts, when it does not condemn.

I have no intention of trying to explain the folksong revival on the campus, in the coffeehouse, in the marketplace. I do want to point out that the widespread interest in folksong has a lot to do with what we may call "folk sound." I grant that it isn't all folk, as those who dub me "purist" know I will. But I know that some academics who now denounce current commercial productions once applauded performers half as authentic as "The Limelighters" or whatever horror you may think of. Much of the current interest in "folk sound" has little to do with scholarship, with serious study of folksong. Much of the interest is misled, much of it is silly. But there is a general if ill-informed interest in live or performed folksongs, and a good part of a new generation with knowledge about folk productions unknown to some scholars. The emphasis on sound, on performance, on personality is making publicly available material previously unknown even in sequestered archives. But the academic tradition remains bookish because so much of the best evidence of the past is bookish. Ideally perhaps the academic scholar should be, if not controlling, at least guiding the revival. Practically it is not possible. Some men whom I consider fine academic scholars are concerned in the revival—though we are not always in agreement on certain compromises involved. But if we can agree that among the plethora of so-called folk-music recordings lie authentic materials which represent the best evidence generally available, I wonder how many academic libraries are gathering the best evidence? And after examining such record holdings as I sometimes find in libraries, I wonder who guided the librarians in their selections. How many students of folksong are encouraged to approach the recording as well as the book? How many scholars know what is on the records? From the revival, the interest in folk sound, a new generation of folksong scholars is emerging, an emergence we permit rather than encourage. It is emerging because the students have found the tradition; the tradition has not found them. They are, unfortunately, only a few in comparison to the potential students who remain in almost total ignorance of the academic tradition, yet stand in need of it. They are interested in aspects of folk tradition—such as performance and style—which the academic tradition has neglected; they lack the discipline, perspective, and larger knowledge which the academic could conceivably exchange with them. What is truly remarkable is that, in spite of the lack of communication, significant work is being done amidst the delusions and commercialism of the folksong revival.

Ironically, one of the studies being furthered by members of the current revival concerns that earlier commercial collection of American folksong neglected by academic scholarship. I am not suggesting a strict parallel between the two commercial operations; they are alike mainly in their importance and their neglect by the academic tradition. It is, I believe, well known that in the early 1920's commercial recording companies began issuing recordings aimed at the Negro and white folk, and that with the help of radio an important musical pattern was established. Yet the significance of this phenomenon eluded and basically still eludes the academic tradition of folk-song study. Alan Lomax, Herbert Halpert, Howard W. Odum, Guy B. Johnson, and others recognized its importance. Latterly such folklorists as John Greenway have repeatedly demonstrated its significance. The materials relevant to this great recording venture provide the most important key to developments in certain areas of twentieth-century American folksong. It is not accurate completely to separate the race—that is, Negro—records from the hillbilly or white records. White and Negro traditions influenced each other here as well as elsewhere. There is a difference in the amount and type of study devoted to the two traditions because the Negro recordings had an aesthetic and sympathetic appeal to an intellectual white audience long before students began to take hillbilly music seriously. The study of country blues is going rather well—little thanks to most folklorists. Like the blues and jazz, hillbilly music was commercial and therefore not folk to romanticist and rationalist alike. It was a low-class commercial production, probably hoked up by city slickers. Even if that were true, subsequent collection has made a study necessary, considering that at least one-third of the contents of any large collection of folksongs from the South can be found—in analogues at least—on hillbilly records, and that many songs can have reached the folk only from the recordings. The same is true of Laws's *Native American Balladry*. And when one begins to trace and interview performers and executives, one reaches quickly the point at which any absolutist distinction between folk and commercial performer becomes totally unrealistic. Yet the materials and support for investigations of this important phenomenon come not under the aegis of academic scholarship, but from private, unsung, and at first fumbling work of individuals who did not know until recently the difference between a Child ballad and a children's song. If a student wants to study this tradition, what folksong archive would we send him to? In what folksong library will he find a copy of *Disc Collector* or *Record Research?* How many folksong scholars could provide our student with a list of authorities?

Let me not belabor my point—which is simply that the approach to folksong must be rational, not rationalistic or absolutist in any form. I have yet to find an approach to folksong from which I have not learned something; I have yet to find one whose dominance is not dangerous.

V. The Transcription and Analysis of Folk Music

GEORGE FOSS

An old man was shown the musical notation of the song which he had just sung. "There is your song," said Mr. Sharp, handing his note-book, and the old man, who could neither read nor write peered thoughtfully at the page of manuscript, carefully scrutinizing the blobs, dashes and dots, and then, shaking his head, said, "Well, I can hardly recognize it."
—Maud Karpeles, Introduction to Cecil Sharp's
English Folk Songs from the Southern Appalachians

THE TURN of this century saw in England an extensive effort by competent musicians to collect and transcribe folk tunes. This was done with the conviction that folksinging was rapidly approaching extinction, and with the aim of pursuing the musical heritage as the literary heritage had been pursued. This work was engaged in by such gifted young men as Ralph Vaughan Williams and Percy Grainger. We must consider Cecil Sharp as the first great figure of the new musicology. Cecil Sharp was a composer, organist, and teacher whose first contact with folk material, at the age of forty, occurred in his search for suitable material for his boys' choir. When World

War I forced a suspension of Sharp's work in England, he traveled to America for an extended lecture tour. Here he was approached by Mrs. Olive Campbell, whose work with settlement schools in the Kentucky mountains had acquainted her with the unusual songs and ballads sung in the rural areas. Sharp was skeptical at first that any worthwhile material was to be found here. However, upon examining Mrs. Campbell's small amateur collection of manuscripts, he left his lecture schedule and began his extensive collections in the Southern Appalachians.

Sharp's collecting trips covered a period of three years, 1916 through 1918, during the months when travel was not made impossible by snow. He covered the Appalachian Range through the states of Kentucky, West Virginia, Virginia, North Carolina, and Tennessee. Since recording devices were much more primitive than they are today and electrical power was almost unknown in the mountain areas, Sharp's work was accomplished almost entirely by dictation. (He made a few recordings on a hand-powered dictating machine.) Sharp was accompanied by Maud Karpeles, who had worked with him in England. It was her duty to note the texts in shorthand while Sharp secured the tunes. In this fashion, Sharp collected some 273 different ballads and songs with variants—some 968 tunes in all, a remarkable achievement in view of the primitive conditions and lack of mechanical aids.

Sharp's training was in Western art music history and theory. In order to avoid the practice of some other collectors, who often altered modal material to fit quaint major-minor piano accompaniments, he expressed his own conscious effort to receive and transcribe only the most elemental and primitive impressions. He considered it, at first, his greatest problem to reject automatic criticism and judgments based on his training in formal musical idioms—mentally modifying odd patterns of rhythm into strict meter and doubtful patterns of melody into tonal frameworks.

In the matter of analysis or classification of the tunes, Sharp was also faced with the necessity of finding new methods. In England, most folk material fell rather conveniently into classification based on the Medieval Church modes. In the Southern Appalachians, however, Sharp discovered such a preponderance of pentatonic and gapped scale material that he considered other methods of classification essential.

Sharp chose as the basic unit for his theories of folksong the pentatonic scale. His theories, admittedly controversial, are thus stated:

> Personally, I believe that it was the first form of scale which was in any way comparable with our modern major or minor scale. Originally, as may be gathered from the music of primitive tribes, the singer was content to chant his song in monotone, varied by occasional excursions to the sounds immediately above or below his single tone. . . . Eventually, however, he succeeded in covering the whole octave, but, even so, he was satisfied with fewer intermediate sounds than the seven which comprise the modern diatonic scale. Indeed, there are many nations which have not yet advanced beyond the two gapped or pentatonic scale, such as, for instance, the Gaels of Highland Scotland. . . . A further development . . . was eventually achieved by the folk singer. . . . The two medial tones required to complete the scale were introduced speculatively and with hesitation. There are many instances in Irish folk music, for example, in which the pitch or intonation of these added sounds is varied in the course of one and the same tune. This experimental and transitional period, however, eventually came to a close, and the final stage was reached . . . when the diatonic scale became definitely settled. But even then, and for a long period after, the mediate sounds remained "weak" and were employed only as auxiliary notes or connecting links, rather than structural or cadential notes, so that the gaps, though covered up, were not concealed.[1]

This, then, was the underlying theory of Sharp's analyzation and classification of his Appalachian collection. Using the pentatonic scale represented by (ascending) C, D, F, G, A (or any transposition having the gapped minor third between the 2nd and 3rd and the 5th and octave degrees), Sharp derived five modes. The first is the scale mentioned, and numbers 2 to 5 the four inversions of the basic pentatonic scale.[2] Sharp elab-

orated the five pentatonic modes in accordance with his theory
to encompass hexatonic (one-gapped) and heptatonic (diatonic) scales. In this elaboration, each pentatonic mode assumes
three subsidiary forms: (a) with one of the two gaps filled by
a "weak" note, (b) with the other gap filled by a "weak" note,
and (a and b), with both gaps filled by "weak" notes. Thus,
having a melody with no sixth degree, we might have a tune
classifiable within modes two or four. If, however, its second
degree were "weak," it would be classified mode 2a; if its third
degree were "weak," its classification would be 4b.

This scheme, while seeming all-inclusive on first glance,
proves upon closer examination to have as many exceptions as
applications. For example, a tune (see Example 1) is classified

EXAMPLE 1

by Sharp as 4b (hexatonic, no 6th, weak 3rd) obviously upon
the basis of the fluctuating pitch of the 3rd degree (B♭, B♮).
This tone, however, is structurally very important. We cannot
be sure that its variable pitch was not a characteristic of the
singer rather than of the tune in the abstract sense. Now note
the occurrence of the 2nd degree. This pitch (represented by
a^1), occurs but on the short note and is in the function of a
connecting tone between the much stronger 3rd degree and
the final. This would tend to indicate a classification of 2a
(hexatonic, no 6th, weak 2), despite the variable 3rd degree.

More obvious concessions are forced upon Sharp in tunes
which do not conform at all with his theories. In Example 2,

EXAMPLE 2

Sharp encounters a tune which he classifies as mode 4b (hexatonic, no 6th, weak 3), but he is compelled to add the modification, "No 2nd degree." This, then, leaves us with a five note scale, and not a hexatonic mode at all. This bit of sidestepping is brought about because the five notes of the tune (G, B, C, D, F) do not conform to the basic pentatonic pattern of whole steps and minor 3rds. This scale might be classified more descriptively as pentatonic 2, with a raised 3rd, or even as Mixolydian with gapped 2nd and 6th.

Sharp's tables of classification do not adequately deal with the occasional appearance of a tune having only four pitches. Within the framework of his ideas, he describes these as, for example, pentatonic mode 3, no 6th. If one is quite familiar with Sharp's methods, the proper note pattern may be deduced, but to label a tune with only four notes as pentatonic is misleading and inaccurate.

Another practice of Sharp which has no place outside elementary academic theory is the arbitrary use of the key signature. For example, in the pentatonic mode 3, having G as the final (G, A, B, D, E), Sharp invariably affixes the signature of one ♯. This, perhaps, to his mind, signified G as the tonal center or final, but the insistence on an F♯ signature to codify a tune in which no F appears is highly questionable. Unfortunately, Sharp makes no mention in his Southern Appalachian collection of his editorial policy in regard to the pitch level at which his material is transcribed. Tunes collected from men and women alike are printed within the confines of the treble clef, and I would assume the material was transposed to eliminate the necessity for the use of many leger lines or multi-accidental key signatures.

As regards the rhythmic factor of the transcriptions, Sharp was very careful to avoid the imposition of strict meter throughout many of the songs. This had been the practice of those who desired to use traditional material in an art song manner. Since Sharp's work was done by oral dictation, it is impossible to verify its rhythmic accuracy. His approach seems, however, as sophisticated and sound as those of some of the best transcriptions done today. This judgment is made primarily on Sharp's treatment of the older ballads (often in the parlando or free meter style), in view of what we understand today to be traditional idioms of performance. It is unfortunate and puzzling that Sharp made no indication of the tempos of any of the material presented. It may be that he considered this more characteristic of the individual performer, and his concern was with the tune in a more abstract sense. It might be argued that a performer is just as likely to alter the mode or scale as he is the tempo to suit his individual liking. Therefore, the one should be considered as reliable a criterion as the other.

A characteristic of Sharp's publication (if indeed not his recording technique) is that only the first stanza of a ballad or song is musically notated. The remaining stanzas must be made to conform to the tune of the first. Since variation is so vital a part of the traditional music and stanzas vary greatly in phrase length and syllabic structure, this representation is quite often inadequate. The practical problems of publication and space must be taken into consideration, and Sharp, after speaking of the essential character of variation, attempts to supply a compromise. This is done by labeling the bar (a, b. c, etc.), which is significantly altered in subsequent stanzas, and giving transcriptions of the alteration after the tune proper. This creates additional problems in that often there is no indication as to which variation applies to which stanza. The number of combinations therefore can become alarming, and any attempt to reconstruct the proper prosody is no more than sheer guesswork.

Many of Sharp's techniques and methods have remained as the standard—now, of course, augmented by modern recording machines. However, some aspects, especially those pointed out, leave something to be desired in constructing a basis for the serious study of our traditional music.

Some indication of the progress made since Sharp's work and of the further progress needed can be gained in a brief comparison of the two works by A. K. Davis: *Traditional Ballads of Virginia*, 1929, and *More Traditional Ballads of Virginia*, 1960. Mr. Davis is a literary scholar, and the literary approach is the predominant one, especially in the first work. This work, for example, contains some 440 ballad texts with only 148 corresponding tunes, these appended in a separate section of the work. Some of the tunes were transcribed by Cecil Sharp during his previously mentioned collecting trips and are the best and probably most trustworthy in the volume. Thus, the tunes are from various sources and informants, undoubtedly varying in capability and musical training. The tunes as printed fall consistently within art song idioms and no attempt is made at representation of traditional styles of performance or analyzation of the material. No mention is made of the editorial policy concerning the pitch level at which the tunes are noted, or of tempo or rhythmic variants necessitated by text differences in various stanzas.

An increasing appreciation of the importance of the music and a careful representation of it is evidenced in the second volume. The ratio is here 101 tunes reproduced for the 148 texts of the book. Here, Davis has secured the editorial assistance of musicians, primarily Ernest Mead, chairman of the music department, University of Virginia. Mead states thus his method, in attempting to overcome the long established practice of noting only the first stanza:

I transcribed all the stanzas and quoted them to arrive at what might

be considered the essential skeleton of the melody. If, after this, the first
stanza seemed, on the whole, characteristic, that stanza was selected for
printing, followed by significant variants that occurred in the remaining
stanzas. In some tunes, the first stanza was either unreliable or not
representative. Occasionally, there was a wide divergence between the
melodies of different stanzas, in which case, the melodies of several representative stanzas are given.[3]

The tunes, although meticulous in their representation, still
seem to function as appendices to the text, the prime object of
interest. Although it is stated that the tunes were fully analyzed
and classified, the designations are not printed in the book.
Davis gives as reasons for omitting a theoretical description of
the tunes the avoidance of controversy in these highly arguable
matters and the wish to avoid discrepancies in classification
with Bronson's *Traditional Tunes of the Child Ballads.* The
first volume of Bronson's work had not appeared at the time
of the completion of Davis' work. It is unfortunate that Mead's
methods are not presented, regardless of any controversy they
might have precipitated.

Mead's approach to transcription seems most practical and
sensible and, to be sure, he represents a great advance over the
oversimplified and art-music-oriented representations of the
first Virginia volume. He offers editorial comments on the
peculiarities of the tunes as well as on the characteristics of the
singer. There is in many of his transcriptions a degree of concern with capturing certain of these performing characteristics.
In this aspect alone, Mead's work is more valuable than that of
most doing traditional music transcriptions today.

The major criticism which could be made of Mead's work
is of his handling of the rhythmic factor of the tunes. Perhaps,
in a deliberate attempt to avoid forcing a tune into a metrical
mold, he has expressed rhythms in an extreme manner, often
using complicated meter changes in every bar. This concept
of fluctuating meter (à la Stravinsky) is undoubtedly farther
from the comprehension of the traditional singer than is regular

meter. This rigid practice of assigning each measure a meter
of its own produces an unnatural effect in many cases, and
leads us to a deeper criticism—that Mead, in representing the
rhythmic pattern as he hears it, in the extremely abstract
fashion, perhaps ignores the effect of the words on melody. This
is a reversal of the old complaint that scholars failed to represent adequately the interdependence of the text and tune.

I have been fortunate in being able to compare Mead's
transcriptions with field recordings from which they were made.
It does seem that Mead's approach was musical to the extent
of excluding literary factors. Example 3 is Mead's transcription

EXAMPLE 3

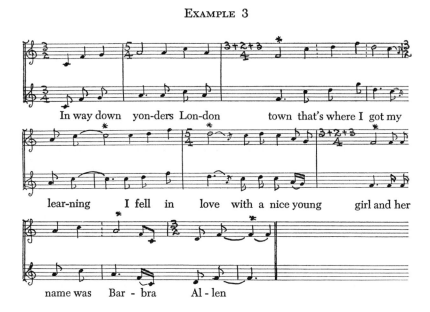

of a ballad tune noted above a transcription done in more
conventional rhythm. There is a discrepancy in duration of
those notes marked *. While these notes are somewhat shortened from the 3/4 example, they do not sound to me as short
as Mead represents them. The singer sings in a slightly fore-
shortened 3/4 meter throughout, and this grouping adheres

more closly to the syllabic structure of the text than does Mead's polymetric notation.

Jan Philip Schinhan, music editor for the huge Frank C. Brown collection of *North Carolina Folklore*, puts forth an interesting view as to the rhythmic properties of traditional music:

> ... meter first came into music when it was found necessary in concerted music to make sure that the different "events" as represented by the individual lines of a polyphonic composition would occur in their proper "order." Meter was and still is a mere convenience which, on the one hand, enables the composer to convey, at least approximately, his ideas and intentions, and on the other, makes it possible for the performer to arrive at an understanding of the music, and thereby realize the intentions of the composer. Rhythm always was first and meter second. Neither in purely monophonic music like Plain Chant, nor in the music of our own day, has there ever been a melody without rhythm, but, as in Plain Chant, the melodies of the troubadours, the Minnesingers and Mastersingers, there was, and still is music without meter.[4]

As Mead's transcriptions can be regarded as an advance over those in the beginning of our traditional music study, Schinhan's methods of analysis may be considered an advance over earlier attempts to apply analytical methods to this material. Schinhan's approach is singular in its thoroughness and overall inclusiveness, for in editing Brown's collection, he has evolved formulae applicable to a vast variety of traditional musical idioms. He writes:

> The present method ... is based on six comprehensive features which, though they sometimes overlap, must be treated separately:
>   1. Scales and modes
>   2. Range
>   3. Melodic line, or interval succession in pitch
>   4. Meter, or interval succession in time
>   5. Structure, or Gestalt; overall rhythm
>   6. Rendition

A brief summary of Schinhan's handling of these six factors follows:

Scales and modes. The terminology used is derived from a number of different tones occurring in a tune and their distribution as regards gaps or skips in the basic scale. To all scales showing a consecutive series of tones, the suffix "chordal" makes this distinction. For instance, a tune comprised of six tones in an unbroken diatonic sequence (C, D, E, F, G, and A; B not used), would be classified as hexa-(six note)-chordal (in diatonic sequence). Likewise, tunes using four tones with the range of a 4th are labeled tetrachordal, five note tunes covering a 5th pentachordal, etc. To designate gapped scale melodies, the suffix "tonic" provides this distinction. Therefore, any tune using but four notes with one or more gaps (for example, D, F, G, A) would be labeled tetra-(four note)-tonic (in broken sequence, or gapped). Realizing the importance and many forms of the pentatonic scale, Schinhan classified these modes I, II, III, IV, and V according to the placement of the gaps derived from the five inversions of the basic C, D, F, G, A scale. This classification corresponds to Sharp's labeling of the five common pentatonic forms. Schinhan explains with greater clarity that although the Ionian mode (for example) corresponds exactly to our major mode tonally, the modal behavior is quite different from what is expected of our familiar major mode. He has, therefore, avoided attempting to assign a modal classification to all heptachordal tunes, and has declined to affix a modal description upon any gapped scale tunes, declaring that this would require an editorial assumption as to which tone would fill the gap. This attitude is both sensible and practical in its avoidance of misleading nomenclature. Schinhan places great emphasis upon the relationship of tones to one another within the melody. This relationship is graphically illustrated in Schinhan's method of numerically expressing the duration of each member of the scale pattern. This is done by dividing the total durations of any given tone into sixteenth notes, and placing this number under the corresponding member of the scale. This provides a ready index to the proportional weight of each member tone to all other tones, gives a mathematically accurate picture of distribution, and avoids arbitrary and often questionable decisions such as are found in Sharp's methods specifying "weak notes."

Range. In dealing with tunes individually, it is easy to see at a glance the range of a particular melody, but Schinhan appends several tables giving the numerical occurrence of all ranges from the smallest (that of a 4th in only one song), to the largest (that of a 13th, occurring also in one song only). These tables, for instance, demonstrate the heavy preponderance of tunes with exactly one octave range, the next greatest frequency, the major 9th, etc.

Melodic line or interval succession in pitch. This approach analyzes the relationship of tones to one another as regards their pitch. There are numerous tables giving rather extensive breakdowns of melodic characteristics, such as the degree of scale on which the tune commences, the initial progression and interval, proportions of step-wise and interval movement, the placing and treatment of the climax and occurrence of repeated tones.

Meter or interval succession in time. Some of Schinhan's ideas of meter were referred to earlier. In addition he supplies tables concerned with the frequency of meters among the songs which definitely fall into a metrical structure. It is interesting to note that in the very early British ballads there is a preponderance of 3/4 first, and 6/8 next. It would provide an intriguing study to determine to what extent these meters (or more properly, mensurations) were adopted from their predominance in art music by early traditional singers, troubadors, and Minnesingers. Schinhan, in giving the occurrence of the common meters, also reveals that the changing meter occurs almost exclusively in the older British ballad forms, and that its occurrence there is only slightly less frequent than 3/4 and 6/8.

Structure or Gestalt: overall rhythm. Schinhan's view of

structure encompasses both melodic and rhythmic characteristics and extends into what might be familiarly called the
form of the whole tune. This representation is achieved in a
fashion familiar to students of music, by using letters to designate small units or periods within the whole, i.e., ABAC, ABA,
ABCD. A variation of a section can be expressed by repeating
the letter plus the figure [1]; i.e., AA^{1}B, ABA^1, ABCB^1, etc. After
each structure formula is given a series of numerals representing
the number of bars of the corresponding lettered segments; thus
ABCB^1 (4, 2, 4, 2) would indicate a four bar phrase, a contrasting phrase, a contrasting four bar phrase, and a two bar phrase
being only a slight variation of the previous two bar phrase.
Such a classification accompanies each tune transcription and
appended tables set forth data on the frequency of all
possible structures.

Rendition. Along with general statements on the characteristics of traditional singers (style, diction, memory, etc.),
Schinhan describes his method for noting peculiarities such as
stanza variation. This is done in the manner of Sharp and Mead.
Little attempt has been made to notate thoroughly stylistic
peculiarities.

Each tune is accompanied by the name of the singer, place
and date of recording, scale, structure, and "tonal center."
Schinhan states that he uses the term "tonal center" to avoid
preconceptions created by the term "tonic," and thence the term
"dominant." Since he has so scrupulously avoided making
academic judgments and arbitrary editorial decisions, his desig-
nation of tone centers seems incongruous. To be sure, most
traditional tunes, excepting pentatonic ones, have a tone easily
recognizable as tonic or the "tonal center"; but in some few
cases such designations cause confusion. In Example 4, as
an instance, we have two tunes to variants of the same ballad
which are markedly similar. In the first, the designated tonal
center is B♭, in the second it is F. Resort to Schinhan's analysis
of the proportional weight of individual tones fails to demon-

EXAMPLE 4

strate that there exist sufficient reasons for the variations in designations.

Though this is not mentioned, it would appear that the editorial policy has been to transpose all tunes so as not to descend beyond B below middle C.

The work of Schinhan leads us logically to the methods of Bruno Nettl, who admittedly patterns much of his work in *Ancient Ballads*[5] on Schinhan's formulae. Nettl's criteria may be briefly summarized as follows:

Structure. Each line or musical phrase (usually corresponding to a line of text) is assigned a letter. Variations are designated by the addition of numbers, i.e., A^1, A^2, etc. More subtle relationships may be indicated as Ba, meaning B has some slight relationship to A. The sequence of numbers relating to measures per phrase is the same as in Schinhan.

Rhythm. Nettl recognizes five rather distinct rhythmic families, the fifth being of irregular or divergent meter:

Contour. Without formal analyzation, Nettl briefly describes the contour or shape of each whole tune (arc, descending, each section arcs, undulating, etc.).

Scales. Scales are described as in Schinhan except that pentatonic scales lacking the half step are further described as "anhemitonic." All heptatonic scales are classified as major, Dorian, Lydian, Myxolydian, and Aeolian. The tunes are transcribed at the pitch in which they were sung. A representation of each tune's scale pattern is printed so as to have g^1 as its final (see Example 5). Rather than describing mathematically the proportional relationship of the tones, Nettl designates this in

EXAMPLE 5

a more general fashion, giving the final g (almost always the tonic) as a whole note, the tone of next importance as a half, other notes of the scale as quarters, and those having only minor significance as eighths.

Nettl prescribes the use of various symbols to augment traditional music notation in order to capture certain peculiarities of traditional music:

✝, ↑	slightly higher than noted
—, ↓	slightly lower than noted
(♩)	uncertain pitch
◊	indefinite pitch
♪	grace note without rhythmic value
ǐǐǐ	weak tones
ᵖ	pulsations
⌢	strong tie
⌢	glissando
⌢•	slightly longer than noted
ᵕ•	slightly shorter than noted

While we are discussing the various methods being evolved to analyze and classify traditional music, it is proper at this point to examine Bertrand Bronson's work *Traditional Tunes of the Child Ballads*.[6] This work has as its aim the mammoth task of presenting all significant examples of melodies ever recorded or noted down along with the proper text variants of the Child ballads. This project is rife with difficulties of an editorial nature. First is the divergence of sources from which the transcriptions come. Many tune transcriptions date from as early as 1600 (Ravencroft's *Mellismata*) and are, of course, impossible to verify as to accuracy and authenticity. Their importance could not be discounted solely on this basis, however, and they must therefore be used alongside the most meticulous and reliable of present-day sources. Bronson states that his only course was to accept all transcriptions available at face value without attempting to correct or affix value judgments. Then there was the divergence of aim within the transcriptions, regardless of period; "One is directed toward the abstract, the song; the other toward the individual act of singing."[7] These, too, could not be altered to conform to one approach or the other and so were used per se. The vast amount of material, already projected into five large volumes, made the inclusion of extensive stanza variations impractical and, indeed, there was no such refinement in most of the early transcriptions, regardless of period: "One is directed toward the tune without words or reference to the specific stanza from which it was transcribed. He states that a knowledge of the tune would suffice and the fitting of the words to a tune skeleton was the cause of the variation to be found in traditional singing. He states further that the attention given to prescribed prosody detracts from the natural flow of words and music. Bronson is certainly correct in these statements but the method does not preclude any intensive study into the ethnic style on tune-text relationship. Considering, however, the scope of the work, the many obstacles that confronted Bronson, and the lack of details available to him, this criticism cannot, in justice, be pursued.

Taking all available tunes to a single ballad, Bronson was faced with the task of classifying them into "tune families," selecting representative specimens, and choosing between significant and insignificant variants. The two criteria used to determine tune-families were "mode" and "contour." The properties of contour are relatively obvious but the problems of modal classifications, in dealing with material from England, Ireland, Scotland, and all parts of the United States, become enormous. A formula which would encompass and codify all the material was evolved. It seems, however, to be rather antiquated in its dependence on the old Church Mode concepts.

This might stem once more from the fact that Bronson's background is primarily that of literary scholarship. His methods seem to rely more on the work of Sharp than on any of the significant methods which have been used since Sharp's time by musicologists.

Bronson uses as a basis for his classifications a table including all the Church Modes. From this he derives the type of hexatonic or pentatonic mode in which a tune is cast. This initial table is constructed of a circle of the modes similar to the circle of tonal fifths which is familiar to all students of music.

(Using as the initial note and transposing all modes to conform)

LYDIAN	C	D	E	F♯	G	A	B	C
IONIAN	C	D	E	F	G	A	B	C
MIXOLYDIAN	C	D	E	F	G	A	B♭	C
DORIAN	C	D	E♭	F	G	A	B♭	C
AEOLIAN	C	D	E♭	F	G	A♭	B♭	C
PHRYGIAN	C	D♭	E♭	F	G	A♭	B♭	C
LOCRIAN	C	D♭	E♭	F	G♭	A♭	B♭	C

The first three modes are bracketed together as π'.

A tune with only six different tones is classified according to its agreement with two modes. Therefore, a tune labeled I/M would agree in all its tones with both Ionian and Mixolydian (i.e., C, D, E, F, G, A, C); the tone not in agreement with both modes (i.e., B) would be missing.

Pentatonic scales are classified according to their agreement with three modes and are represented by $\pi 1$, $\pi 2$, $\pi 3$, $\pi 4$, and $\pi 5$. Pentatonic mode 1, for example, agrees with modes Lydian, Ionian, and Mixolydian. These five pentatonic modes then would be as follows:

$\pi 1$	C	D	E	–	G	A	–	C (Sharp mode 3)
$\pi 2$	C	D	–	F	G	A	–	C (Sharp mode 1)

$\pi3$	C	D	–	F	G	–	B♭	C (Sharp mode 4)
$\pi4$	C	–	E♭	F	G	–	B♭	C (Sharp mode 2)
$\pi5$	C	–	E♭	F	–	A♭	B♭	C (Sharp mode 5)

This method does not require the editorial intrusion of determining "weak notes" as did Sharp's, but final judgment as to its overall value will have to be withheld until more of the work is completed. The impact on others in the field cannot yet be gauged, but it seems unfortunate that such a comprehensive and important work should revert to dependence on the "modal" concepts when the direction of musical scholarship (at least in this country) was in other directions.

In surveying styles and techniques of transcription only, we turn to the work of Bela Bartok. In 1934, Milman Parry of Harvard University did extensive collecting in Yugoslavia in an effort to reconstruct the probable styles of the ancient Homeric chants. His collection of Serbo-Croatian traditional songs and epic ballads was turned over to Bartok after Parry's untimely death. Bartok's work on this material has become a model of ultradetailed and perfectionist transcription as well as the most penetrating analyzation.[8] We shall not include a discussion of Bartok's analyzations and classifications because of the wide difference in the Serbo-Croatian material and Anglo-American tradition, which is our prime interest here. As one example, Bartok elaborately systematizes the arrangement or order of presentation for the tunes according to melodic characteristics and syllabic formulae, whereas it has been a hundred-year tradition to arrange the presentation of Anglo-American material on the basis of literary content.

Bartok's approach to transcription, while never unrealistic, is so thorough and demanding on editor and reader as to be termed idealistic. Some of his policies, however, might well be adopted and made applicable to Anglo-American traditional music.

All tunes are transposed so as to have the note g^1 as their final. (While there can be argument as to what note is tonic or tonal center, there can be none as to which tone is the final, and in the great majority of Anglo-American tunes, they are one and the same.) In order to refer to a particular tone within a melody, Bartok assigns numerals to all notes from g below middle c to b². The tone g¹ is assigned to the Arabic numeral 1, and the ascending diatonic notes numbered consecutively to b² designated 10. G below middle c is designated by Roman numeral I, and all notes through f numbered consecutively, f being designated VII. (See Example 6.) Accidentals placed before the number designate an alteration of that tone; i.e.,

EXAMPLE 6

bVI means e♮ above middle c. A method devised to designate visually the contour of a melody utilizes this system. The last phase of a melody terminates on g¹, or in Bartok's system, 1. This is inevitable because of transposition and need not be designated. The figure ☐ designates the main (or in most cases of Anglo-American tunes, the middle) caesura or phrase ending. The figure ⌐ indicates the minor caesura preceding it, and the figure ⌐ indicates the minor caesura following it. Thus, the symbols ‾3‾ ☐5☐ VI would indicate a four-part melody having b¹ as the final tone of its first phrase, d² as the final tone of its main caesura, e¹ as the final note of its third phrase, and, of course, g¹ as its final. Another method of describing phrase structure is similar to those already discussed of Schinhan and Nettl, using A B A C formula. There are these modifications: A⁵ (A⁴, A³), a fifth (fourth, third) higher than A.

> . . . A₅, a fifth lower than A
> . . . A₆, a sequence one tone lower than A;
> . . . Aˢ, one tone higher

In all cases, the setting of bar lines is done with particular consideration to the rhythmic structure of the text. In parlando material, that is, the extremely free melodic movement characteristic of much Serbo-Croatian music, no meter is indicated, and the bars are set purely according to syllable emphasis. If a tune rigidly adheres to meter, both musically and textually, the fact is indicated. When meter varies from bar to bar, because of differing periods of emphasis, such changes are noted by meter signatures within parentheses. Bartok further makes it a practice to present each line of text as a separate staff line of music. This greatly aids in the graphic representation of the interdependence of text and tune. As to the choice of values, Bartok has, as a general rule, used the quarter note for values between M.M. 50-130 and the eighth for M.M. 100-200. Any deviations from constant pulse, such as accelerando or ritardando, are indicated exactly by a change in note values or, if this becomes overly complicated, a change in the metronome marking.

Signs in the current notation which have a more or less vague meaning (the hold, the trill sign, the mordent, comma, and so forth) should never be used; instead of the hold and a comma, the exact measurement of the value, and instead of embellishment marks, the exact pitch of the ornamental tones should be used in the notations. Perhaps only four exceptions are permissible: the use of a wavy line above the note (for the vibrato), or semicircles for slight lengthening or shortening, and of the short grace note.[9]

Other practices of Bartok include: (1) The wavy line connecting two notes indicates glissando; above or underneath a group of notes it indicates a blurring of the group; and above a single note, it represents vibrato. (2) Arrows above a note pointing upward or downward indicate raising or lowering the designated pitch up to the extent of a quarter tone. (These may be used in conjunction with flats or sharps and remain valid as long as the accidentals.) (3) Beams are used to connect groups of eighths, sixteenths, etc., instead of the old-style

separate flags for notes sung to different syllables. The slur
is used to group several notes to which only one syllable is
sung. As to key signatures, only those sharps or flats occurring
consistently within the melody are included in the signature.
Therefore, a Phrygian type tune, lacking the sixth degree and
having g as its final, would have the signature B♭, A♭. Bartok
introduces some innovations in handling ornamental notes, both
singly and in melismatic groups. He contends that most melismatic groups contain a major or heavy tone. This note is represented in a conventional manner surrounded by its subsidiary
notes, represented by "small head" notes. The values of the
small head notes are subtracted from that of the major tone.
For example, ♪ ♩ ♬ equals ♬♬; ♩ ♬ equals ♪♬ ;
♩♪ equals ♩♪, etc. Sometimes, these groups are connected
by beams and no additional rhythmic adjustment need be made.
Grace notes, having no definable rhythmic value, but having definite pitch, are represented ♪; those of indefinite
pitch, ♪.

In Bartok's work at least three, and often all, stanzas are
transcribed. This, of course, gives full justice to stanza variation.
When, however, partial variation is required, the specific
stanza requiring variation is labeled and printed along with
prosody of the text, and direction is given as to the closest
relationship to the stanza of those fully transcribed.

The following suggested axioms are put forth with the aim
of encouraging a more consistent approach to the transcription
and analyzation of traditional music. These represent a dis-
tillation of the most meaningful techniques discussed above
plus techniques which the writer could wish might become
common practice among folksong scholars. Consistency of
technique, of analyzation methods, and of terminology has been
notably lacking in the rather new musicology of Anglo-American folksong. The basic and ultimate aims of transcribers,
scholars, and collectors have also varied greatly. It is hoped

that the following outline will come a bit closer to "pleasing everyone" and creating interest in some mutually beneficial standardization.

Each text and tune should be preceded by the name of the informant and the place of recording or transcription (if transcription is made without mechanical aid in the field).

The full text should be given in the commonly accepted poetic format. Points needing footnotes or clarification should be numbered and such clarification made separately.

Prior to the tune the metronome marking of the performance should always be given. The quarter note should be used as a unit of measure as consistently as possible. The quarter note is convenient from about 70 to 135 pulses per minute. Faster than this the values may be halved and the quarter note restored as the unit of measure at 70 or more. If different recordings of the same informant vary in tempo, the extremes should be indicated, for example $\rfloor = 74 - 90$. If the tempo changes within a performance this may be indicated $\rfloor = 74 + -$, and the exact nature of the changes indicated in the transcription itself.

Preceding the tune there should be given the actual pitch of the performance. The final of the tune represented as a whole note and the upper and lower extremes of range should be given in small black notes. If pitch level varies from performance to performance, the extremes should be given. Variance of pitch level during a single performance should be mentioned and indicated in the transcription itself.

All tunes should be transposed so as to place their final at g^1. The selection of g^1 is not entirely arbitrary since it places most tunes within the scope of the treble clef, thereby avoiding excessive leger lines. The use of g^1 also precludes the use of extreme key signatures. Transcribing tunes at a common pitch level (or at least with a common level for the final) greatly facilitates comparative study of variant versions, scales or modes, and ranges. Since traditional singers often vary pitch levels, we should not be bound to transcribe at the pitch level of a particular performance. The indication of actual pitch of the performance given prior to the complete transcription should suffice even the most serious student.

Key signatures should be used to indicate only consistent characteristics of the tune. Key signatures should not be used to connote major or minor properties in gapped or modal scales. Practices of assigning a signature to tunes in which one note of the signature is missing, or of consistently altering notes involved in the signature with accidentals or naturals, should be avoided.

Meter signatures, like key signatures, should be used to indicate only consistent metrical characteristics. In tunes which are very free or erratic throughout, no meter need be indicated, and barring and grouping should be accomplished solely by the stress of the melody (usually closely interdependent with the text phrasing). In tunes which adhere throughout to a metrical pattern, the meter should be indicated in conventional fashion. The transcriber should limit himself to as few of the common signatures as possible. Such meters as 3/2 and 6/4 might just as easily and accurately be transcribed as 3/4 and 6/8. In a tune which is fairly consistent throughout, but with slight variations, the basic meter can be given in parentheses. This would relieve the transcriber of the obligation to limit any one bar to a specific number of unit values or to fill out bars not having enough signature prescribed value. It would further eliminate the need for exotic meter signatures at points throughout the transcription which are obviously outside the idiom of the traditional singer. For example, the slight foreshortening of the basic 3/4 meter mentioned in Example 3 could be indicated without the necessity for strict adherence to the meter signature, if such signature had been given in parentheses. (See Example 7.)

In the initial transcription each line of text should be represented by one staff of music. This will, in most cases, place equal phrase lengths beneath one another and make phrase relation-

EXAMPLE 7

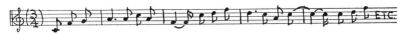

ships more readily apparent. This technique will further stress tune-text relationship. Each bar should be numbered.

This transcription should be as accurate a record of the performance as possible, including ornamental tones, rhythmic oddities, and stylistic peculiarities of the singer. Here techniques and peculiarities of notation should be consistent among transcribers. Since the notation employed by Bartok meets the demands of transcribing a traditional idiom more ornate than our own, it provides more than adequate basis for our needs. Signs and indications (fermatas, ritard, accelerando, etc.), being merely approximations, should not be used, but their exact values should be indicated by precise notation. Other approximations, for example, grace notes for ornamental tones, should be allowed only if precise representation of value is impossible. The use of separate flags, long traditional in vocal music, should be abandoned for the instrumental idiom of barring across groups of rhythmically related notes (eighth, sixteenth, etc.). The assignment of several notes to a single text syllable can be indicated by the slur. Characteristics of notation particularly useful in transcribing Anglo-American traditional music are indicated below:

↑ higher (up to a quarter tone) than the pitch given

↓ lower (up to a quarter tone) than the pitch given

↨, ↥ a quarter lower or higher than the pitch given

⌇ signifies a glissando of all microtones between the pitches indicated or a blurring of the notes indicated into one another

Ornamental tones of equal volume with the more important tones of the tune should be notated with their proper rhythmic values. Weak tones are to be represented by "small head" notes. These are not grace notes of indeterminate length but rather must be specified accurately. Small head notes indicate a lower level of volume or lack of clarity rather than rhythmic uncertainty. For example,

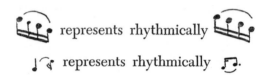

represents rhythmically ... (image shown)

Separate small head notes are subtracted from the large note to which they are connected.

Following a complete transcription of the first stanza there should be full transcriptions of each succeeding stanza sufficiently different to warrant complete representation, and transcriptions of any stanza fragments containing variation from the initial stanza. These fragments should be carefully labeled as to stanza and bar number and given with the corresponding fragments of text.

After detailed transcriptions of the first stanza and all variants, there should be given a "skeletal" tune. This should be determined after the methods of Mead and based on comparison of all stanza variants. The characteristics found most often in the separate stanzas should be projected into the skeletal tune. This tune outline should be an abstract expression of the tune and printed without words. All classifications and analyses should be made from the skeletal tune.

From the skeletal tune there should be given an analysis of the scale. After the method similar to Schinhan, the scale should be given with a numerical expression of the "weight" of each member tone. The unit of number should equal the smallest value to be found in the skeletal tune and this value note should be shown in parentheses prior to the analysis. For example, a sixteenth note in parentheses (♪) would mean that the number under any member tone of the scale would indicate how many sixteenth note values are given that tone in the tune. If a tone had the number 12 under it, this would indicate that the particular tone occurs in the tune for a duration of 12 sixteenth notes; i.e., three full beats.

The scale should be classified from the reduction discussed above. Pentatonic scales may be classified 1 to 5 according to the inversion of the "basic" pentatonic scale given by Sharp.

Pentatonic 1 c d f g a	(transposed with g final)	g a c d e
Pentatonic 2 d f g a c		g b♭ c d f
Pentatonic 3 f g a c d		g a b d e
Pentatonic 4 g a c d f		g a c d f
Pentatonic 5 a c d f g		g b♭ c e♭ f

The terms "chordal" and "tonic" may be used to indicate diatonic and gapped scale systems respectively. Modal classification should be made only if all seven tones of the scale are used and the *modal characteristics are consistent throughout.* Gapped scales (pentatonic or hexatonic) should be given no modal classification. A scale having the tones g b c d e f should be labeled "Hexatonic, no second degree" and not "Mixolydian, no second degree." Assignment of a tone center or tonic is unnecessary. In most instances this would correspond to the final, but in some cases (especially with pentatonic scales) this is a highly questionable matter. The numerical breakdown of the scale will be of greater use than an arbitrary assignment of a tonic. Likewise the labeling of "weak tones" can be omitted. The scale analysis will demonstrate which tones are "weak" and to exactly what extent. The terms "authentic" and "plagal" are founded in Church Mode theory and have been used in many ways over the centuries. Since their original meaning referred to a specific behavior as well as the range of a given mode they have no real meaning in our context. The distribution and range of tones in relation to the final will be readily and completely apparent from the numerical analysis of the scale.

In designating structure, three factors will be indicated in combination. First, the relationship of individual phrases will be given, with letters (A B C, etc.) to represent differing musical content. Above the phrase symbol shall be given the numeral corresponding to the final tone of the phrase. This technique is taken from Bartok and the numerals are the same found in Example 6 above. The symbol ⨆ should indicate a phrase ending prior to the principal caesura of the tune, and the symbol ⨅ should indicate phrase endings following the main caesura. The main caesura should be indicated □. Below the letter symbols should be given the number of bars contained in the phrase indicated. All phrases which are identical musically should be identified by the same letter, contrasting phrases by different letters. Phrases markedly similar but with some slight variation may be expressed A, A′, A″, etc. Small letter symbols may be used to indicate phrase segments or periods within a larger phrase. As an example, the structural representation of the tune for "The Two Sisters" version No. 35 in Bronson (p. 157) would be:

$$
\begin{array}{c c c c c c c | c c}
- & \boxed{V} & \boxed{V} & \boxed{V} & \boxed{5} & \boxed{2} & \boxed{V} & 4 & \\
 & A & (B) & A & (C) & D & E & (F) & a + b \\
 & 2 & 1 & 2 & 2 & 2 & 2 & 4 & 2 \quad 2
\end{array}
$$

This would indicate a tune in seven parts or phrases: the first phrase is two bars in length and ends a fourth below the final; the second phrase is but one bar in length and is of contrasting musical material ending a fourth lower than the final; the third phrase is an exact repetition of the first phrase musically; the fourth phrase is of new material, two bars in length, and its final tone is the main caesura of the tune (a fifth above the final); the fifth and sixth phrases are each of two bars length and present new melodic material; the fifth phrase ends a tone above the final, and the sixth ends a fourth below the final; the last phrase (F) is four bars in length and may be considered to consist of two subdivisions of two bars each (represented by a and b). These sub-phrases end upon the tone a fourth higher than the final and of course the final itself. I have in addition enclosed the second, fourth, and last phrases in parentheses to indicate that these phrases are refrains and not the text proper. Any additional comments as to the structure, contour, or angularity of the tune may be added in prose.

Matters dealing with the rendition should be included as footnotes. These might include:

Explanations of corruptions or idiomatic language in the text.

Asides and information given by the singer concerning the learning of the song, relating local customs or history, and statements indicating when the song would most likely be sung.

Description of accompaniment including the name of instrument used, style of playing, use of instrumental interludes, and tuning.

Mention of any stylistic peculiarities of the singer.

Mention of any related occurrences such as gestures which are meaningful to the song.

The date of the recording or transcription should be given. If several recordings had been made of the same informant this should be noted.

The name of the transcriber and recorder should be included.

References to related material (text or tune) in standard works or journals should be given to facilitate cross study and comparison.

NOTES TO I

1. *Harvard Studies in Comparative Literature* (Cambridge, Mass., 1960).
2. See Mody Boatright, Wilson M. Hudson, and Allen Maxwell (eds.), *Singers and Storytellers* ("Publications of the Texas Folklore Society" XXX [1961]), pp. 30-45.
3. Chicago, 1961.
4. New York, 1957.

5. "Bibliographical and Special Series of the American Folklore Society" (Philadelphia, 1960), XI, see No. 12, 7.

6. *Native American Balladry*, "Bibliographical and Special Series of the American Folklore Society" (Philadelphia, 1950), I, 214.

7. Phillips Barry, *Bulletin of the Folk Song Society of the Northeast*, "Bibliographical and Special Series of the American Folklore Society" (Philadelphia, 1960), XI, see No. 7, 5.

8. Copied from the *Delaware* [Ohio] *Gazette* by Ernest Amy. Sent to me undated in typescript, from a September or October, 1910, issue.

9. See my note in the *Journal of American Folklore*, LXVIII (July-September, 1955), 282.

10. See John W. Draper, *The Funeral Elegy and the Rise of English Romanticism* (New York, 1929), p. 95 and associated notes.

11. Francis J. Child, *The English and Scottish Popular Ballads* (5 vols.; New York and Boston, 1882-1898).

12. See G. Malcolm Laws, Jr., *Native American Balladry* and *American Balladry from British Broadsides*, "Bibliographical and Special Series of the American Folklore Society" (Philadelphia, 1957), VIII.

13. For readily available examples, see Horace P. Beck, *The Folklore of Maine* (Philadelphia and New York, 1957), pp. 103-6, and the Ring Mss. as printed in *Journal of American Folklore*, LXVI (January-March, 1953), 63-64.

Notes to II

Works Cited

Chase, Richard. *Quest for Myth*. Baton Rouge: Louisiana State University Press, 1949.

Goldstein, Kenneth S. "The Unfortunate Rake: A Study in the Evolution of a Ballad." New York: Folkways Records Album FS 3805, 1950.

Hewes, Gordon W. "Mexicans in Search of the 'Mexican.'" *American Journal of Economics and Sociology*, XIII (1954), 209-23.

Lomax, Alan. "Folk Song Style," *American Anthropologist*, LXI (1959), 927-54.

Radin, Paul. *The Trickster: A Study in American Indian Mythology*. London: Routledge and Kegan Paul, 1956.

————. *Winnebago Hero Cycles: A Study in Aboriginal Literature*. ("Indiana University Publications in Anthropology and Linguistics," Memoir 1.) Baltimore: Waverly Press, Inc., 1948. Supplement to *International Journal of American Linguistics*, XIV, 3.

Thompson, Stith. "Advances in Folklore Studies," in A. L. Kroeber, *Anthropology Today*. Chicago: University of Chicago Press, 1955, pp. 587-96.

Utley, Francis Lee. "Folk Literature: An Operational Definition," *Journal of American Folklore*, LXXIV (1961), 193-206.

Notes to III

1. Archer Taylor, *"Edward" and "Sven i Rosengaard"* (Chicago: University of Chicago Press, 1931), p. vii.

2. *Ibid.*, pp. vii-viii.

3. Two major comparative studies from the Scandinavian area preceded

Professor Taylor's work; these were Sofus Larsen's two books *Niels Ebbesens Vise* (Copenhagen: H. Hagerup, 1908) and *Ebbe Skammelsons Vise* (Copenhagen: H. Hagerup, 1923). More recent years have seen significant studies in the English language. There have been, for instance, Paul Brewster's study *The Two Sisters* (Helsinki: Suomalainen Tiedeakatemia, FFC No. 147, 1953), Iivar Kemppinen's prolix *The Ballad of Lady Isabel and the False Knight* (Helsinki: Kirja-Mono, 1954), and Holger Olof Nygard's more exacting study of the last-named ballad entitled *The Ballad of Heer Halewijn* (Helsinki: Suomalainen Tiedeakatemia, FFC No. 169, 1958). In addition, five or six studies of less comprehensive nature have appeared in the various folklore journals in recent years, and two analyses have been published in which ballads (or narrative folksongs at least) have given impetus to literary or historical studies—Paul Christophersen's *The Ballad of Sir Aldingar* (Oxford: Clarendon Press, 1952) and Américo Paredes' *"With His Pistol In His Hand"* (Austin: University of Texas Press, 1958).

4. Julius Krohn, *Suomalaisen Kirjalisuuden Historia [A History of Finnish Literature]* (Helsinki, 1897).

5. Kaarle Krohn, *Die Folkloristische Arbeitsmethode* (Oslo, 1926).

6. In addition to the well-known bibliographical guides such as Tristram P. Coffin's *The British Traditional Ballad in North America* (Philadelphia: American Folklore Society, 1950), Malcolm G. Laws, Jr., *Native American Balladry* (Philadelphia: American Folklore Society, 1950) and *American Balladry from British Broadsides* (Philadelphia: American Folklore Society, 1957), there are, of course, the only slightly less well-known volumes by Margaret Dean-Smith, *A Guide to English Folk Song Collections* (Liverpool, 1954) and Leiv Heggstad and H. Grüner Nielsen, *Utsyn yver gamall norsk Folkevisedikting* (Kristiania [Oslo], 1912). None of these, however, serves as more than a starting point when one is tracking down texts.

7. Ernst von der Recke, who occupied himself for many years with regrouping and analyzing the materials found in Grundtvig's *Danmarks gamle Folkeviser*, which he published in four volumes with the title *Danmarks Fornviser* (Copenhagen, 1927-29), also compiled a manuscript concordance of Danish ballads with references to some of the other major Scandinavian collections in Norway, Sweden, Iceland, and the Faroe Islands. This manuscript, copies of which can be found at the Norsk Folkeminnesamling in Oslo and at the Dansk Folkemindesamling in Copenhagen, is arranged according to the subject matter of published ballad texts. It is especially useful for finding parallel stanzas and phrases.

8. The indexed materials and broad themes found in F. J. Child's *The English and Scottish Popular Ballads* were included in Stith Thompson's *Motif-Index of Folk-Literature*, but individual texts and later variants were not included.

9. Reed Smith, *South Carolina Ballads* (Cambridge, Mass.: Harvard University Press, 1928), p. 69.

10. Tristram P. Coffin, *The British Traditional Ballad in North America* (Philadelphia: American Folklore Society, 1950), pp. xv, 4-5, 11.

11. D. K. Wilgus, *Anglo-American Folksong Scholarship Since 1898* (New Brunswick, N. J.: Rutgers University Press, 1959), pp. 396-97, *note* 88.

12. Phillips Barry, Fannie Hardy Eckstorm, and May Winslow Smyth, *British Ballads from Maine* (New Haven: Yale University Press, 1929), p. 224.

NOTES TO IV

1. *The Ballad Revival* (Chicago, 1961), p. 227.

2. See my *Anglo-American Folksong Scholarship Since 1898* (New Brunswick, N. J., 1959), pp. 33-35, 38-41.

3. *Ibid.*, pp. 97-98.

4. *American Balladry from British Broadsides* (Philadelphia, 1957), pp. 120-22.

5. Al Craver, Columbia 15031-D; Vernon Dalhart, Banner 1613, Bell 364, Broadway 8047, Challenge 160, 318, Columbia 15064-D, Conqueror 7068, Edison S1609, 51714, 51609, and cyl. 5049, Emerson 7364, Gennett 3197, Herwin 75502, Okeh 40623, 40584, Paramount 3012, Pathe 032144, Perfect 12223, Regal 9916, Silvertone 2683, Supertone 9227, Victor 19779, 19821, 19997; Frank Evans, Oreole 490; Tobe Little, Okeh 40568. Many of these were pressed from the same matrix.

6. In addition to Jenkins and Carson they are: Gloria Greer (Vaughn DeLeath), Cameo 805; Charlie Oaks, Vocalion 15099; Red River Dave (McEnery), Musicraft 286; Harry Smith, Okeh 45260 (I have not heard this performance).

7. The information concerning Brockman and Jenkins was obtained from tape-recorded interviews with Mrs. Irene Futrelle and Polk C. Brockman in Atlanta, July 10, 1959, by Fred G. Hoeptner and Bob Pinson, and August 8-9, 1961, by Archie Green, Ed Kahn, and D. K. Wilgus; and from manuscript material generously provided by Mrs. Futrelle, the stepdaughter of Andrew Jenkins.

8. Albert B. Lord, *The Singer of Tales* (Cambridge, Mass., 1960).

9. *Journal of American Folklore*, LXXIV (1961), 97-112.

10. *Op. cit.*, p. 120.

NOTES TO V

1. Cecil J. Sharp, *English Folksongs from the Southern Appalachians* (2d ed.; New York, 1952).

2. *Ibid.*, pp. xxxii ff. All examples in the discussion of Sharp's methods come from this source.

3. Arthur Kyle Davis, Jr., *More Traditional Ballads of Virginia* (Chapel Hill, 1960), p. xix.

4. Jan Philip Schinhan (ed.), *North Carolina Folklore* (Durham, N. C., 1957), IV, xxxi.

5. Bruno Nettl (ed.), *Ancient Ballads Traditionally Sung in New England* (Philadelphia, 1960), p. xx.

6. Bertrand Bronson, *Traditional Tunes of the Child Ballads* (Princeton, 1959).

7. *Ibid.*, p. xxvii.

8. Bela Bartok, *Serbo-Croatian Folk Songs* (New York, 1951).

9. *Ibid.*, p. 12.

Contributors

ROGER D. ABRAHAMS, who received the Ph.D. at the University of Pennsylvania, was the first to give a general course in folklore at the University of Texas. Working with the files of Archer Taylor, he has been studying riddles recently.

RILEY AIKEN for many years taught modern languages at Kansas State College, Emporia, and spent much of his vacation time traveling among the *gente* of Mexico. He is now retired and is living at Norman, Oklahoma.

JOHN Q. ANDERSON is chairman of the English department at Texas A.&M. He has contributed articles to past annuals of the Texas Folklore Society and to other publications, and has edited a valuable Civil War diary.

E. BAGBY ATWOOD, for some years professor of English at the University of Texas, published *The Regional Vocabulary of Texas* in 1962. He died in the fall of 1963.

TRISTRAM P. COFFIN is secretary and treasurer of the American Folklore Society. He has written or edited some half-dozen books including *The Ballad and the Critics,* of which Mac-Edward Leach is coauthor.

J. FRANK DOBIE, through his many books, has made the American Southwest known all over the world. For twenty years he was editor for the Texas Folklore Society, and he likes to contribute to each annual. His next book will deal with cow people he has known.

GEORGE FOSS is a full-time member of the National Symphony Orchestra in Washington, D.C., and a part-time collector, with a special interest in ethnomusicology.

KENNETH GOLDSTEIN collects folklore and teaches at the University of Pennsylvania. Among his important services have been the production of folksong albums, of which he has issued some two hundred, and the republication of important works out of print.

JOHN GREENWAY, a member of the anthropology staff at the University of Colorado, is the new editor of the *Journal of American Folklore*. His *American Folksongs of Protest* is perhaps his best-known work. He has received several grants, one of which took him to Australia.

GEORGE D. HENDRICKS is at work on an extensive collection of popular beliefs and superstitions in the Southwest, which will be assimilated into the multivolume "Dictionary of American Popular Beliefs and Superstitions." He is the author of *The Bad Man of the West*, now in its third edition, and of numerous articles contributed to learned journals. He teaches at North Texas State University.

WILSON M. HUDSON has assisted in editing the annuals of the Texas Folklore Society since 1951 and is the Society's newly elected Secretary and Editor. At the University of Texas he teaches, among other courses, Life and Literature of the Southwest, which was originated by J. Frank Dobie. He is studying myth as it exists at present in nonprimitive settings.

JAMES M. LACY is professor of English at East Texas State College. He received a doctor's degree at the University of Denver, with a dissertation on Spanish Americans in Anglo-American literature.

E. HUDSON LONG, chairman of the English department of Baylor University, has published books on O. Henry and Mark Twain. He has wide literary interests and is currently president of the Texas Institute of Letters.

EDISON RICHMOND, bibliographer for the *Journal of American Folklore* and editor of *Midwest Folklore,* teaches courses in the ballad at the University of Indiana.

D. K. WILGUS' scholarly reputation was firmly established by the appearance of his *Anglo-American Folksong Scholarship Since 1898,* published in 1959, when he was teaching at the University of Kentucky. He has since joined the staff of the Folklore and Mythology Group at the University of California at Los Angeles.

Index